Praise for *For...*

"The book opens with a scoop [...]
hypocrisy of western governments."—*Los Angeles Times*

"The charges made by [Brisard and Dasquié] deserve close
scrutiny."—U.S.Representative Ron Paul calling for an investigation of charges made in the book on the House floor

"This has got a cast of characters in it that is fascinating. We've
got a former CIA officer, Christina Rocca, who is now in the State
Department who went to Afghanistan weeks before September
11, and to Pakistan, and talked with the Taliban, a group that we
did not recognize, and you now know what we have done to
them. You have got Laili Helms, the niece of the former head of
the CIA, who was a public relations agent hired by the Taliban.
And you've got oil, and this is a fundamental thing. Let us not lose
sight of this basic reality. The population of the United States of
America represents 5 percent of the population of the world. Yet,
we use 40 percent—40 percent of the world's oil. So oil is a big
issue, and as we were saying yesterday, there is very substantial oil
in Central Asia. And to get that out to the sea, the best possible
way to do it would be to build a pipeline across Afghanistan. So
that's the web, Paula, and I don't think we're being told all of the
facts. There are denials, claims that meetings didn't take place,
when clearly they did. The most interesting thing those French
authors told us today is that they had seen archives. That means
records of diplomatic conversations that took place."

—Former UN Arms Inspector Richard Butler to Paula Zahn,
January 9, 2002, CNN. Discussing *Forbidden Truth*.

FORBIDDEN TRUTH

FORBIDDEN TRUTH

U.S.–TALIBAN SECRET OIL DIPLOMACY AND THE FAILED HUNT FOR BIN LADEN

JEAN-CHARLES BRISARD
and GUILLAUME DASQUIÉ

Translated by Lucy Rounds
with Peter Fifield and Nicholas Greenslade

Introductions by Joseph Trento and Wayne Madsen

Thunder's Mouth Press/Nation Books
New York

FORBIDDEN TRUTH: *U.S.-Taliban Secret Oil Diplomacy and the Failed Hunt for bin Laden*

Copyright © 2002 by Jean-Charles Brisard and Guillaume Dasquié
Translation © 2002 by Avalon Publishing Group
Introduction p. ix © 2002 by Joseph Trento
Inroduction p. xiii © 2002 by Wayne Madsen

Published by
Thunder's Mouth Press/Nation Books
161 William St., 16th Floor
New York, NY 10038

Nation Books is a co-publishing venture of the Nation Institute and Avalon
Publishing Group Incorporated.

Library of Congress Cataloging-in-Publication Data is available for this title.

ISBN 1-56025-414-9

9 8 7 6 5 4 3 2 1

Printed in the United States of America
Distributed by Publishers Group West

CONTENTS

Introduction

Forbidden Truth is the story of the greatest foreign policy blunder of the past thirty years. This important book delves into the aftermath—the blowback—of the United States and Saudi Arabian policy of creating an Arab Islamic force to bring down the Soviet Union by miring it in a war in Afghanistan. *Forbidden Truth* is the story of how that force turned against its creators with effectiveness and vengeance.

In the pages of *Forbidden Truth* are all the leftovers from this ill-conceived U.S. policy: Saudi front men, the ruins of BCCI, Saudi and Pakistani intelligence. They all came together to assist Osama bin Laden in retooling the Arab fighters of the Afghan war into an Islamic Frankenstein. All of this happening under the nose of a CIA unwilling to revisit an array of forces that once had been allies.

On September 11, 2001, the world saw three thousand lives destroyed. President George Bush reacted with confusion, anger and resoluteness and began to lead the country and a handful of allies into the war on terrorism. The United States went into war mode. As a result, everything in government has deferred to the war—especially the truth.

Young George Bush did not have the luxury of time to consider if the chickens from his father's foreign policy misadventures had come to roost. Fortunately, for all of us, authors Jean-Charles Brisard and Guillaume Dasquié did take the time. The result is the most important explanation of the secret history of how the United States came to be attacked and who was responsible. The answers the authors uncovered will and should make you very angry. Many of the same men around young George Bush now, played a major role in the original failed scheme.

Forbidden Truth is the first comprehensive revelation of how the foreign policy of the President's father and the cozy relationship with the Royal Family of Saudi Arabia exploited and created an extremist Islamic mercenary army that eventually turned on its creators.

In the pages of *Forbidden Truth* are the awful details that our government understood that the Saudi government was financing bin Laden's Al Qaeda through Islamic charities years before the attacks.

Like Shakespearean characters, the "evil-doers" and young American President had a dark thread connecting them: a common benefactor—the Saudi Royal family. Their wealth had helped Prescott Bush and his sons grow rich and powerful over the years. It had also kept opposition to the Royal family at bay at home by funding for decades the most extreme forms of Islam.

Few would imagine that these sophisticated partners—the Bushes and the Royal Family—would together create the conditions and opportunity for terrorism to grow into a worldwide network. As CIA Director, the President's father, George Herbert Walker Bush, joined with a Saudi Prince to create a bank for covert operations to fight the Soviets through the Islamic cause in

Afghanistan. The Bank of Commerce and Credit International collapsed in scandal, but its personalities and pieces became the vessels and conduits of the terrorist network. These same personalities were George's partners in policy, and in some cases, private business.

The then Vice President, George H. W. Bush, introduced the bin Laden family to William Casey to help the United States "win" its proxy war in Afghanistan. When the Saudis sided with Kuwait in a long festering dispute about stealing oil, President Bush turned Saddam Hussein from a friend to a foe. He put the full force of the United States with his old friends. The United States fought a war to save two kingdoms. Our reward was that our soldiers and state department employees were not allowed to publicly worship in Saudi Arabia.

Bush lost the presidency, but the Saudis took care of his family. When the scion who would be the next Bush in the White House needed help with Harken Energy, old friends again came to the rescue.

As Bill Clinton dealt with the indifference of the Saudis to their support for Islamic extremist, bin Laden blew up our barracks at Kohbar. The Saudis hindered our investigation and denied the truth: that bin Laden and his forces had begun to move against the Royal Family inside Saudi Arabia. Their motivation was money. Their methods came straight from organized crime: extortion. Pay us protection or more threatening faxes will come on the King's private fax line. Then worse. Pay us our tribute or the revolution will be at home, not in Afghanistan or Yemen.

The Arab princes and their hangers on made the decision to pay.

Now, nearly a year after the horrors of September 11 and the consequent bombing of Afghanistan, with neither bin Laden nor

Mullah Omar captured, with more and more Saudis showing up in the terrorists' ranks, more bad news: Missed signals, missed warnings: The FBI and CIA tied to out blame each other. The day after the 9.11 attacks vice-president Cheney call the senate majority leader Tom Daschle trying to talk him out of any major probe into the intelligence failure. There could be no serious investigation because a serious investigation in the end would reveal that money and oil were more important than protecting Saudi Arabia or the United States. A serious investigation would reveal that bankers, politicians, and family friends in business suits support Al Qaeda. A serious investigation would demonstrate that George Bush's father was the midwife to the birth of this monster. A serious investigation would demonstrate that Middle East oil money still helps support members of the Bush family.

The real terror for George Bush will come when he reads *Forbidden Truth*. *Forbidden Truth* is the only serious investigation available to us up to now. Only then will he finally connect the dots. Perhaps he will ask his father to come in for that long overdue talk. To be President you need to know how to handle the guilty knowledge that comes with power. Sadly, Bush has more than his fair share.

—JOSEPH TRENTO
Author of *The Secret History of The CIA*
Managing Director of National Security News Service

Introduction

Long before the world first heard of the FBI's Minneapolis, Phoenix, and Oklahoma City memoranda on what was known to U.S. law enforcement prior to "9-11", Jean-Charles Brisard and Guillaume Dasquié presented in the first French edition of *Forbidden Truth* a unique insight into what the U.S. and other governments "knew and when they knew it" concerning the future plans of Bin Laden's Al Qaeda network. After three years of painstaking research, the authors succeeded in "connecting the dots" in revealing the behind-the-scenes maneuvering preceding the September 11 terrorist attacks on New York City and Washington, DC.

Particularly gripping is the tale of John O'Neill, the former deputy director of the FBI's New York office who spent years tracking bin Laden and his confederates. As the chief counter-terrorism agent within the bureau, O'Neill focused on the Al Qaeda network following a series of terrorist attacks aimed at Americans, particularly in Saudi Arabia and East Africa. In October 2000, Al Qaeda set off a bomb amidships the *USS Cole* in Aden harbor. O'Neill describes his frustrations in dealing with an uncooperative U.S. ambassador to Yemen who, along with her CIA and State Department interlocutors, was more interested in placating Saudi and American oil interests than in bringing the Al Qaeda perpetrators to justice.

It is not often that a book provides an unintentional last testament. But in *Forbidden Truth*, O'Neill provided the authors with his virtual last words on the subject of his investigation of bin Laden's network and his thoughts on cover-ups reaching high into the echelons of political power in Washington, Saudi Arabia, and the oil company headquarters in Texas. On September 11, 2001, after an illustrious career with the FBI, O'Neill died while carrying out his new duties as director of security for the World Trade Center. Fortunately, Brisard and Dasquié have provided for the historical record the words that O'Neill may have himself penned had he survived the September 11 attack.

There has been a general tendency in the media and among America's political and military leaders to begin the Al Qaeda and Taliban timeline on September 11. Brisard and Dasquié explode this myth by describing the close economic ties between the Bush and Clinton administrations, U.S. Big Oil, and the Taliban and their Saudi patrons. In connecting the dots between Taliban-controlled Afghanistan and the United States, Brisard and Dasquié reveal the main principals involved in negotiating a lucrative but controversial oil and gas pipeline deal with the mullahs of Kandahar. The reader is introduced to Laili Helms, an Afghan-American with ties to the former Afghan royal house, the mujaheddin, the Taliban, and most interestingly—the CIA (her uncle by marriage is former CIA Director Richard Helms). In the weeks prior to the September 11 attack, Laili Helms was orchestrating high-level meetings between senior members of the Bush administration and emissaries of Mullah Mohammed Omar, the main benefactor of Osama bin Laden.

Brisard and Dasquié successfully connect the dots to an even degree. They explain the actual motivation behind the United Nations' "6+2 Group"—pipeline politics—not the ballyhooed aim of bringing about a ceasefire between the Taliban and their Northern Alliance rivals. The authors reveal that it was at a May 15, 2001 meeting in Berlin that a U.S. official ominously presented the following ultimatum to the Pakistani delegation (who were the Taliban's interlocutors at the meeting), "Either you accept our offer of a carpet of gold, or we bury you under a carpet of bombs." It was a statement that would take on even greater meaning after the September 11 event.

When *Forbidden Truth* was first published in France in November 2001, skeptics inside and outside the U.S. government scoffed at the authors' contention that French intelligence had warned the FBI about the terrorist connections and on-going flight training in the United States of Zacarias Moussaoui, the so-called "20th hijacker" who was arrested on a visa violation in Minnesota on August 17, 2001. These skeptics were later confronted with an incontrovertible validation of this information when FBI Minneapolis Chief Division Counsel Coleen Rowley, a 21-year veteran agent, wrote in a blistering letter to FBI Director Robert Mueller, "the French Intelligence Service confirmed [Moussaoui's] affiliations with radical Islamic fundamentalist groups and activities connected to Osama bin Laden."

Rowley's concerns, along with those spelled out in a July 10, 2001 warning from the Phoenix FBI agent Kenneth Williams concerning the activities of Arab flight students and a May 1998 report from the Oklahoma City FBI concerning similar flight training by Middle Eastern men in that city, fell into the laps of what Rowley described as "flippant" FBI bureaucrats in

Washington. The FBI headquarters, including two special units tasked to investigate religious extremists and bin Laden—the Radical Fundamentalist Unit and the UBL Unit, respectively—refused to authorize a full investigation, including critical electronic surveillance, of the suspected terrorists.

The world of intelligence in which the truth is not always the truth and lies are not always lies has been characterized by some observers as a "hall of mirrors." But the failure to "connect the dots" and fuse and analyze critical intelligence before September 11 cannot merely be blamed on the staggering nature of analyzing disparate pieces of information from a multitude of oftentimes questionable sources. In addition to the French intelligence that came to senior U.S. law enforcement and intelligence officials, we now know that similar hard intelligence came from the intelligence and police agencies of Egypt, Morocco, Jordan, India, Israel, Russia, Germany, Kazakhstan, Canada, the Cayman Islands, and Italy. The Italian counter-terrorism police had recorded a conversation in the summer of 2000 in which a Yemeni sheik described what sounded like the plans for September 11, saying an attack was planned that would be "one of those strikes that you never forget . . . [a] terrifying thing, it will move from south to north, from east to west. He who made this plan is a madman, but a genius. It will turn you to ice."

Skeptics continue to deride any notion that the Bush administration had advanced warning of September 11. But Brisard and Dasquié lay out one of the most important clues in tracking any criminal enterprise-the money trail. It is a trail that connects Osama bin Laden to other members of his family involved with construction and financial projects throughout the world—the so-called "good bin Ladens." Yet, the links do not merely end with the greater bin Laden family—they involve the House of Saud, the Pakistani Inter Service Intelligence agency, other wealthy Saudi bankers and merchants, Islamic charities and *madrassas*, U.S. oil tycoons, and U.S. defense contractors like The Carlyle Group. The links even extend into the very heart of the administration and include President George W. Bush (a prior recipient of bin Laden family investment money), his father (an advisor to Carlyle and its major client, the Binladin Group, and Vice President Dick Cheney (a beneficiary of Saudi monetary largesse as the head of the oil services company Halliburton).

While President Bush portrays himself a leader with a myopic world view—from referring to Pakistani President Pervez Musharraf during the 2000 presidential campaign as "General, General" and believing he was elected to being under the impression that the Taliban was a Bavarian brass band—his coterie of friends and business partners certainly see the Middle East and South Asia with perfect 20/20 vision. And it is this view that should have alerted them to the dangers of dancing with the likes of the Taliban, corrupt Pakistani generals, and Saudi sheikhs.

While brave and selfless FBI agents like John O'Neill saw the dangers posed by Al Qaeda and their Saudi and Pakistani friends, the U.S. oil-intelligence complex was contented with "treating with the enemy."

Forbidden Truth answers a number of questions concerning the failure by the "world's only remaining superpower" to prevent one of the most tragic days in American history. During the Cold War, when my colleagues and I stood watch in Navy facilities monitoring the movements of Soviet submarines, such lapses in vigilance would have had dire consequences, and we knew it. In those days, there was no tolerance for such mistakes. This tenet has been largely lost on today's bloated intelligence and law enforcement infrastructure, which has more money and resources available to it now than at any time in our nation's history.

Brisard and Dasquié have laid the groundwork for future investigations into terror assault that shook the world. As the history books are written about September 11 and as reports of government committees and possible commissions are issued, *Forbidden Truth* will remain a seminal reference point for all those who are compelled to look beyond the veil of secrecy thrown around the events leading up to America's worst and most costly terrorist attack.

—WAYNE MADSEN
May 2002

PREFACE TO THE AMERICAN EDITION

It is May 2002, and Osama bin Laden and his lieutenants are as well known as Bill Gates and his software: the irony of infamy. I remember walking in London[1]—it must have been about a year ago—in the company of a banker, a specialist in fund management whose services were greatly appreciated by his wealthy clientele from the Persian Gulf. On that day, we were having our fourth interview, I think; by this time, we had reached an understanding and were no longer just discussing the secrets and sins of a Middle Eastern businessman. As we strolled toward St. James's Park, he told me about the everyday life of his parents, somewhere in a village overlooking the Mediterranean, to the north of Beirut. Boisterously and with great animation, he complained about his father's inability to converse normally with his daughter, an English schoolgirl who was a passionate militant in an environmentalist group. Further on, in Pall Mall, after having walked past the walls that shelter the legendary Travellers Club, which he sometimes frequented—that place in London where mercenary aristocrats and adventurous diplomats can be found—suddenly, he began to speak in hushed tones, occasionally turning around. He began to recount family stories of how the financing of Islamic terrorism had succeeded.

We talked about the accounting operations of a credit establishment in the United Arab Emirates, and his trips to Islamabad, in particular to the bank used by the Pakistani secret service to support the Taliban and Al Qaeda. As always, it was the concern of a Saudi religious chief, allied with one of the 4,000 princes who make up the royal family, and whose right-hand men had organized a financial circuit from Dubai to the British Virgin Islands for the profit of Osama bin Laden. Officially, bin Laden was then an *ordinary* terrorist, albeit one who had blown up two U.S. embassies and attacked the USS *Cole*, sought naturally by the FBI, but in whom most diplomats beyond the frontiers of the West were not interested. The multiple oil contracts with Saudi Arabia then necessitated a certain understanding of the specificities of the religious dictatorship operated by King Fahd and Prince Abdallah. Clearly, one did not crush such an invaluable ally in the name of seizing a bandit. Therefore, at that time, these enterprises were mentioned only *sotto voce,* even by the two peaceful pedestrians walking under the London drizzle. Especially under the London drizzle. The city is home to dozens of fortunes built around the oil wells of the Gulf.

Since 1998 the professional newsletter *Intelligence Online*[2] had published several investigations of these charitable associations and companies with Saudi, Pakistani, and United Arab Emirates origins, which, without giving too much away, financed Al Qaeda. Each time, our sources trembled. Some begged us to promise them that we would no longer cover the subject. But September 11 changed everything. Osama bin Laden and his lieutenants became public figures, their story was shown on hundreds of television programs, and, gradually, the reasons behind the emergence of their movement and its expansion over the course of the past ten years became fundamental questions for our understanding. After asking, "How was it possible?" everyone wanted to know, "Why was it possible?"

This book, *Forbidden Truth*, sought to bring together the first brief responses. Published for the first time in France on November 14, 2001, it brought together three years of investigations on how political channels, financial networks, oil stakes, and secret diplomatic deals slowly created room for maneuver for this group of nostalgic terrorists of the holy war with their crude ideology, swearing as much by the Koran as by the Kalashnikov. After the attacks, we tried to publish it as quickly as possible because, at the moment when the military operations were getting under way in Afghanistan, it seemed important, precisely, not to focus on Afghanistan. It was more a matter of looking closer to home. We wanted to decipher this badly controlled nexus without which Osama bin Laden and his companions would have remained just distant, armed cranks praying in the desert. We wanted to dissect this entanglement of negligence and political interests and calculations from the parquet floors of the Foreign Office in London to the marble floors of Texas oil companies in Houston and to the fitted carpets of fiduciary companies in Geneva.

In fact, Appendix VII of this book—originally commissioned by the French intelligence services—was the basis of a French parliamentary report that resulted in the closing of several so-called Islamic charities. The report was handed over to George Bush by Jacques Chirac during his first visit to the United States in the wake of September 11.

But at no time did we imagine the consequences of the revelations contained in these pages. What's worse, we never once wanted this book to become party to the investigations that were going on right under our eyes. That would have been a waste of time and effort. But its contents overtook us. We had taken stock of it in December 2001, when, several days before Christmas, a committee of special inquiry of the Security Council of the United Nations moved to hear us. Its mission: to reconstruct the money trail thanks to which bin Laden had been able to pursue his activities. The hearing took place in Paris in a quiet annex at UNESCO headquarters. It focused exclusively on the financial networks and parallel diplomacy that had allowed the Taliban and Osama bin Laden to gain an aura of power. What transpired was two hours of tight, technical discussion in the presence of eight diplomats who had recently discovered the extent of these collusions, and who did not hide their embarrassment before the seriousness of the charges leveled at Saudi Arabia. From India to the United States, this panel of investigators represented the gamut of leading nations, all of which at one time had gone greedily fishing, opting to preserve their relationship with the monarchs of the Gulf or their pipeline projects in Central Asia over the fight against terrorism. But, henceforth, they forced themselves to examine it, sometimes to the point of fear.

As the book has been covered by the foreign press, reactions of a different sort have reached us—aggressive ones, sometimes in the form of insults. French bankers, American oil companies, and Persian Gulf businessmen luxuriously ensconced in financial paradises in Europe or the Antilles did not take well to such a spilling of the beans. These were the men whose fortunes derived from family secrets and maybe a few words exchanged on the tarmac at private airports. One of them, and not the least, Yeslam bin Laden, brother of Osama, a Swiss citizen of just one year, head of an arborescence of offshore companies, stepped up litigation, using all the possibilities afforded under Swiss freedom-of-press laws to stop the book's publication on the grounds that he disapproved of our general approach. The court that pronounced the act of censorship did not seem to have taken into account the text's content. This is proof that not all truths should be spoken, especially in the land of secret banking. Nevertheless, despite the unexpected support of the Swiss justice system, Yeslam bin Laden did not escape an investigation. A money-laundering watchdog at the French finance ministry spotted suspicious transfers being made through one of his accounts.[3] An action was quickly brought in March 2002 by magistrate Renaud Van Ruymbeke, a specialist in financial cases, at which we were asked to appear as witnesses in our capacity as authors of this book. Swiss police carried out searches across the country on March 27 probing the money-laundering allegations. The operation involved searches at the headquarters of nine companies and four homes in Geneva, Berne, Zoug, and Zurich, A week earlier, bin Laden's villa in Cannes in the South of France was also searched at Van Ruymbeke's request.

Beyond these developments, we felt that after September 11, with investigations like this one (there are others), something was transformed: perceptions perhaps, a sense of urgency, a general impression that from now on world affairs were of more interest. After finally terrorizing us, the terrorists have surrendered some of their vigilance to our societies. With the endless debates and exchanges provoked by this book, it seems to us that a new wisdom for the long term was essential. People will no longer joke about the power struggles and petty rivalries that plague our planet. Everyone must be mindful of the consequences of a hatred left to rot on the other side of the world just because there was no immediate interest to keep a rich country there.

However, over there, in "that other world" where the unthinkable emerged, where educated, then fanatical, young boys became capable of flying airplanes into large buildings—in that part of the world, what has changed? Nothing, or very little. Certainly there is a plethora of military options under way to destroy the terrorist camps. Certainly the contemptible Taliban regime has disintegrated, having benefited for too long from the benevolence from some Western quarters and the generosity of oil companies. Evidently even in the middle of the Afghan mountains, deprived of powerful political and financial connections, their one-time allies now rectifying their mistakes, the masters of the country became once again masters of their goats.

With the spectacle of the fall of the Taliban and the bombardment of the final trapped Al Qaeda legion in Afghanistan, a conviction seizes us. We witnessed the rightful vengeance inflicted on this rabble. And still, not quite. How does one erase that vision, almost burlesque, of the head of the Taliban, Mullah Omar, saving himself (that is, running away) from a city on a simple moped in a country that had been, for several weeks, under the control of the Western allies?

The executors of low deeds have been routed, but their paymasters remain unpunished. Who are they? Islamic banks located in the United Arab Emirates, those chief clerics installed as the ruling spiritual powers in Saudi Arabia whose intrigues we describe, several Saudi princes close to the royal palace whose hidden alliances we divulge, those in charge in Pakistan eager to promote a strong Sunni regime on the other side of the border, in particular. The bald truth, ugly but undeniable, in that Arabic peninsula that is home to the main supply of oil reserves consumed by the industrialized nations, is the power rests in the hands of dictators of the sands whose penchant for nepotism and gerontocracy guaranteed us fifty years of reliable and easily corruptible middlemen, who were able to fill their coffers on our fuel purchases and their arms acquisitions. In the region, these emirs and kings that keep their people in a permanent state of submission and fear have always held up the Koran to legitimize their position, and have always been prepared to compromise with the most radical clerics to ensure that no one dislodges them from their palaces. Here they are now, acting shocked and surprised to learn that one of the faithful soldiers of one of these mullahs, Osama bin Laden, is behind the New World Disorder that so vexes their rich Western partners.

It's the mesh of these secretive relationships, it's the influence of religious extremists in those countries on which the health of our trade rests, it's our willful blindness before these sovereigns whose very archaism debases Islam, it's the inconsistency of them financing their radical aims throughout the world through foundations aided by the petrodollars we throw at them—these are the realities that explain in depth the growing power of Osama bin Laden. At the same time, they bring to light the irresponsibility of what, euphemistically, we call in our country *parallel diplomacy*—as if to convince ourselves that the misdeeds that it necessarily incorporates remain parallel to our concerns, that one should not be confused with the other. Herein lies our mistake.

PROLOGUE

The interview took place at the Oak Bar in the New York Plaza hotel, a place as dark and austere as the lives of those who, behind the scenes, are leading the fight against terrorism. In late July 2001, I met with John O'Neill on business.[1] O'Neill was the former head of antiterrorism in the United States who had become deputy director of the FBI's New York office in charge of national security. At the age of forty-nine, after having dedicated half his life to the FBI, he joined the New York "flagship office," a position coveted by all FBI agents.

We had first met a month earlier in Paris. A group of French antiterrorist experts and I had met O'Neill to share information on Al Qaeda's financial networks. We had dinner at Chez Benoit in the Le Marais area, at the same table occupied not long before by Hillary Clinton; Madeleine Albright; the deputy director of the Direction de la Surveillance du Territoire (DST) in charge of antiterrorism; and Alain Marsaud, the former chief prosecutor of terrorists for the Parquet de Paris, the highest prosecution authority in France. I gave O'Neill my report titled "The Economic Network of the bin Laden Family"[2] of which he had heard, during the dinner, and we agreed to meet in New York the following month to discuss the report.

New York had become John O'Neill's territory. He knew every nook and cranny, from the historic steak houses to the China Club, from Little Italy to the bars frequented by movie stars and film directors. Following him through the city, one would think he owned the place. He was welcomed everywhere as a friend. He was also never "off duty," constantly juggling his cell phone and PalmPilot as if to remind himself of his central mission. Accompanying him on his rounds was also an opportunity to discuss our business together.

John O'Neill was a rebel in a world where the president and his administration called the shots. In charge of investigating acts of terrorism by the Al Qaeda organization, he went to Yemen in October 2000 after the attack on the USS *Cole,* in which seventeen U.S. servicemen died. He lambasted the obstructionist attitude among American diplomats there. In the course of the investigation, it became clear that diplomats from the State Department and FBI investigators did not share the same approach. The diplomats wanted to comply with the Yemenite regime in order to calm political relations, while the FBI wanted to solve the crime and find those responsible for the attack as quickly as possible. It was apparent that these two visions—these two cultures—could not coexist. After another dispute over the FBI agents' carrying of arms and the turning over of second-level suspects to the American authorities, the American ambassador to Yemen, Barbara Bodine, forbade John O'Neill and his team (of "Rambos," as the Yemenite authorities called them) from entering Yemen.[3] This despite the fact that, according to O'Neill, the FBI had in hand all of the evidence needed to implicate Osama bin Laden's terrorist network in the attack.

Sitting in the China Club at the top of a building overlooking

Manhattan, John O'Neill recounted the heated exchange with the American ambassador, his disappointment in the State Department's impotence—feigned or not—and above all the threat of Osama bin Laden. For him, everything originated in Saudi Arabia, and everything could be explained and solved through this prism. "All of the answers, all of the clues allowing us to dismantle Osama bin Laden's organization, can be found in Saudi Arabia," he told me, emphasizing "the inability of American diplomacy to get anything out of King Fahd" concerning terrorist networks.[4] The reason? There was only one: corporate oil interests. Could this single explanation keep the United States from investigating one of the principal terrorist networks in the world? Yes—for the simple reason that the American administration had refrained from using the investigation as a means of putting pressure on its Saudi friends.

Since George W. Bush's election, "the FBI was even more politically engaged," O'Neill said, and that could be felt "even on [his] own investigations" regarding Osama bin Laden. "Saudi Arabia has much more pressure on us than we have toward the kingdom," he said, considering the United States's dependency on its oil and thus the State Department's need to have a "secure and stable" Saudi Arabia.

During investigations into the attack on a military installation in Dhahran on June 25, 1996, which killed nineteen American soldiers, O'Neill went to Saudi Arabia himself to convince King Fahd to get the Saudi authorities to cooperate. But that was a lost cause, because Saudi officials interrogated the principal suspects themselves, while the FBI was relegated to collecting material evidence from the bomb site. As for the relations between Al Qaeda and Saudi Arabia, the conclusions of my report[5]—which was commissioned by the French intelligence service—did not surprise O'Neill, and he confirmed that bin Laden had close ties with "high-ranking personalities and families of the Saudi kingdom" in July 2001, contrary to their public statements. He believed, however, that the chances of getting the Saudis to cooperate were slim, and he called into question the FBI's extremely "political" stance in this area, as well as that at the interior level.

Coming from one of America's top specialists in these matters, John O'Neill's revelations shed light on the potential danger of Osama bin Laden. They tell us in clear terms that the fight against terrorism was not the government's number-one priority. It was essentially out of resentment, and because he knew that nothing would change his strong beliefs, that O'Neill left the FBI in August 2001 to take a position as director of security—at the World Trade Center.

On September 11, he was at a meeting on the subject of security at the Twin Towers when the first plane hit the building. He left to call for help and to coordinate the arrival of the police, before going back into the building to help evacuate the occupants—as if to save the thousands of New Yorkers who were so dear to him. He died in the effort.

John O'Neill's testimony continues to be an essential piece of the puzzle in the fight against terrorism. It sheds light on the two principal stumbling blocks for the West in confronting these networks: oil and its geographically strategic importance; and Saudi Arabia and its religious and financial ambitions.

FOREWORD

In Washington on January 22, 2001, America appeared to be
delivered. After weeks of controversy over how to read punch bal-
lots, the United States presidential election was finally over. On
this day, George W. Bush took up residence in the White House
and, even more important, in the Oval Office. Members of the
international press watched skeptically as the governor of Texas
was sworn in.

That same evening, on the top floor of the National Press
Club building on 14th Street, several European reporters gathered at the bar. Opinions flew, castigating the new administration's Texan culture, while only a stone's throw away the
Republican team was settling into its new home. The journalists engaged in lively conversation with members of the
American press, mostly from the *Washington Post,* whose offices
are a few blocks away. The Europeans, who had witnessed the
jubilation of the inauguration, worried about the new president's lack of international awareness; his penchant for wide
application of the death penalty, which had been abolished in
so many countries; his limited knowledge of the Israeli-
Palestinian conflict; and his arrogant declarations of American
Empire which had offended many old-world observers and

decision-makers. Perched on massive barstools, surrounded by the endless cherrywood bar of the National Press Club, some of the more prudent members of the French and German press revealed their contrasting opinions, foreshadowing many more debates to come.

Others contented themselves with listing a few truths. To wit: Before the presidential campaign, Bush Junior had traveled outside the United States a total of three times; his knowledge of foreign politics was limited to that which concerned Texan oil companies—which, while they may be the most powerful of their kind in the world, were also among the biggest contributors to his campaign—and finally, the new president showed major gaps in his knowledge of the world's most vulnerable regions, especially Central Asia. Proof of this had come when he was unable to name the president of Pakistan during an interview in the middle of his presidential campaign: Pervez Musharraf, a veritable ally of the Pentagon who had to reckon with a population largely hostile to the United States.[1] Since his victory, Bush had learned how to spell at least his last name.

Of course, journalists are professionals of fragmented commentary, and sometimes incapable of complexity. For sure, young Bush never traveled the globe, and didn't figure in the ranks of the elite diplomats, but even so, he wasn't completely ignorant of world affairs. He had still been living close to his parents when his father was director of the CIA,[2] and very early on, like so many children of wealthy Texan families, George W. Bush had developed small service companies in the oil industry with strong ties abroad. These activities led him to work with businessmen from the Middle East—in particular from Saudi Arabia—as was the case when he was a director, stockholder, and paid consultant of

Harken Energy.[3] What's more, the president's close advisers benefited from considerable experience in managing world affairs, also acquired from their contact with Bush Senior and Texan oil companies. First in rank was the placid, enigmatic Condoleezza Rice. Even glossy celebrity magazines are interested in her, listing the same pedigree each time: professor at Stanford, Soviet specialist, and former security counselor (under Bush Senior) in charge of Soviet affairs. Meanwhile, from 1991 to 2000, Rice was a director of the Chevron group[4]—one of the leading oil companies in the world—in which she notably dealt with questions related to developments in Kazakhstan.[5]

On that twenty-sixth of January 2001, the men and women moving into the White House were not the isolationists we believed them to be, even if their taste in international relations possessed a vague odor of petroleum. Several thousand miles away from Washington, some people had already taken note of this.

On February 5, 2001, a thunderbolt exploded in the ordinarily quiet milieu of international diplomacy. At the United Nations Security Council, the usually restrained functionaries were flabbergasted. Less than two weeks after the American inauguration, an unexpected message had come from Kabul, though no one had yet realized the connection between the event and George W. Bush's election. On this day, for the first time in their short history, the Taliban said they were prepared to negotiate for international recognition. The "religious students" would drop their hard line.[6] The man making this announcement was none other than the foreign minister for the Taliban, Wakil Ahmad Muttawakil. To make the desired impact, he conveyed his message to a reporter from the *Times* of London, rather than a major Arab newspaper. His target audience was therefore Anglo-Saxon.[7]

As well as widespread famine, Muttawakil's country was suffering from international sanctions that were beating down with greater intensity since the United Nations Security Council's decision on December 19, two months earlier, to slap an arms embargo on the Taliban and tighten diplomatic, financial, and travel sanctions on its leaders for harboring Osama bin Laden and other wanted terrorists.[8] The Afghan foreign minister was looking for sympathetic and powerful interlocutors to help loosen the stranglehold on his country; obtain financial assistance from the IMF; and return to the conditions that had officially prevailed since 1996, when Saudi Arabia and the United States had encouraged the Taliban in their military enterprise, considering them a source of stability in Afghanistan.[9] In exchange, Minister Muttawakil was prepared to yield on many sensitive issues, the first being the extradition of bin Laden.[10]

Sanctions were severe, of course, but to what extent did the Taliban know their message would be heard by the new American administration? Had Republican representatives and the Taliban already met privately before this spectacular announcement?

What we do know for sure is that from February 5 to August 2, 2001, the United States engaged in private and risky discussions with the Taliban concerning geostrategic oil interests, among other things. These discussions involved the Taliban betraying Osama bin Laden, though at the time the Americans did not know the extent of the religious leader's power over the Afghan rulers. The suicide attacks of September 11 were possibly the outcome of this initiative. That needs further investigation. The pages that follow, however, describe this fervent conflict, largely led by the Saudi monarchy and provoked by the cynicism of a fringe group of the Republican party.

Why did some of the key players, whose responsibility in the matter is slowly being revealed, appear to be blind to the danger? The situation in Afghanistan will help answer this question.

Afghanistan is essential for any country wanting to exercise its supremacy in Central Asia, and has long been coveted by Russia, the United States, and, above all, Saudi Arabia. In Washington, it is considered the best transit zone for the extraction of Central Asia's petroleum and natural gas. In Riyadh, for members of the Al-Saud family, who control the Saudi kingdom with an iron fist, the Taliban's accession to power was ideal, since it represented an extension of their zone of influence in Central Asia. Their Wahhabite brand of Sunni Islam goes very well with the kind of Islam espoused by the Taliban. From the beginning, they have regarded these holy warriors as religious brothers who have allowed them to extend their oil-business interests in that part of the world, and above all to contain the hegemony of their neighbor, Iran, whose Shiite values they are trying to combat.[11]

Such a small territory, ruled by a group of religious fanatics, linked by so many energy interests, marked by struggles of power with international repercussions—how could it not become the crucible of the crisis that marked the beginning of the twenty-first century?

I.
SECRET LIAISONS:
THE UNITED STATES AND
THE TALIBAN

1. LAILI HELMS: LOBBYIST FOR THE TALIBAN

Even though she has been portrayed as a suburban soccer mom living in New Jersey, Laili Helms has seen her share of the world's darkest places. An American of Afghan origin, she grew up amid and got caught up in the tumultuous relations between her native and adopted countries. Her two grandfathers were ministers in Afghanistan's last royal government, and, by marriage, she is also the niece of Richard Helms, former CIA director and American ambassador to Iran. In the 1980s, while living on the East Coast, she took up the cause of the Mujahedeen, the warriors who at the time were fighting Soviet invaders. By the age of twenty-two, she was already executive director of American Friends of Afghanistan—a nongovernmental organization looked upon kindly by the State Department and the White House—whose purpose was to favorably influence public opinion regarding the Afghan Mujahedeen. She was a sort of Occidental representative in the holy war being waged against the USSR.[1]

In that capacity, the young Laili Helms organized a visit to the United States by the Mujahedeen leader Sayed Ahmad Gailani from March 20 to April 5, 1986. (During his trip, the Afghan guerrilla leader also had a lengthy discussion with then vice president George H. W. Bush, on March 21, 1986.)[2]

It was partly circumstances of history, partly her grace in dealing with Afghan religious leaders, but also her important contacts that turned Laili Helms into the "unofficial ambassador" for Afghanistan in America's powerful political circles. A product of U.S. policy in that region of the world, she had long supported the Islamist leaders favored by the American administration. By the mid-90s, she was one of many representing Taliban interests in Washington. At the time, the regime was preparing to take power in Kabul, with the blessing and financial backing of Saudi Arabia and the cautious support of the U.S. State Department.

Over the last six years, Helms had spearheaded several initiatives on the Taliban's behalf, principally with the United Nations. Her activities with the Taliban continued even after 1996, when the Taliban's leader, Muhammad Omar, gained notoriety in the eyes of the American government after carrying out summary executions. Her efforts continued even after the Taliban welcomed the fundamentalist leader Osama bin Laden in 1997, and after 1998, when bin Laden was found guilty of orchestrating the attacks against American embassies in Nairobi and Dar es Salaam. In February 1999, Helms, among others, was invited by NBC's *Dateline* to provide footage of women in Afghanistan for a report on the lives of Afghan women. For this project, the station provided her with a camera. The result: a propaganda film presenting the lives of Afghan women in a particularly optimistic light. NBC used about thirty seconds of it in their twenty-minute segment, which also included an interview with Helms.[3]

After the Taliban's request for official recognition on

February 5, 2001, Laili Helms, quite naturally, was given the job of orchestrating new relations between Afghanistan and the United States. Within a few weeks, she had worked her diplomatic magic to make sure the most important members of the Bush administration met Mullah Omar's emissaries. Within the Bush administration, her former partners from the anti-Soviet war in Afghanistan were extremely valuable contacts. In the Republican camp, officials who had strongly supported the Islamist guerrillas in destabilizing Russia held key positions yet again. Precious allies of circumstance, indeed.

The fruit of this came two months later. Between March 18 and March 23, Mohammad Omar's itinerant ambassador and personal adviser, twenty-four-year-old Sayed Rahmatullah Hashimi, made a brief trip to the United States. His visit came just after the Taliban's destruction of the centuries-old Buddha statues in Bamiyan. Despite the tense context, Helms organized several meetings for the young Afghan dignitary, including ones at the Directorate of Intelligence at the CIA,[4] and the Bureau of Intelligence and Research at the State Department.[5] Even better, Helms got her client interviews on two influential media channels, ABC and National Public Radio. This was a perfect opportunity to improve the Taliban's image, and thus facilitate negotiations. [6]

However, it wasn't all plain sailing for Hashimi. He was exposed to tough questioning on the PBS *News Hour* and on National Public Radio's *Talk of the Nation*.[7] ABC broadcast images of Hashimi's surly response to a pointed question from a female journalist, "I'm really sorry for your husband. He must have a very difficult time with you"[8] But the print media—including the *New York Times*,[9] *Washington Post*[10] and the *Wall Street Journal*—seem to be quite charmed. Nora Boustany in the *Washington Post* noted "[Hashimi's] smooth, sharp and sometimes sarcastic message from the country's rulers in fluent, idiomatic American English." He was "cynical, irreverent, even witty at times [swaggering] into Washington's most prestigious think tanks and newspapers that week with a striped silk turban and matching scarf draped over his shoulders."[11]

It wasn't hard to detect a sympathetic tone in George Melloan's *Wall Street Journal* piece either. "The 24-year-old Mr. Hashimi is a big improvement over past Taliban representatives in that he speaks excellent English and is adept at conveying Taliban anger over the U.S. and Russian making common cause against his country."[12]

In fact Melloan seemed to think that it was the Clinton administration's close relations with Russia that was the cause of Afghanistan's dire predicament. "The U.S. was Afghanistan's ally in the 1980s. But Bill Clinton cut off commercial contact with the Taliban in July 1999 and later that year joined with the Russians to persuade the United Nations to ground the Afghan national airline, Aryana, cutting off Afghanistan from the outside world. All this because of a Taliban refusal to hand over suspected terrorist Osama bin Laden to the U.S. Mr. Clinton launched a cruise missile attack on Afghanistan in 1998 at the height of the Lewinsky crisis, ostensibly to kill bin Laden but killing nineteen other people instead . . . the ham-handed policies of the previous administration have done a good job of alienating the leaders of a country that was once a strategic ally."

This visit provoked concern and criticism in Washington—especially from the women's movement—over how Hashimi obtained a visa, a plane ticket, security clearance, and access to American institutions—including the State Department and the National Security Council—despite travel restrictions on the Taliban leadership imposed by U.N. sanctions (the official answer was that Hashimi fell below the rank of senior official covered by the sanctions).

In fact it was only figures from the women's movement—the most consistent and principled foe of the Taliban, inside and outside of Afghanistan—who were able to suss out the purpose of Hashimi's trip: "Hashimi's visit appeared to be a public relations ploy—an attempt to create a smoke screen to mask the atrocities that the Taliban has committed against the Afghan people and especially Afghan women."[13]

Furthermore: "Possible motivations for a State Department meeting with Hashimi include the desire to keep other Muslim sects from engaging in drug, gun, and terrorist activity in Afghanistan in order to clear the way for a proposed oil pipeline from Central Asia, through Afghanistan, to Pakistan. The pipeline project has been planned by American companies since the mid-1990s."[14]

In reality, from the beginning of 1999 until August 2001, there was a concerted effort to resolve the Afghan question. The only notable progression was the Republican decision to speed up the process begun by members of the Clinton administration. For sure, there were differences of emphasis. The Bush administration deliberately played down the bin Laden factor—as the *Wall Street Journal* reported—for fear of burnishing his reputation in the Islamic world. "[The Bush administration] hope that will make it easier to win support within the Islamic world to force Afghanistan to shut down the camps supported by his organization, Al Qaeda."[15] Ironically, this approach almost dovetailed with the Taliban's public ambitions. Hashimi complained on his trip to the U.S. that the emphasis on bin Laden as public enemy number one made it harder for the Taliban to think about turning him over. "For us, it's not easy. This man has become a hero. He has become world famous because of these cruise missiles. He was nothing before." But it was the old game of appeasing the Taliban through a carrot-and-stick approach. The Taliban foreign minister's declaration on February 5 simply indicated that the leaders of Kabul—hammered by sanctions—were eager as well to come to an agreement quickly.

Both sides understood the interests at stake. In the name of energy policy, Washington would support a progressive effort for international recognition of the Taliban. In exchange, the Taliban would adopt a more peaceful brand of politics, stop harboring Osama bin Laden, and agree to stay in line with the other Sunni fundamentalist states.[16]

For the last two years, Washington had dispatched some of its most senior figures to ensure this trade-off was accomplished. For example, in January 2000, U.S. Assistant Secretary of State Karl Inderfurth met with Taliban Ambassador Amir Khan Muttaqi in Pakistan.[17] Muttaqi also met with Tom Simons, the former U.S. ambassador in Islamabad, who, as time went by, played a leading role in facilitating these discussions. From Washington's point of view, the talks came down to getting their former allies to finally fall into line.

For the White House had not always abhorred the Taliban regime. On the contrary: For several years, it was even considered a providential movement. From 1994 to 1998, the United States was relatively benevolent toward the Taliban. Of course, observers in Washington, sheltered inside the plush buildings that overlook the Potomac River, have a unique way of gauging a country's ups and downs. In financial, political, and military headquarters—from the World Bank to the Pentagon—staff members follow world affairs by watching screens filled with information on markets of primary goods, and by reading diplomatic telegrams that summarize the world's latest upheavals.

Of Afghanistan, such indicators were taken seriously. The key to Central Asia's energy reserves, the country had to be run by a strong and uncontested government in order for the United States to peacefully profit from the situation. Which is why, even after the attacks in Nairobi and Dar es Salaam in 1998—when the Taliban was openly protecting Osama bin Laden—the negotiating continued.

2. THE STATE DEPARTMENT: SPONSOR OF THE TALIBAN

It became clear that the emergence of these so-called "religious students" in 1994 was inseparable from oil and gas interests in the region. This explains why so many states and large oil corporations bet on this group of religious soldiers, whom they saw as the only ones capable of establishing a strong government, a source of stability and security.[1]

Just beyond the Afghan mountains to the north lie the rich subsoils of Turkmenistan, Uzbekistan, and Kazakhstan, a pipe dream for any oil executive were it not for the daunting geographical terrain he or she would face along the way. To extract and sell this oil and gas would require either routing it from the west through Russia and Azerbaijan to Turkey; or from the southwest through Iran; or, finally, from the south through Afghanistan. And so, it was decided that the pipeline project Chardzhu-Gwadar[2] would cross Afghanistan, passing through the city of Herat. In the same way, the pipeline project between Daulatabad (ending in Turkmenistan and linking other gas installations in the region) and Multan (Pakistan) would run through the Afghan valleys, most notably near Kandahar. Clearly the Afghan solution represented a major political interest for a number of Western oil companies and their governments, especially the United States. It was an ideal alternative to the routes that flirted with Russia or went through Iran. Those solutions would require negotiating directly with Moscow or Teheran and put the United States in the position of having to ask for favors—a nightmare situation for Washington, which was pushing for initiatives that would restrict these countries' influence in Central Asia.[3]

In southwestern Afghanistan, the city of Kandahar—famous long ago for its oasis—was now known as the birthplace of the Taliban movement. The city was a religious center for the Pashtun ethnic group, which is the majority in the country, as opposed to Kabul, the administrative and commercial hub more open to the outside world.[4] From the first hours of resistance to the Soviet invasion in 1979, it was Kandahar that attracted a number of clans ruled by Muslim warlords determined to resist the Red Army.[5]

After Soviet troops withdrew in 1989, the city attracted the leading warlords of different Pashtun movements, who espoused a Sunnism more radical than ever. For the Mujahedeen who returned to this southern valley, the guerrilla war against the Soviets was above all a holy war. Saudi Arabia provided ample amounts of money and military advisers (the highest-ranking being the young Osama bin Laden, honorable servant of the General Intelligence Department, the Saudi secret service). While the civil war with other ethnic groups was taking place in Kabul and other northern cities,[6] many Pashtun warriors put down their Kalashnikovs for a while in order to study religious teachings in local schools. After jihad, they were intent on perfecting their knowledge of the Koran, and entered various *madrassa* in the Kandahar region. Many of these schools maintain spiritual and material ties to the powerful Koranic school Deobandi, located in India and known both for its radical positions and for its proselytizing in favor of a pure Islam (the cult of saints is notably prohibited).[7]

A young Mujahedeen leader, Mohammad Omar, belonged to one of them. Upon his return in 1990, at the age of twenty-seven, Omar exuded the image of a war hero, a courageous soldier willing to give his life for the fight against the Soviets. Such bravery cost him his right eye after he was hit by rocket fire in 1989. He personified the future of Afghanistan, a country where women were not allowed to hold office, and where legendary tribal chieftains either perished or fled the onslaught. For Omar, these years of studying the Koran were part of a natural progression of events. Up until that point in his Mujahedeen career, he had followed a very militant Islamic structure;[8] he fought in the mountains for General Younis Khalis's Hezb-I-Islami (Islamic Party). But now he wanted to become a spiritual leader, and to shed his military clothes, which were too restricting for his taste.

From this point in Omar's career, there are several different versions of the story, many of them legends spread by Taliban propaganda. The "official" story is as follows: Between 1992 and 1994, Mohammad Omar, overcome with a sense of spiritual piety and devotion, decided to help defend the poor people in the valley of Kandahar by fighting the warlords who were leading a way of life contrary to Islam. During this time, he was regarded as a kind of Robin Hood.[9] It is said that he defeated a sodomite warlord and slit the throat of a depraved

Mujahedeen soldier. He quickly became the charismatic leader that all of the "friends" of Afghanistan were hoping for. In other words, their Pakistani neighbors and a few businessmen in the oil industry.

Pakistan had been concerned about the Afghan situation ever since the outbreak of civil war after the Soviet withdrawal, in 1989. Since its creation in 1947, Pakistan has grappled with endemic diplomatic crises with its Indian neighbor. The two countries have been waging constant battles over the disputed province of Kashmir. For Islamabad, it was vital that its Afghan neighbor to the north stay in the hands of a friendly government that could exercise real authority. If not, it would risk being smothered between two zones of instability. Pakistan's national interests were therefore at stake. From that moment on, Pakistan used the Taliban as a pawn in a deadly regional balancing act.

Though they could have chosen to side with any other group within the Afghan mosaic, the Taliban's Pakistani supporters thought the group had many good, and strategic, qualities. In Pakistan, the Jamiat Ulema Islami party, which played a key role in Parliament, regarded them as religious brothers and encouraged the authorities to support them. The Pakistani Inter-Services Intelligence (ISI) regarded them as the true heirs of the 1980s Mujahedeen, whom they had trained, and still exercised control over. This was not the case with other Afghan groups, who kept their distance. In Riyadh, King Fahd's Saudi government, the leading financial supporter of the ISI, encouraged the movement.[10] Saudi leaders were concerned about the chaos prevailing between 1989 and

1994, because they saw Afghanistan as an opportunity to extend their zone of influence and spread their pure form of Islam, Wahhabism.[11]

There were other, more earthly issues at stake as well. Saudi religious leaders were always watching out for Iran, which borders Afghanistan and adheres to the Shiite sect of Islam.[12] In Riyadh, the Minister of Cults made appeals that could not be ignored by the king and his crown prince. If Teheran managed to take over Kabul, their enemy Shiite brothers would hold the key to Central Asia.

Washington shared this analysis. After the 1979 hostage crisis at the American Embassy in Teheran, the State Department's most important objective in the region was to support the pro-Western monarchies and weaken the Islamic Republic of Iran.[13] From then on, American security analysts wanted to contain the Shiite sphere of influence in that region; supporting radical Sunnites like the Taliban was an excellent way of accomplishing that. Other, more economic, reasons drove them to such a position. Starting in 1991, various American oil companies, including Chevron, became heavily involved in Kazakhstan, Turkmenistan, and Kyrgyzstan. As it happened, Russia refused to allow them to use its pipelines to transport these energy resources to oil terminals.[14]

By 1994, all of the elements were in place to transform the Taliban into the peacemakers everyone had been waiting for.

3. A PIPELINE FOR
   THE TALIBAN

One man would meet these expectations and was instrumental in soliciting outside help to bring the Taliban to power. Naturally, it was an oilman. But Carlos Bulgheroni is not Saudi Arabian, or Pakistani, or American; he is Argentinean. He is the president of Bridas, the fourth-largest energy group in Latin America, based in Buenos Aires and founded after World War II.[1] In the 1970s, Bridas became a world player. With India and Pakistan on the brink of war in 1991 and 1992, Bridas executives recognized the necessity of forging partnerships with new executives in the former Soviet republics, especially in Turkmenistan. From their offices in Islamabad, they envisioned a stable Afghanistan run by leaders who were willing to cooperate with them so they could build oil and gas pipelines connecting Turkmenistan to Pakistan. Bulgheroni struck his first deal with the government of Turkmenistan in January 1992 to exploit a gas field in Daulatabad.[2] On March 15, 1995, he brought together Pakistani and Turkmen officials, who signed an agreement in principle for the construction of a pipeline crossing Afghanistan. [3]

At that point, Bulgheroni invited other oil companies to

join his business venture, including Unocal, one of the largest oil corporations in the United States.

The Union Oil Company of California was founded in Santa Paula in 1890, and changed its name to Unocal Corporation in 1983. One of the success stories of the energy industry, it became, under the direction of its president, Roger Beach, one of the "world's largest independent oil and gas producers" in the 1990s.[4] A savvy businessman, Beach immediately recognized the potential of Carlos Bulgheroni's offer—so much so that he decided he could do without Bridas's services and invest in the region without their help.[5] To improve his bargaining position and get financial backing, he enlisted the help of another group, the Saudi company Delta Oil.

On October 21, 1995, executives from Unocal and Delta Oil signed an agreement with the president of Turkmenistan, Saparmurad Niyazov, based on gas exports evaluated at $8 billion—which included a plan for the construction of a gas pipeline that would cross Afghanistan.[6] The cost of the undertaking was estimated at $3 billion.[7] At that point, support for the Taliban was not only geostrategically important, it was an economic priority.

Meanwhile, the Saudi secret services of the GID, led by Prince Turki Al-Faisal, decided to give massive financial support to the Taliban—most important, providing them with communication networks, but also with dozens of Japanese-manufactured black pickup trucks with tinted windows.[8] Saudi Arabia withdrew support for ethnic Uzbek and Tajik factions, who quickly found themselves without means and lost ground. With unanimous support, the fundamentalists stormed Kabul and took power on September 27, 1996, much to the general satisfaction of those around. "If this leads to peace, stability, and international recognition, then this is a positive development," said a delighted Chris Taggart, a Unocal vice president.[9]

The months between Unocal and Delta's deal with Turkemistan and the Taliban's takeover of Kabul saw an unusual amount of interest from the U.S., which had left the region for dead after the Soviet withdrawal in 1989. They were represented by the likes of Robin Raphel, then U.S. assistant secretary of state responsible for South Asia, and U.S. Republican senator Hank Brown, a supporter of the Unocal pipeline project as well as a recipient of campaign donations from it,[10] a longtime friend of Pakistani interests on the Senate floor, and a member of the influential Senate subcommittee on foreign relations. Both justified their interest by expressing their fear of regional instability and humanitarian disaster. Brown toured Afghanistan's rival strongholds, spoke with all warring sides, and invited them to attend a conference in Washington later that year. At that conference—which Unocal helped fund[11]—he said, "The purpose is to seek advice" about how to rebuild U.S. interest in Afghanistan and "help the Afghanis develop their own peace initiative."[12]

Raphel, expressed similar sentiments when she visited Afghanistan a few months before the Taliban seized power in April 1996: "We continue to be concerned about the humanitarian situation here and we are particularly concerned about the political instability and the potential for it spreading in the region."[13]

Another comment of hers, however, suggests that the

United States's renewed interest wasn't entirely humanitarian: "We are also concerned that economic opportunities here will be missed if political stability cannot be restored."[14]

Perhaps what she had in mind was what Marty F. Miller, vice president of Unocal, told the *Washington Post* when he revealed that his firm had plans to build "two mammoth pipelines across Afghanistan to carry oil and gas from Turkmenistan to Pakistan," but all potential sources of financing "have consistently advised us that there will have to be a single entity governing Afghanistan that has international recognition" before they will invest any money.[15]

While the United States may have positioned itself as a independent mediator, the Kabbani government, then besieged by the Taliban, accused the U.S. of ignoring Pakistan's support for the Taliban. "What is important is that the United States, despite the fact they knew Pakistan was arming and supplying the Taliban, remained silent on the issue," Kabbani said.[16]

Their silence ended tentatively after the Taliban's takeover. Glyn Davies, a State Department spokesman, said the United States could see "nothing objectionable" about the brand of Islamic law the Taliban had imposed on the regions it controlled, while Senator Brown chimed, "These fellows are deeply religious and strongly anti-Soviet." And as the journalist Richard McKenzie recounted in the *New Republic* two years later, "[In] one encounter a few months before the Taliban entered Kabul, a mid-level bureaucrat at the State Department perched on his couch and tried to convince me that the Taliban was really not such a bad bunch. 'You get to know them and you find they really have a great sense of humor,' he said."[17]

This, a movement that even the government of Iran denounced as "medieval."[18]

Back in the United States, members of two of the most influential foreign policy research institutes took up the Taliban cause: Barnett Rubin, an Afghanistan specialist at the Council on Foreign Relations, had this to say in October 1996: "The Taliban do not have any links to Islam's international radicals. In fact, they hate them."[19] While Zalmay Khalilzad, a senior strategist at Rand Corp. who had served in the State and Defense departments in the Reagan and Bush administrations, and a Unocal consultant, urged the United States to engage the Taliban: "Based on recent conversations with Afghans, including the various Taliban factions, and Pakistanis, I am confident that they would welcome an American reengagement. The Taliban does not practice the anti-U.S. style of fundamentalism practiced by Iran—it is closer to the Saudi model. The group upholds a mix of traditional Pashtun values and an orthodox interpretation of Islam."[20]

How eloquent! Only one month after taking power, the Taliban were already talking about the Islamic Emirate of Afghanistan, and how they owed their spectacular ascent to the Saudi fundamentalist dictatorship that supported them financially—and especially to the religious leaders of that country, who espoused an ultra-orthodox and reactionary brand of Islam. Mohammad Omar proclaimed himself Spiritual Leader and assumed the title of mullah. Then the Taliban summarily executed the former pro-communist president

Mohammad Najibullah, who had taken refuge at UN premises in Kabul.

At the end of a terrible Afghan winter in 1997, the Taliban's call seemed to be heard. With the religious militias controlling almost 90 percent of Afghanistan, oil experts and diplomats posing as businessmen were already on-site. The pipeline project was on its way to realization. Unocal expanded its teams in Islamabad, sending several representatives to Kabul and especially to Kandahar, the stronghold of their new and precious allies. The oil company didn't skimp on expenses in any area.[21] It offered $900,000 to the Center for Afghani Studies at the University of Nebraska, which spent the money funding various education infrastructure projects in Kandahar.[22] Eminent figures joined the charitable enthusiasm. Among them was Gerald Boardman, the former director of the Peshawar office of USAID (U.S. Agency for International Development), who opened a school to train "some 400 Afghan teachers, electricians, carpenters and pipe-fitters to help Unocal lay the pipeline."[23] Robert Oakley, former U.S. ambassador to Pakistan, was hired to oversee the diplomatic division of this "Afghan gold mine."[24] He set up shop in Islamabad in the offices of CentGas, a local consortium created by Unocal.[25]

On the Saudi side, in addition to Delta Oil, all of the princely families wanted to profit from the new Taliban leadership, which was bringing order to the region. As for Bridas, after Unocal's betrayal, the Argentinean company was eager to find new partners. It approached Ningharco, a Saudi company with close ties to Turki Al-Faisal, director of intelligence for the GID.[26]

4. MULLAH OMAR: A TROUBLESOME ALLY

Just when all the political and business deals were progressing so well, when Taliban representatives were being wooed by their respective suitors with trips to Houston and Buenos Aires, fierce fighting erupted in the spring of 1997 in northern Afghanistan, in the city of Mazar-e-Sharif, the opposition stronghold of Uzbek general Rashid Dostum, after the Taliban tried to retake this vital northern city. The Taliban were initially successful when they allied with General Malik Parwalan, Dostum's deputy and most bitter rival. Dostum fled Mazar-e-Sharif after Mailk's betryal, but the Taliban's ambitions backfired almost immediately, as Malik realized that the Taliban were using him as a foil to impose their complete control on the city. As the Taliban tried to impose order by declaring *sharia* law (Koranic law) and trying to disarm the locals, Malik and the locals turned on them. The ensuing insurrection ended with the Taliban's humiliation and the slaughter of its soldiers. This only helped to compound the Taliban's siege mentality.[1] To the great disappointment of Unocal and Bridas, the Taliban made several abhorrent political mistakes that "officially" put them on the radar screen of the international community, forcing their interlocutors to distance themselves.

There were reports of the Taliban mobilizing Afghani and Pakistani teenagers to replenish the Taliban's frontline forces outside Mazar-e-Sharif. There were reports too of opium production booming under the Taliban, something the Taliban did little to hide. "We let people cultivate poppies because farmers get good prices," the chief of the Taliban's drug control unit told the journalist Ahmed Rashid in April, 1997.[2] There were also the ghoulish public executions of criminals in soccer stadiums, where thousands of adult men would gather in the stands in silence as they witnessed the relatives of the crime victim mete out Taliban-style justice with a Kalashnikov against the accused.

And there was this announcement from the Department for Promoting Virtue and Preventing Vice: "Stylish dress and decoration of women in hospitals is forbidden. Women are dutybound to behave with dignity, to walk calmly and refrain from hitting their shoes on the ground, which makes noises."[3]

It was their severity toward women that made the international community gradually take notice. Perhaps September 28, 1997, was a turning point. On that day, Emma Bonino, the commissioner of the European Union in charge of humanitarian affairs, visited Afghanistan to see things for herself. She was struck immediately by the Taliban's reactionary ways. Accompanied by several journalists and directors of humanitarian organizations, she assessed the Taliban's damaging effects, especially on women, education, and civil liberties. "This is an example of how people live here in a state of terror," she said after several journalists in her entourage were arrested after taking photographs in a woman's hospital ward.[4]

Meanwhile, as the Taliban showed their true colors, Osama bin Laden entered the scene.

For almost two years, Sunni fundamentalists of Saudi origin had identified the United States as their main enemy. In their headquarters in Khartoum, Sudan, and with the help of their auxiliaries in Yemen, they planned their first attacks on the American imperialists, whom they accused of contaminating their homeland and the sacred sites of Islam. Bin Laden was one of the plan's leading advocates. Stripped of his Saudi nationality in April 1994 after having sharply criticized the ruling monarchy and its submission to the United States (to the delight of religious authorities), he was accused of instigating the attack on an American military residence in Khobar, Saudi Arabia, on June 25, 1996.[5] Saudi Arabia's rulers feared that, with his vast financial resources, bin Laden would start a radical Islamic movement to fight the corruption of the monarchy, and use veterans from the war against Russia in his endeavor. Around the same period of the attack, bin Laden was spotted in Afghanistan on several occasions, in the city of Jalalabad, territory of the fundamentalist leader Gulbuddin Hikmatyar, his former comrade-in-arms during the guerrilla war against the Soviets and—more important—Mohammad Omar's former right-hand man.

Bin Laden's trip back to Central Asia in May 1996 was his first since 1991, and was prompted by his expulsion from Sudan after his protector, the Sudanese head of state Omar al-Bashir, came under pressure from the Saudis to expel bin Laden.

Even though bin Laden had been linked to terrorism since

the 1993 World Trade Center bombing, that his name had started to crop up in CIA reports as a financier of terror,[6] the Clinton administration became fully aware of the scope of bin Laden's operations only after General Wayne Downing completed an "informal" report at the request of the deputy secretary of defense, John White. An antiterrorism expert,[7] Downing had just retired in February of 1996, after having directed the Special Operations Command of the U.S. Army for several years. After the attack in Khobar, when authorities in Riyadh refused to allow FBI agents to investigate the site, the Pentagon chose General Downing to privately conduct research on the situation, and to do so outside of any judicial context.[8]

Oil companies, diplomats, and the Department of Commerce were increasingly troubled by the Taliban regime's evolution and its relationship with the new enemies of America. In November of 1997, Secretary of State Madeleine Albright openly criticized Afghanistan's new regime during a visit to Islamabad, condemning its treatment of women and children as "despicable."[9] Washington then officially distanced itself from the Taliban, claiming "neutrality" in the civil war and pressing Pakistan to cut off the Taliban's food and fuel supples.[10] Conflict mounted in the months that followed, and finally came to a head in the summer of 1998.

At the end of July, in Kabul, the Taliban forced all nongovernmental organizations to leave the country in a fit of pique after aid groups failed to comply with a Taliban order to relocate to new premises. This followed two years of suspicion that aid groups were undermining the Taliban's policy toward women.[11] In the north, they silenced the opposition and seized the city of Mazar-e-Sharif.[12] From then on, only a handful of relentless fighters, under the command of Massoud, continued to resist the new regime. But they controlled less than 5 percent of the territory, and were cut off from the rest of the world in the secluded mountainous region. The Taliban committed numerous atrocities during the takeover of the city, including the execution by firing squad of ten Iranian diplomats.[13] Political leaders from around the world viewed this act as the point of no return. But that wasn't all. On August 7, 1998, the American embassies in Nairobi and Dar es Salaam were attacked, killing 257 people. Osama bin Laden commanded the assaults with the logistical support of two Islamic terrorist groups well established in East Africa: Jihad and Jamaat-I-Islami. On August 20, the United States retaliated with seventy-five cruise missiles targeting the regions of Khost and Jalalabad, where Al Qaeda camps were located, and one pharmaceutical factory in Sudan. The next day, Mohammad Omar condemned the U.S. attacks and announced that his country was happily harboring Osama bin Laden.[14]

Act One had now ended. The American administration stopped all direct relations with Kabul—for only six months.

The consequences: For the time being, the oil project had collapsed. In the United States, the Feminist Majority Foundation intensified its campaign against Unocal,[15] accusing the company of supporting a dictatorship whose social policy included the subjugation of women. Hillary Clinton publicly gave her support to the organization, and Unocal gradually pulled its teams out of Afghanistan and Pakistan and closed its offices there. In Washington, the State Department's Bureau of South Asian Affairs expressed regret at the unfortunate turn of events. No one lost sight of the enormous opportunities waiting in Afghanistan if only a friendly government could take control and stabilize the country—as they hoped the religious students would have done. The idea of favoring a more moderate Taliban regime gained ground—a cynical and self-destructive tactic indeed. For many, the country was too important to give up, especially over a little disagreement with some fundamentalists who were just too accustomed to waging war.

5. NEGOTIATING AT ALL COSTS

Elsewhere, other countries might have imposed a draconian embargo, besieged the local rulers, and supported a democratic opposition. But in Washington, this was not an option. Instead, on February 1, 1999, the State Department went back to the drawing board to find a solution that would satisfy both sides. Deputy Secretary of State Strobe Talbott along with Rick Inderfurth, visited Islamabad personally to meet several Taliban representatives: He showed them proof of Osama bin Laden and Al Qaeda's culpability in the attacks in Nairobi and Dar es Salaam, gave them a letter that officially requested bin Laden's extradition, and hinted that there would be "economic rewards" if the Taliban cooperated (the caveat being that from then on the U.S. would hold the Taliban responsible for any terrorist acts by bin Laden).[1]

Too many countries were showing interest in the situation and interfering with the debates. Therefore a less visible forum was used. At the initiative of Russia and the United States, the international group 6+2 had been formed in the fall of 1997, which took shape under the auspices of the United Nations. The group was composed of the six countries bordering Afghanistan—Pakistan, Iran, China, Uzbekistan, Tajikistan, and Turkmenistan—as well as Russia and the United States. It was a true legacy of Cold War–era strategy. Outside of any restrictive legal framework but with the benediction of the UN, once again—twenty years later—Washington and Moscow were determining the fortune of Afghanistan. The only notable differences: This time, the two governments were dealing directly with each other, taking into account the strategic objectives of the neighboring countries, and were not clashing with each other by way of Afghan intermediaries. The 6+2 group however had been hobbled by internal feuding between Pakistan and Iran and derailed by the crises of 1998. But Lakhdar Brahimi, the seasoned diplomat chosen by the UN secretary general to organize and supervise relations with the Taliban was unleashed again. During his UN service, Brahimi was considered a key figure by all of the players in the Afghan arena. At the UN headquarters in New York, American and Russian ministers spoke highly of him. Quite naturally, he was chosen to lead the 6+2 project. In early 1999, he could be seen everywhere in the valleys of Kandahar, in Pakistan, and especially in Riyadh.[2] He met King Fahd there in February of that same year, and probably Prince Turki Al-Faisal as well, who equipped and armed the Pakistani secret services of the ISI, the Taliban legions, and the first Mujahedeen militants who counted Osama bin Laden among them in the 1980s.[3]

Following Brahimi's shuttle diplomacy a 6+2 summit took place on July 19, 1999, in Tashkent, Uzbekistan,[4] in the presence of Taliban representatives, one month after the FBI placed Osama bin Laden on its list of the ten most wanted criminals of the U.S. Justice Department. But by August UN officials were casting doubt on the process, frustrated by the fact that "outside support for the warring parties has not diminished" and disunity among members of the group (of whom some were still materially supporting the belligerents). A month later Brahimi resigned. "I am going to withdraw from the mission . . . because of the meagerness of the results achieved after two years of fruitless effort . . . by their continuous support for ceratin Afghan factions, some members of the 'six plus two' appear mostly to be paying lip service to their stated intentions."[5]

At that point, the United States still hoped to tame the Taliban. On July 6, 1999, Clinton banned all commercial and financial dealings with the Taliban and froze all their U.S. assets, in response to the Taliban's continuing to provide refuse to bin Laden.[6] Two days earlier Pakistani prime minister Nawaz Sharif visited President Clinton while New Delhi and Islamabad were battling over Kashmir.[7] The two men spoke about it and came to an understanding. Sharif was given a deadline of several weeks to order his troops out of the Kashmir mountains, where they were training and advising groups of Islamist combatants who had been recruited and trained by the secret services of the ISI.[8] He would then ask the director of the same ISI, General Khawaja Ziauddin, to go to Kandahar to plead in favor of Osama bin Laden's extradition. Around October 5, Ziauddin spoke with Mullah Omar, who then—incredibly, it seemed—agreed to cooperate. With shutting down terrorist camps and repatriating Islamic militants to Pakistan, who were wanted for sectarian murder.[9] However, Omar made no mention of bin Laden in his public statements[10] and he apparently turned down Ziauddin concerning the extradition of bin Laden.[11] On October 7, the prime minister asked the ISI to close all of its Islamic fundamentalist camps near the Pakistani-Afghan border, notably in the region called the "tribal zone."[12]

On October 12, a military coup occurred in Islamabad. The chief of staff of the Pakistani army overthrew Nawaz Sharif and took control of the country. His name: General Pervez Musharraf.[13] Though the coup was sparked by Sharif's attempt to sack Musharraf, it was the fruit of two and a half years of animosity between the military and the government. Sharif's personal corruption and political megalomania was an issue,[14] but there were concerns that Sharif was dancing too eagerly to Washington's tune on Kashmir and Afghanistan. When Musharraf took power he canceled a top secret mission being planned with the U.S. to send commandos using ISI intelligence into Afghanistan to capture bin Laden.[15] He advocated a moderate brand of Islam and immediately adopted a careful political discourse on foreign matters. The United States stayed optimistic about its power in the region, despite the fact that this sudden change essentially reduced Sharif's efforts to nothing.

In this context, on October 15, 1999, after intense pressure from the U.S. and Russia the UN Security Council passed Resolution 1267 demanding the extradition of Osama bin Laden and instituting major economic sanctions against Afghanistan, including the grounding of its national airline.

In January 2000, following signs of goodwill from Mohammad Omar, Clinton's diplomatic advisers deemed it safe to take up discussions again. On January 20, the assistant secretary of state in charge of Asia went to Islamabad. Karl Inderfurth's visit was the first contact between the administration and General Musharraf, Pakistan's new president. There, Inderfurth met two high-level Afghan leaders: the Taliban information minister Amir Khan Muttaqi, and the ambassador to Pakistan, Saeed Mohammad Muttaqi.[16] The topics of discussion were the extradition of Osama bin Laden and the normalization of relations between the Taliban and the international community.

The timing of this visit could not have been entirely unintentional. Two days earlier, UN Secretary General Kofi Annan had named a new overseer for the Taliban dossier. Francesc Vendrell earned the title of Special Representative to the Secretary General in Afghanistan.[17] From that point on, he centralized all informal talks with the Taliban and aimed to bring Osama bin Laden to justice. Based in Islamabad, Vendrell traveled all over the region, meeting representatives of the 6+2 group, the leaders of the Taliban and its opposition, pushing for a cease-fire between the groups in order to prevent the usual resumption of spring hostilities. There were talks in Jeddah in March at the Organization of the Islamic Conference (OIC), where the Taliban's Wakil Ahmad Mutatkawil voiced support for a negotiated settlement. It was not enough, however, to prevent the outbreak of fighting between the Taliban and its rivals in the next months. Nevertheless, with a drought threatening to devastate Afghanistan, the White House increased its humanitarian aid from $70 million and $100 million.

At that moment, optimism prevailed for the first time since August 1998. Vendrell traveled back and forth between New York and Kabul. That summer, 6+2 meetings took place in Washington for the first time. What's more, the participants aimed to support a reform government in Kabul, bringing together Taliban and Northern Alliance leaders. They made such good progress that Vendrell decided to invite the two enemy parties to participate directly in these discussions.

On its side, the State Department did not want to be left out, and decided to start up bilateral negotiations with Kabul again. It was soon clear how excited everyone was about these renewed relations. On September 27, 2000, the Taliban's deputy foreign minister, Abdur Rahman Zahid, attended a conference at the Middle East Institute in Washington.[18] In the course of the event, he demanded that the United Nations recognize the legitimacy of his government. No one in the audience protested this lobbying. In order to appease the crowd, he delivered promising news about the bin Laden case. The Afghan minister stated that religious leaders in his country had created a special investigative commission to look into bin Laden's involvement in the various attacks, and that his eventual extradition was possible.[19]

One month later, on October 18, 2000, the State Department recognized the work being done by 6+2, as well as the pursuit of negotiations with the Taliban in the name of pacifying Afghanistan.[20] Two weeks later, the negotiations seemed to be on the verge of conclusion. Francesc Vendrell announced that for the first time the Taliban and the Northern Alliance were considering a peace process under the guidance of 6+2.[21]

The West's great hopes for Afghanistan's stability seemed, more than ever, on the verge of being realized, and Osama bin Laden would be driven out of his sanctuary.

In the month that followed, however, these promising developments were obscured by the U.S. presidential election and the dramatic uncertainty of the result that followed. By the time Bush was declared winner by the Supreme Court the Afghan situation had changed radically. In less than a month, the diplomatic equilibrium between the Taliban and the West had been broken. Negotiations were now out of the question, as were the discussions led by 6+2. Remarks on both sides were violent and full of suspicion, even anger. On November 12, the Taliban's ambassador to Pakistan, Mullah Abdul Salam Zaeef accused Vendrell of interfering in Afghanistan's internal affairs after he suggested that the Taliban return the city of Taloqan—a former stronghold of Masoud's anti-Taliban forces—back to the Northern Alliance.[22] Then Taliban foreign minister Wakil Ahmad Mutawakil acused the UN of impartiality, following the UN's decision to allot Afghanistan's UN seat to the anti-Taliban alliance led by Burhanuddin Rabbani. Mutakawil also disagreed with Vendrell's proposal for a government of "neutral people" to rule Afghanistan.[23]

Most inflammatory—from the Taliban's perspective—was Russia's call to harden sanctions against the Taliban,[24] and the UN Security Council resolution that the U.S. and Russia were drafting that proposed banning sales of weaponry to the Taliban but not to the opposition. The Taliban's U.S. representative, Abdul Hakeem Mujahid, fuming about such one-sidedness, said, "The Russian Federation is trying its best to keep instability in the region and [to justify] their military presence in the newly independent states of Central Asia. If the United States supports this Russian conspiracy, it will not be for the benefit of the people of the United States."[25] On December 12, 2000, before the House Committee of Judicial Affairs, Michael Sheehan sharply accused the Taliban of supporting terrorism and called on the international community to impose new sanctions against Kabul.[26] On December 19, Sheehan's demands were granted.[27] The UN Security Council passed a measure for new economic sanctions against the Taliban and a freezing of part of their financial aid. This vote represented one of the last diplomatic decisions made by the Clinton administration.

However, as soon as George W. Bush took office, there was yet another sudden change in tone.

6. CHRONICLE OF A
FORBIDDEN NEGOTIATION

(February 5, 2001–August 2, 2001)

This was the environment Laili Helms, public relations flack for the Taliban, found herself in at the beginning of 2001. After a curious declaration in the *Times* of London on February 5,[1] which invited the new administration to take up negotiations again, Helms organized a trip to the United States for Sayed Rahmatullah Hashimi, the itinerant ambassador and personal adviser to Mullah Omar. Obviously, the latest round of sanctions were hurting the Taliban. But what was it that led to the new administration's engagement?

For sure, the Bush administration's strong ties to the energy industry are cause for speculation. Like their predecessors, Republican leaders clearly understood the economic stakes involved in the stabilization of Central Asia, and no one could forget the recent pipeline projects in Afghanistan. And Texan oil and gas companies were the leading contributors to the Bush campaign.[2] Once in office, the new administration remembered its supporters' generosity. The president decided to reopen oil and gas drilling in Alaska's natural reserves on

March 29 and rejected the Kyoto Protocol on polluting emissions that was so hated by the energy sector.[3] A look at the new administration's past experience explains a great deal.

For many years, Vice President Dick Cheney was the chairman and CEO of Halliburton, one of the world's leading service contractors for the oil industry—a position he left when he agreed to run as Bush's running mate. Condoleezza Rice, director of the National Security Council—the supreme body overseeing all intelligence agencies—spent nine years at Chevron. She was a director of the oil giant from 1991 to 2000, and often dealt with issues concerning Central Asia.[4] Specifically, she worked on projects in Kazakhstan, where Chevron is well established, using her expertise on Soviet affairs (she had already worked for the National Security Council under Bush's father). Commerce secretary Don Evans,[5] who is also a close friend of George W. Bush, spent the greater part of his career in the oil sector (as CEO of Tom Brown), as did energy secretary Spencer Abraham. Kathleen Cooper, undersecretary for economic affairs, had been the chief economist for Exxon.[6] The pedigrees are much the same at more subordinate levels in the cabinet ministries.

Ultimately, Cheney's team wanted a flexible energy policy. Just four days after Bush took office, Cheney organized an informal group for this purpose, the Energy Policy Task Force.[7] Naturally, journalists and observers covering the administration's first one hundred days in office were very curious about the group's activities. On May 16, Cheney agreed to disclose a summary of the team's energy program, but only presented its general objectives. Among the task force's priorities was the development of new partnerships in Central Asia. The summary gave no more details. Piqued by this secrecy, Congress's General Accounting Office[8] sent a stern request to the White House asking for the release of details from the Energy Policy Task Force's program and of the names of its participants. The office's controller, David Walker, planned judicial proceedings in order to get the information.[9]

No one knows what influence the task force had on the Afghan project. But industry professionals only had to congratulate themselves for the White House's prompt willingness to speak to the Taliban. For the oil industry, which had just earned an even more privileged place in Washington, it was unthinkable that Central Asia be relegated to the status of so many Third World countries, useful for dumping military stockpiles. This fear became even more real when the cards changed: Moscow and Beijing were multiplying their agreements for pipelines that would exclusively control the transport of Central Asia's reserves. What's more, the Russian pipeline transporting oil from the Caspian opened that summer, while the competing American route from the West— leading into Ceyhan in Turkey—was still only in the development stage. At this pace, it wouldn't take much for the oil and gas fields of Kazakhstan, Turkmenistan, and Uzbekistan, which belonged to American companies, to be linked to Russian- and Chinese-controlled pipelines.[10]

When the United Nations had finally imposed strict sanctions on Kabul on December 19, 2000; when no one was tolerating the Taliban's tactics; when the former head of antiterrorism came to the conclusion that the religious students would continue to support terrorism; when all of the evidence was revealing itself, the administration still decided to negotiate with the Taliban. Laili Helms's mission was to paint the Taliban in a less negative light, while the White House and the State Department took care of the rest.

In European circles, diplomats tried to keep up with it all. There were murmurs of informal meetings between U.S. officials and Qazi Hussein Ahmad, a senior official from the Jamaat-I-Islami, which had merged its forces with Osama bin Laden's in the Khost valley.[11] At the State Department, these high-risk talks with the Taliban were assigned to the assistant secretary of state for South Asian affairs, Christina Rocca, who was already familiar with the region. Between 1982 and 1997, she had worked with the CIA as an agent reporting to the director of Intelligence Operations.[12] In this capacity, for several years she coordinated relations between the CIA and the Islamist guerrillas, and supervised some of the deliveries of Stinger missiles to the Mujahedeen fighters. Starting in May 2001 the former underground U.S. employee reopened her files, started up a dialogue with her contacts again, and entered the slightly less shadowy world of diplomacy.[13]

The recently stalled activities of the 6+2 group were suddenly of great interest again now that the Bush administration was up and running. Officially, leaders claimed to support the group for humanitarian reasons. It was on this pretext that, on February 12, the American ambassador to the UN, Nancy Soderberg, stated that—at the request of Francesc Vendrell—the United States would try to develop a "continuing dialogue" with the Taliban,[14] of which Vendrell would be in charge of its administration. In this capacity, between April 19 and August 17, he made five trips to Kabul and Kandahar to talk with the Taliban.

There was a difference from the 6+2 meetings that took place that July in Berlin. The gathered representatives from those 6+2 countries did not hold official positions in their representative countries; instead, these were figures who had distinguished careers in the diplomatic field, former ambassadors, career diplomats, ex–foreign secretaries, many who had known each other as opposite numbers in their careers. This was what was known as "level-2" diplomacy, an excellent way for foreign ministries to float ideas, test waters, while using trusted but unofficial intermediaries so not to compromise each respective government. This secretive "sub-group" was composed of Robert Oakley, former U.S. ambassador and Unocal lobbyist; Tom Simons, former U.S. ambassador to Pakistan; Nikolai Kozyrev, a former Russian special envoy to Afghanistan; Saed Raja Khorrasani, former Iranian representative to the UN; and Niaz Naik, Pakistan's former foreign minister. According to Niaz Naik, at least three rounds of meetings took place in Germany, under Vendrell's authority, in November 2000, and then March and July 2001. The meetings focused on getting the Taliban to sign an armistice with the Northern Alliance, creating a government of national unity, and obtaining the extradition of Osama bin Laden. "We would . . . try to convey to them that if they did certain things, then, gradually, they could win the jackpot—get something in return from the international community."[15] The objective was to convince the Taliban that once a broad-based government of national unity was installed and the pipeline project was in the works, there would be billions of dollars in commission—of which the Taliban, with their own resources, would get a cut.

Everyone involved wanted the radical regime to peacefully cede some of its power, and to subscribe to U.S. priorities. But the deal fell short. In Berlin on July 17, a third secret meeting was supposed to occur. Two days earlier, on July 15, the weekly newspaper *Focus* announced that a meeting was scheduled to take place in the German capital between the Taliban foreign minister and his counterpart in the Northern Alliance, Abdullah Abdullah. But the Taliban representative never showed up. In fact, ever since a certain stormy meeting took place on May 15 in Brussels, he had refused to sit in an assembly—even an informal one—organized by the same UN Security Council that was imposing sanctions on his country. The Taliban's complaint was a familiar one. The UN was being "one-sided." In early July, at the delightful seventeenth-century manor house in Weston Park in Shropshire, England, a meeting was held between the Afghan opposition, Pakistani diplomats, senior staff from the British foreign office, and— according to one report—twenty-one countries with an interest in Afghanistan [16] "under UN auspices for private teach-ins on the Afghan situation."[17] A compromise based on the return of Zahir Shah, the Afghanistan king exiled in 1973, to oversee a coalition government was approved, with especial enthusiasm by the Northern Alliance.[18]

In the course of these last talks in Berlin, and in the absence of Taliban representatives, according to the Pakistani representative Naiz Naik, the small American delegation mentioned using a "military option" against the Taliban if they did not agree to change their position, especially concerning Osama bin Laden. Naik recounted that a U.S. official had threatened, "Either you accept our offer of a carpet of gold, or we bury you under a carpet of bombs."[19] U.S. representative Tom Simons denied that any such straightforward comments were made on the subject. When the French daily *Le Monde* contacted Simons to ask him to comment on the allegations made in the French edition of this book, he said, "We said in July to the [Pakistani] delegates that we were investigating the attack against the USS *Cole* on October 12, 2000, in Yemen, and that since there was solid evidence of bin Laden's involvement, one had to expect a military answer. Now, one can always inflate such a declaration to see this as a global threat against the Taliban. But the American declaration related only to the USS *Cole* investigation. As for carpets of gold and carpet bombs, we actually discussed the need for a plan to rebuild Afghanistan, which would follow a political agreement." Simons added: "It is possible that an American participant, acting mischievously, after some glasses, evoked the gold carpets and the carpet bombs. Even Americans don't avoid the temptation to act mischievously."[20]

Lee Coldren, a member of the U.S. delegation, confirmed the broad outline of the American position at the Berlin gathering: "I think there was some discussion of the fact that the United States was so disgusted with the Taliban that they might be considering some military action."[21]

Naik claims however that he was told that Washington would launch its operations from bases in Tajikstan, where American advisers were already in place. He was told that Uzbekistan would also take part and 17,000 Russian troops were also on standby.[22]

Whether we rely on Naik's testimony or the former U.S. ambassador's, which doesn't necessarily contradict Naik's, one has to focus on the Pakistani representatives' knowledge regarding the statement. It is clear that in July 2001, a U.S. representative, speaking an an informal meeting, but mandated by their government to do so, in specific or general terms, whether mischievous or not, whether drunk or not, evoked the option of a military operation against Afghanistan.

And no doubt, the Pakistani delegation reported back to the foreign ministry and to the secret services, and word reached the Taliban. "In late July, Islamabad and Pakistani military circles were buzzing with rumors of war," Pierre Abromovic reported. "According to a semi-official source at the Quai d'Orsay [French foreign ministry] it is possible that, by inflating what Simons had said, the Pakistani secret service were trying to pressure the Taliban to expel bin Laden."[23]

On July 17, yet another point of no return was crossed. In a short statement, the French minister of foreign affairs acknowledged the failure of the Berlin meeting, without any further explanation. After September 11, however, this statement took on a whole new meaning: "Mr. Hubert Vedrine met this morning with Mr. Francesc Vendrell, special representative to the Secretary General of the United Nations and overseer of the special mission in Afghanistan. Mr. Vendrell informed him of the deadlock in the political situation. The two leaders explored options that would lead to favorable developments, in particular the support that the international community could bring to the king's efforts to bring together representatives of Afghan society."[24]

What king? Naturally, at that point, no one (or very few) knew what this was about. The events that followed would explain that the French minister's statement was referring to the former king of Afghanistan, Zahir Shah, who had been called upon months earlier to take the Taliban's place in Kabul, and to eventually include them in his unified government. In fact, starting on May 16, Francesc Vendrell was discussing matters with the king in Rome and examining the conditions of his return to Kabul.[25]

Thus, during the same period, in July, the religious students received two messages from the West: One, an option was being considered against them in order to capture Osama bin Laden; And two, discussions were under way with the former king for him to take power in Kabul. All of these elements, taken together, were proof that the West was rejecting the Taliban, once and for all. They were already talking about successors. Was the Taliban taken by surprise? Perhaps. In Islamabad on August 2, the tireless Christina Rocca spoke with the Taliban ambassador and demanded the extradition of bin Laden.[27] Was this the ultimate bravado?

Since 1999 Mohammad Omar's constant flip-flops and obscurantist politics proved that he wasn't really planning to take the democratic route, or to relinquish support of his ally and religious brother bin Laden. And besides, who really knew which of these two men exercised more power over the other? The fundamentalist millionaire, educated in one of the wealthiest Saudi families, who traveled the Arab world mobilizing extremist leaders everywhere? Or the Pashtun peasant, educated by the Mujahedeen in the remote mountains of Afghanistan, in favor of a radical Islam and capable of training his comrades-in-arms? No one knows. But since September 11, everyone regrets not having wondered about it sooner.

We pause to take a deep breath. Naturally we hesitate to speculate about whether the Taliban and its Al Qaeda supporters might have tried to anticipate a military action against them by launching a devastating and horrendous attack on U.S. soil on September 11, 2001. Bin Laden, after all, knew he was being hunted long before July 2001, and there had been a continual tug-of-war between the U.S. and the Taliban. Moreover, given the nature of the September attacks, on the surface it appears that many months, if not years, of planning went into them. Nevertheless, we now know that the Taliban was under the influence or control of bin Laden, that he and his organization were more than just guests living under Taliban control. And at the beginning of August 2001 the Taliban and its terrorist allies knew their days were numbered. Was the statement made in Berlin and relayed to the Taliban by the Pakistanis, understood as a signal by them? Did they launch a preemptive strike? We have no clear answer to that, but the months from February to August 2001 must be independently investigated, in the same way that such an investigation also needs to focus on to what extent the Bush administration knew (or didn't know) and whether the right steps were taken to avoid this tragedy.

7. THE IMPOSSIBLE INVESTIGATION

February 1996. Three months after the attack against the National Guard building in Riyadh that claimed five American lives, the United States intelligence services were intensifying their investigations into the network of the man who had already been identified as the ringleader: Osama bin Laden.

From that day onward, bin Laden, who until that time had simply been observed from a distance, now became a major target for investigators. Everything was set in motion to identify his network and destroy its operational structures.

Certainly, there were diplomats who disapproved of this inquiry, preferring instead to negotiate with some of bin Laden's protectors, even if it meant their not being put on trial, but the political powers-that-be seemed to have decided to "fight it out." President Clinton, for instance, signed a counterterrorism bill in April 1996 that expanded the federal government's power to fight terrorism, and thus combat the Al Qaeda network.[1]

For the United States, these measures did not seem to contradict the dialogue with the Taliban and the unconditional support given to Saudi Arabia. The superpower believed that it could conduct two distinct policies leading to two different objectives, which in reality were intimately tied: the political stabilization of the Taliban regime and the war against Al Qaeda, which had availed itself of Afghanistan that May.

As the investigation advanced, these two objectives turned out to be incompatible and irreconcilable, since the United States could not accommodate itself with the Taliban and at the same time let the FBI point a finger at the warlords and the support they gave to terrorism.

In the face of this contradiction, the United States made the historic choice to favor diplomacy over security. It persuaded itself that bin Laden was a lesser evil, "under control" in a country that was offering him temporary refuge. It also believed that bin Laden did not constitute a direct and immediate danger to the country's security. His scope of action, it was thought, was politically and geographically limited. Certain countries insisted on this line, countries that had no interest in seeing a vast international investigation launched that could shed light on their own complicity. Even recently, the Saudi interior minister, Prince Nayef, declared that bin Laden was nothing but an "instrument" and doubtless not the commander of the attacks on September 11.[2]

The United States turned to its allies in the European intelligence community and spun a similar story: that bin Laden was a renegade from the Saudi kingdom, that he was isolated, that he had no relations with his family or that he had little support from them, especially in the heart of the Arab world. The idea that the Arab world would be indifferent to bin Laden's message was a dangerous one and, as we now know, ultimately fatal.

A former FBI agent described the paradox of the Clinton years succinctly: "In eight years of the Clinton administration, we took one single initiative against the terrorists. We sent sixty-six Cruise missiles into an aspirin factory in Sudan and into a camp in Afghanistan."[3] The agent was no doubt exaggerating, but his comments expose the United States's neglect toward a network described at that time as one of the most "structured" in the Islamic fundamentalist universe.

After that, the investigators were confronted with two kinds of obstacles: external ones, linked to the absence of cooperation between states such as Saudi Arabia or Yemen; and internal ones, linked to the absence of will from the U.S. administration.

Such was the case in 1996 with an investigation that concerned two relatives of Osama bin Laden, Abdullah and Omar, who lived in Virginia near Washington at the time. On February 23, 1996, an investigation was opened by the FBI about the ties of the American office of the World Assembly of Muslim Youth (WAMY), a charitable organization based in Falls Church, Virginia. (Four of the hijackers who attacked New York and Washington are listed as having lived a couple of blocks from WAMY's tiny basement office in Falls Church.)[4] The FBI suspected WAMY of being a "terrorist organization." Abdullah bin Laden at the time was president of WAMY, which was alleged to have maintained relations with several members of the Al Qaeda network.

Founded in 1972 in Riyadh to combat the "corrupting" ideas of the West that were alleged to be seducing Muslim youth and directed by Mania Al-Johani, WAMY has thirty-four offices worldwide and is funded by religious taxes from Saudi Arabia.[5] Officially, it runs holiday camps and conferences and publishes works of research. But the FBI in 1996 was suspicious of the organization's objectives, and the apparent support it gave to the terrorist networks.

The investigation of Abdullah bin Laden is a prime example of how dichotomized American thinking was: supporting the Saudi regime, yet calling into question some of its organizations.

The decision was ultimately made to close this investigation in case it called into question or simply embarrassed their Saudi ally. A high-placed intelligence source told the journalist Greg Palast that "there were always constraints on investigating the Saudi."[6] To this day, no conclusive evidence has been found to implicate WAMY despite the expulsion of several of its members by Pakistan, suspicions weighing on its Indian subsidiary's involvement in organizing attacks in Kashmir, and accusations against its members in the Philippines.[7]

As the FBI document published in the Appendix VI—which comes straight from the central files of the FBI—reveals, an investigation was opened by the FBI's Washington office into Omar and Abdullah bin Laden on February 23, 1996, and was closed without explanation, as chance would have it, on September 11, 1996.[8]

There is the case too of Mohammed Khileri, the Saudi dissident who defected to the U.S. with 14,000 documents that he claims implicates Saudi citizens in financing terrorism. The FBI refused to look at them.[9]

There was another series of surprising events. The former

mediator between the United States and Sudan, Mansoor Ijaz, a member of the prestigious Council on Foreign Relations, revealed that between 1996 and 2000, the U.S. authorities spurned on several occasions the offers of the Sudanese government to help in the fight against Al Qaeda. In order to relax the economic sanctions weighing on Sudan, President Omar Hassan Ahmed Bashir offered to extradite Osama bin Laden to Saudi Arabia or seize bin Laden's economic network in Sudan. In February 1996, several Sudanese officials visited the United States to press their case. In the face of American refusal, Sudan settled for demanding the departure of bin Laden to Afghanistan in May of the same year.

The Sudanese offer was renewed in 1997 and 1998. Mansoor Ijaz affirms that the U.S. authorities again refused all offers of help from Sudan, even when Sudan's intelligence services offered to hand over dossiers compiled on bin Laden. Among these documents were intelligence on the activities of a Syrian businessman who frequented the same mosque in Hamburg, Germany, as two of the suicide pilots of September 11. An identical offer was made again in vain in July 2000, after the attack against the USS *Cole* in Yemen.[10]

Blindness or realpolitik? Incapacity to perceive the reality of the threat, or to contain it by the very fact of ignoring it? All this helped nurture the bin Laden phenomenon during these years. The characteristic bureaucracy of the U.S. intelligence services clearly did not help define a clear position on this matter and reduced the evidence gathered to a series of faint signals that the administration was incapable of integrating into its analytical process.

Aside from bureaucratic obstacles, political or analytical blindness, the principal factor that explains America's poor response to the fundamentalist phenomenon is cultural. This was in evidence during a hearing before Congress, when the CIA director declared that "it would be wrong to separate the possibility of Iranian or Iraqi state terrorism" concerning the attacks of September 11.[11] So, the myth of state terrorism, of which Al Qaeda is precisely the counterexample, continues to enjoy favor in American government circles. Operationally we know it is on its way out, yet it continues to hold sway as a political argument—as if nothing had changed since the Cold War, as if bin Laden had never breached the narrow frontiers of the United States. It's as if the United States were incapable of taking into account the considerable mutation of terrorism in the past twenty years, or rather, as if certain people were looking for useful political scapegoats to justify a planetary war against "the axis of evil."

Contrary to their European counterparts, in particular the French, the U.S. security services appreciated the dangers of Islamic fundamentalism only when it was too late. To the initial inadequacy of investigative methods, add the administrative constraints to which the relevant organizations were subjected. While the French antiterrorist struggle had been born out of a crisis situation, the U.S. effort, by contrast, was merely integrated as another line of inquiry among existing fields of operation.

The considerable strides made by the French security services in the penetration of these terror networks was dictated by necessity to act quickly and decisively to combat the threat. Also, the antiterrorist fight was confined to a handful of specialists who through their experience in the field had rapidly acquired a unique understanding of the phenomenon. These were men and women who, confronted by the immediacy of the attack, always put the interests of the antiterrorist fight before all other political, diplomatic, or economic interests and because of this always enjoyed the attentive ear of government

One single but striking example can illustrate this cultural difference: the case of Zacarias Moussaoui, the French citizen arrested in the United States on August 17, 2001—less than a month before the attacks—for visa violations, who turned out to have been enrolled since February 2001 in a flight school in Oklahoma frequented by several of the suicide pilots of September 11.[12] The so-called twentieth suicide bomber, whom the world discovered after the attacks on the World Trade Center, was not unknown to the Western intelligence services. It is even certain that officials of these services, among them the director of the CIA, had him in mind when these murderous attacks occurred. Indeed, the director of the CIA admitted having a thick file on the suspect one month before the attacks.[13]

Officially, however, neither the FBI nor the CIA had serious evidence that would allow Moussaoui to be interrogated before the attacks. As proof of this, a request for special surveillance as part of an antiterrorist procedure had been refused to the FBI on the grounds that evidence for his involvement in terrorism was insufficient. Moussaoui was therefore held at an Immigration and Naturalization Service

(INS) location in Minneapolis and wasn't transferred to FBI custody until after September 11. The European intelligence services, notably the French, had already alerted the FBI to the Moussaoui case, at least once in August 2001—but the information sent, according to the Americans, was insufficient to put him under surveillance. This official version is acknowledged freely. The FBI did not hesitate in certain cases to contact investigative journalists about the matter in order to assure them, without material proof, that the information in their possession was if not insufficient, at least inadmissible.[14]

We can reveal, however, that one month before the attacks of September 11, French counterintelligence services relayed evidence, the "insufficiency" of which remains to be proven. History will judge. Indeed, according to corresponding accounts taken from highly placed sources who have seen the relevant files, the French alerted the Americans about Moussaoui at this stage—"and not for the first time"—and passed on unambiguous intelligence, leaving no doubt as to the suspect's terrorist links. It was shown to the Americans via the usual channels that Moussaoui had made his way to Afghanistan, that he was trained in 1998 in a camp controlled by Al Qaeda, and that a strong possibility existed that he had been in contact with members of its network in Europe. Another twenty-page document that includes an interrogation of his brother, which confirms this information, was also sent to the American services.[15]

So, nearly one month before the September 11 attacks, or at least since the arrest of Moussaoui on August 17, the U.S. authorities had two fundamental pieces of evidence before them: They knew that the suspect apprehended on American soil was linked to the Al Qaeda network, which in itself should have been cause enough for prompt serious investigations; and they knew that he had taken part in flying lessons for civil aircraft.

Were the legal responses of the INS and FBI until September 11 appropriate? Could they have acted differently? No one can really know, except to acknowledge that what is at issue is the method of data processing. Intelligence is a business of gathering facts, and some might come to the conclusion that the information provided by the Europeans was "insufficient" to signal an immediate threat, while others would have taken the necessary measures to erase the slightest doubt, or at least would have taken time to analyze and confirm all suspicions. As far as they are concerned, the French believe that, placed in the same situation as their counterparts, they would have registered and investigated this information, however fragmentary.

No one can pretend that the attacks of September 11 were foreseeable, but at least we can now talk about the bureaucratic if not legal obstacles that hampered any forewarning of these plans. It's not a question of blaming one service or another, or one person or another, but of doing away with certain regulatory, legislative, or legal red tape—and to recognize that intelligence gathering is not an exact science and remains an essentially human activity, which is fallible, and the faint signals hinting at the September 11 attacks can never be considered as significant as the events themselves.

With September 11, everything changed in the United

States, or so one would think. Washington unleashed a world war against terror networks and their supporters, whoever they may be, or so we were told. So on December 4, 2001, within the framework of the fight against the financial networks of terrorism, President George W. Bush announced, amid a great media fanfare, the freezing of assets of several charities in the United States and of two Palestinian financial companies believed to be support structures for the Hamas terrorist movement. One among these, the banking institution Al Aqsa Islamic Bank, was described as the "financial branch of Hamas" by the American authorities.[16] Since 1998, however, Israel had refused to approve the bank, citing its obvious ties with Hamas. At the beginning of 2001, several antiterrorist authorities from that country even visited Citibank's headquarters in New York—Al Aqsa's partner in the United States—to warn its directors of the nature of the bank's activities. According to the Israelis, monies destined for Hamas originated from the U.S.-based Muslim charity Holy Land Foundation for Relief and Development, whose assets were frozen as part of the same measures taken in December 2001.[17]

The most astonishing point is not the foreknowledge of the intrigues of the financial institution and the tardy nature of the response but the ineffectiveness of the measures for combating the financial terror networks beyond their announcement. In effect, the bank was established with $20 million in capital by several financial groups or institutions of the first order, the highest of these being the Jordan Islamic Bank and Dallah Al Baraka (of whom we'll being hearing more in the following chapters). The Jordan Islamic Bank is the property of the Saudi Dallah Al Baraka Group, led by Saleh Abdallah Kamel, shareholder of the same bank Osama bin Laden controlled in Sudan via local subsidiary companies. To this day no measure has been taken against the assets of this powerful character from the Saudi kingdom, as if the antiterrorist fight stopped inevitably at the doors of the Arabic peninsula, even after September 11.

For those who still doubt the Saudi presence in these networks, what are we to make of the searches undertaken in Virginia in March 2002 aimed at several charitable organizations (including the Saar Foundation, Safa Trust, and the International Institute of Islamic Thought) as well as companies directed by the same people (among them Marjac Investments, Sterling Management, Sterling Poultry, and Sanabel Inc.) suspected of having given their support to terrorism?[18]

The Saar Foundation was created in 1983. Its president is Yaquk Mirza and its treasurer is Mohammad Jaghlit.[19] It turns out that Cherif Sedky, who is a trustee of the Saar Foundation, is the legal counsel to Khalid bin Mahfouz, one of the principal supporters of Osama bin Laden (see Chapter 12), and has recently presented himself as Khalid's spokesman. What's more, Cherif Sedky is a member of the board of two companies belonging to Khalid bin Mahfouz, Nimir Petroleum (once associated with the Unocal consortium to construct a pipeline in Afghanistan), and the Credit Libanais SAL bank.[20]

At the same time, according to the American authorities, the Saar Foundation and its partners appear to have been financed by the Al Rajhi Saudi family, whose patriarch,

Sulaiman bin Abdulaziz Al Rajhi, heads up an important investment bank in Riyadh, Al Rajhi Banking & Investment Corp.[21] It also turns out that Yaqub Mirza is directly tied to these interests, since he heads Sanabel Inc., at the same Virginia address as the Saar Foundation. The Al Rajhi family controls the Saudi holding company Sanabel Trade & Agricultural Industries Co. Ltd.[22]

It's not surprising to discover that the Al Rajhi family holds stock, alongside the Binladin Group and Khalid bin Mahfouz, in the Arabian Cement Company in Jeddah, whose president is none other than . . . Prince Turki Abdulaziz Al Saud.[23]

In a second round of measures, the American authorities also searched the American offices of the charitable organization called the International Islamic Relief Organization (IIRO), led by Suleiman Al Ali in Washington and Mohamed S. Omeish in Virginia.[24] Omeish is also vice president of the American Muslim Foundation, which is led by Abdurahman Alamoudi.[25] Alamoudi registered an association called Free Dr. Ashgar/Elbarasse Committee[26] at the same address in Virginia as an association already known to the FBI, since it was suspected at the time of being tied to a terrorist organization—namely the aforementioned World Assembly of Muslim Youth (WAMY), led by Abdullah bin Laden and then by Sameel Al-Moabbir.[27]

If the United States had followed the WAMY trail at that time, a certain number of pieces of evidence would have rapidly appeared about the central role this organization played in the promotion of Islamic fundamentalism.

As it is, the United States charged the principal leader of

the Benevolence International Foundation Inc. (BIF), Ennam M. Arnaout, on April 29, 2002.[28] The trial brought to light the support given the Al Qaeda network by this Illinois-based organization, especially in Chechnya and Bosnia, its frequent contacts with operatives from the terrorist network, and its financial participation in the 1993 attacks against the World Trade Center.[29]

The organization was founded by Adel Abdul Batterjee, who directed it with another member of his family, Shahir A. Batterjee, as well as Mazin M. Bahareth, from an office in Plantation, Florida.[30] There was also another office in New Jersey. The Batterjee family is one of those Saudi families that controls powerful corporate interests, holding the upper hand in the Saudi Arabian National Development Company in Jeddah.[31]

Shahir A. Batterjee, Mazin M. Bahareth, and Hassan Bahfzallah established the Triple-B-Trading-GmbH textile company in 1995 in Rethwisch, Germany. The leadership of the company was insured by a certain Abdul-Martin Tatari, who also insured the leadership at the same address of the Tatex Trading GmbH, established in 1978, of which Mohamad Majed Said of Syria is a shareholder.[32]

But the most surprising fact is that Adel A. Batterjee was until 1992 the Saudi Arabian president of the World Assembly of Muslim Youth (WAMY). There it is again. He declared in 1992 in an interview in the *New York Times* that "if a member of a charitable organization decides to join the ranks of the warriors, we cannot stop him."[33]

In order to make the connection between these organizations, established in the United States, and their Saudi sponsors, it would have been necessary only to read this prestigious American daily.

No one will ever be able to state that if one single Western service had known about the preparations for the attacks of September 11, those attacks would not have occurred. On the other hand, there are a number of factors indicating an overdue realization on the part of the United States, but one that was always subject to petty political, diplomatic, and economic interests. It remains to be seen if the American authorities really intend to attack the very sources of this fanaticism. One may doubt it in regard to the numerous examples put forth in this work.

Upstream from the "axis of evil" evoked by George W. Bush, there remains much to do on a financial, logistical, and political level to counter this form of terrorism. Beyond fancy political sound bites, the reality of these networks and their support groups forces us to consider an urgently needed revision of our diplomatic interests. The pages that follow show just how compromised one of the United States's greatest allies in the Middle East really is, and the almost insurmountable task the United States faces if its security interests are dictated by corporate necessity. As the late John O'Neill told one of the authors of this book, "All of the answers, all of the clues allowing us to dismantle Osama bin Laden's organization, can be found in Saudi Arabia."

II.
SAUDI ARABIA, KINGDOM OF MANY DANGERS

8. OF OIL AND KORAN

Religion has always played a decisive role on the Saudi Arabian peninsula, surrounded as it is by the Red Sea to the west and the Persian Gulf to the east.

In Mecca, in the year 569, Muhammad was born. Son of Abdallah and Amina, of the Quraych tribe, he became a shepherd, then a shopkeeper. At the age of forty, while he was on the mountain of light where he liked to meditate, he received the revelation from the Angel Gabriel, who announced that he had been chosen as a *rasoul* (messenger) by God. Little by little, the angel dictated the words of the Koran, which he would bring to men. The revelation took twenty-three years. It was in the year 630 that Mecca's population converted to Islam, and the Prophet died shortly after, in 632.

But this cradle of the Islamic world would not necessarily become the site of a new civilization. Mecca was indeed the place of pilgrimage where all good Muslims had to travel, but it could not compete with the gleaming Emirate of Cordoba, stretching across the Arab-Islamic world from the Pyrenees to India.

The Prophet's land was arid, as if abandoned by God. Flanked by unwelcoming deserts to the north and south, it was made up of a succession of sandy plains and a plateau

3,300 feet high, where cold and rainy winters were followed by dry and suffocating summers.

The dry climate forced many nomad populations to migrate north to Iraq and Syria, and west to Egypt and North Africa. For ten centuries, these territories so hostile to man, where rare tribes of nomad shepherds lived, passed from hand to hand before falling under the division of the Ottoman Empire in the sixteenth century, with the exception of the region of Najd, the plateau of Central Arabia.

It was there, in the heart of Najd, that the future Arabian kingdom, cradle of Islam's holy sites, was born. Around 1745, Muhammad bin Abd al-Wahhab, a religious dissident who had been chased out of his native oasis for his radical interpretation of the Koran, found refuge in Dir'iyyah, an oasis controlled by the Al Saud clan. His ideas collided with the softness he saw in the local religious practices. The leader of the tribe, Muhammad bin Saud, adopted Wahhab's strict faith and literal interpretation of the *sharia* (Koranic law). Poetry, music, tobacco, jewels, and anything considered a novelty were prohibited.[1] And so, the reformist movement of Wahhabism was born. Its central belief is the unique singularity of God, the only entity the faithful should worship. It rejected all other cults believing in intercessor spirits or saints. Anyone violating the word of the Koran was severely punished.[2]

Wahhab the religious leader and Saud the warrior—who would give the country his name—became allies, making a sacred pact to spread the cause and lead the faithful on a path to God. And so it was, from the very beginning, that faith and power were intimately connected. They brandished the saber high in order to impose their interpretation of the Koran. The first demonstrations of force were attacks against the worshipping of objects, such as trees, rocks, and tombs, which the locals believed to have magical properties. They stoned adulterous women, cut off the hands of thieves, and made sure the five daily prayers were scrupulously observed.

Muhammad bin Saud trained his warriors to conquer Arabia, and eventually the Al Saud territory grew larger. But it took forty years to unify the immense region of Najd. The Saudi influence quickly stretched into Shiite territory to the heart of Oman and Qatar, though Kuwait and Bahrain resisted. Muhammad's grandson, Saud, known as al-Kabir the Great, took over Yemen, the Syrian desert, and Southern Iraq. In 1801, the Saudi forces conquered the holy Shiite city of Kerbala, in Iraq. It wasn't until the beginning of the nineteenth century that the Ottoman Empire began to fight back against this amputation of its territory. In 1811, Turkey sent 8,000 soldiers there. The battle lasted seven years and ended with the destruction of Dir'iyyah, the Al Saud capital. Abdallah, descendant of the Al Saud dynasty, was delivered to the Ottoman court and executed in Constantinople.

But the little state was not so easily destroyed. It rose from the ashes in 1824 in the new capital of Riyadh, while Istanbul watched carefully, trying to contain its smaller neighbors expansionist attempts. However, internal power struggles weakened the Al Saud state, which fell again in 1880, and Riyadh became attached to the pro-Ottoman city of Hail in the Northwest. The region then came under the dual influence of Turkey and the United Kingdom.

Another descendant of Muhammad bin Saud had been in power during the collapse of the second Saudi state. It was clear from the first conquests that the Al Saud tribal leadership was a family affair. More precisely, it was an affair of two families with convergent interests. Wahhab and his descendants were responsible for religious matters, making sure the people stayed obedient to the ruling power by legitimizing it, while Saud and his descendants exercised the political authority, making Wahhabism the state religion. Temporal and spiritual powers went hand in hand, and both benefited from the arrangement.

The Saudi Arabian kingdom of today was born from the upheavals of World War I. But before that, in the beginning of the twentieth century, Muhammad bin Saud's descendant Abd al-Aziz, who was barely twenty years old and had been exiled in Kuwait, recaptured the former capital of Riyadh. He won back his ancestors' power with the help of a commando team of just fifty men in 1902. With the help of the British and Lawrence of Arabia, who led the Arabs in a revolt against the Turks, the young prince hoped to conquer all the territories where his ancestors' flag had once flown. In 1918, the emirate became autonomous again in the region of Najd. In 1921, Abd al-Aziz defeated the tribal coalition of Chamar, and in 1924 took control of the sacred city of Mecca. The Al Saud-Wahhabis detroyed the tombs of the Hashemites, who were descendants of Muhammad and rivals of the Al Saud for religious power. In 1925, Medina fell as well. From 1923 to 1925, Abd al-Aziz annexed the kingdom of Hijaz. Recognized as sultan of Najd and proclaimed king of Hijaz, he formed in 1927 the "Kingdom of Hijaz, Najd and its dependencies."

The takeover was swift. Perhaps too swift. In outflanking the territories of Jordan, Syria, Iraq, and Yemen, the Saudis jeopardized the fragile equilibrium restored by the British, who controlled the protectorates in the Gulf region. Abd al-Aziz heeded the warning, and bowed to the boundaries set by the United Kingdom, leaving his dreams of conquest behind. But the Ikhwan Wahhabis, a fringe group of recently settled Bedouins, wanted to continue to spread the faith, and challenged the king. In the battle of Sibila, Abd al-Aziz defeated the Ikhwan, marking the end of the expansionists.

In September 1932, the Saudi Arabian kingdom was created, unifying the kingdoms of Najd and Hijaz. Its definitive borders were set in 1934. Thirteen provinces make up this ocean of sand between Africa and Asia, which spans an area four times the size of France and occupies almost the entire Arabian peninsula. Without a written constitution at the time, the kingdom was governed by the Koran. Abd al-Aziz, a towering figure at more than six feet tall, became the absolute monarch. The man who conquered the lands of his ancestors and proved himself to be a master of desert war wasn't the type to share power. In his mind, there would be no government, and especially no political parties. The authoritarian king's only concept of government was himself. Meanwhile, the British let him be, remembering how he had stayed in line in 1915. Though he encouraged the settlement of the Bedouins and constructed the beginnings of a road network, the king did not necessarily plan to lay the foundation for a state worthy of the name. Rather than lead his young nation down the path to modernization, Abd al-Aziz preferred to go slowly, mindful of the fact that such rapid development could break up a society consisting mostly of shepherds. Lawrence of Arabia's territory still remained an immense desert flanked by a few small, unchanged towns along the more hospitable coasts.

Though Abd al-Aziz was a perfect autocrat, the ulama, the religious leaders who were qualified to interpret the divine law, played an important role in the new regime, especially the descendants of Abd al-Wahhab, who remained the guardians of dogma. Religion was the state. The most rigorous kind of Islam was *de rigueur.* The country was run on a system mixing the *sharia* and customary law. All other cults were simply banned. After all, the country was home to the holy sites of Islam, where each year thousands, later hundreds of thousands, of followers went on pilgrimage. But a new subject of adoration would soon appear: oil.

The first concession was granted in 1923, even before the country's creation, to a group of British investors, the Eastern and General Syndicate. Since there had yet to be a drop of oil discovered in the region, the company didn't really know what to do with this concession, and hoped to sell its exploitation rights. But no other British companies would bite, and the concession fell null in 1928. Europe would end up paying for that mistake over the years as it lost its influence in the region. Soon after, American and British companies discovered oil in the Persian Gulf. Standard Oil Company of California was the first to obtain a concession to explore the black gold, first in Bahrain in 1932, then in Arabia in May 1933.[3] The original concession, a sixty-year agreement, called for an annual fee of

5,000 pounds sterling until the discovery of oil. To exploit this concession, the American company created California Arabian Standard Oil Company.

The first deposits were found in March 1938, 4,727 feet deep, in a well near Damman in the Persian Gulf. In January 1944, the company changed its name to Aramco, the Arabian American Oil Company. In addition to Standard Oil Company of California, the corporation controlled Texaco and eventually opened Standard Oil Company of New Jersey and Socony-Vacuum in 1946.[4]

From the moment Aramco started drilling for oil, the president of the company was virtually the American ambassador in Saudi Arabia. What's more, the company certainly had to play a role in the organization of the country if it was going to exploit its subsoil. Roads and ports needed to be constructed in order to transport the oil, which was beginning to overflow. Water wells needed to be drilled for the workers. Hospitals and offices needed to be built. The American influence was officially recognized on February 14, 1945, with the Quincy Accords. The meeting took place a few months before the end of the war, between President Franklin Roosevelt and Abdul Aziz Ibn Saud on the *Quincy* off Jeddah. It marked the beginning of the monopoly granted to the United States for the exploitation of Saudi oil. The British had, without a doubt, missed the boat.

Soon the Americans would install a military base in Dhahran—a close flight to any of the Gulf emirates—and become the privileged partners of Saudi Arabia and its king, who, thanks to the royalties he received from the oil exploitation, soon became one of the richest men in the world. The "heroes of liberty," the new world superpower combating Soviet totalitarianism in Europe, had just invented, under the Tropic of Cancer, a petro-monarchy—a mix of political and religious absolutism with a new universal currency, the dollar. With this new foul-smelling liquid, the East Coast and the Persian Gulf—including the oil port of Damman and Dhahran, and awaiting the hotels in Al Khobar—became the materialist counterpart of the West Coast, symbol of Islamic spiritualism and home of the minarets of Mecca, Medina, and Jeddah, where (according to legend) Eve's tomb lies, next to the Red Sea.

It was after the 1950s and the extraordinary increase in oil use that Saudi Arabia became a bona fide state with a recognized place in the international community. Tall, thin, with an aura of certainty, King Faisal, one of the thirty-six sons of Abdul Aziz, already had experience when he took the throne. As prime minister, which does not hold the same meaning as in Western democracies, he had had to take charge of the kingdom in order to compensate for his brother Saud's discrepancies. Saud had taken the throne after the death of their father.[5]

Even before the creation of Arabia, Faisal had held the position of minister of foreign affairs, which exposed him to power at a very young age. In November 1964, he replaced his sick and incompetent brother, who had been deposed by the royal family. Brought up in the tribal tradition, Faisal governed the country as a tribal leader would, taking advice only from a small circle of ministers and family members, all of whom held leadership positions within the government. But he was smarter than his brother, whose fatal error was to hoard all the power for himself.

Saud thought he could continue to act like an absolute monarch, mixing public finances and personal fortune.[6] As for Faisal, he made sure his family profited from the regime's income. From its members' point of view, the Saudi state and the Saud family were one and the same, to the extent that they gave it their name—a symbol if there ever was one—of the patrimonial concept of Arabian power and riches. A profoundly religious man, he implemented a literal interpretation of the laws of the Koran according to the strict precepts of Wahhabism. It was nonetheless under his reign that the hybrid and somewhat incoherent Kingdom of Saudi Arabia became a modern and slightly better structured state. At least, its stature in view of other Gulf states was restored, though its progressiveness proved to be nonexistent.

In the country that witnessed the birth of the Prophet, religion was everywhere. The Koran, the Sunna, Al Ijmaa, and Al Ijtihad remained the four pillars of the *sharia*.[7] Life in Saudi Arabia revolved around the five daily prayers, when all good Muslims had to kneel and face Mecca. The country's rapid development from pastoral to mono-industrial never diminished the importance of religion, which was omnipresent.

And Saudi Arabia remained a leader in the Islamic world. The pilgrimage to Mecca that every Muslim man must make was a fundamental part of the kingdom's identity. Each year, close to two million believers, of which one quarter were Saudi Arabian, flocked to the black stone given to Abraham by

Gabriel. They went in order to follow, fourteen centuries later, the same gestures as Muhammad. Though the huge crowds of pilgrims gathered each year could be overwhelming, Saudi authorities used the pilgrimage to leverage influence in the Islamic world. The Saudis also took advantage of the pilgrimage to make contact with the Islamic leaders present. And each year, with the modernization of transportation, the crowds gathering in the holy city grew larger and larger.

In the 1980s, the Saudi government imposed national quotas so that every Muslim country could send pilgrims. Apart from this official explanation, it was also a way for the monarchy to anticipate the presence of religious extremists from places like Egypt and Iran, who might use the pilgrimage to speak out against enemies of Islam. Such was the case in 1987, when Iranian Shiites denounced America, the West, and Israel as the "Great Satan." The clash between the Saudi police and the pilgrims ended in a bloodbath, leaving hundreds dead.

This escalation wreaked havoc in a country whose flag proclaims, "There is no God but Allah, and Muhammad is his prophet." Saudi Arabia was like a mosque, which made it easy for authorities to legally justify the banning of all other religions. To ensure successful proselytism, the ulama and imams created the "Committee for the Propagation of Virtue and Prevention of Vice," which was nothing more than a religious militia in charge of policing the state's 18 million inhabitants. Canes in hand, 4,000 to 5,000 Mutawwaeen had the job of enforcing the *sharia*. They hunted down women who dared to wear clothes that were too Western, or anyone who consumed alcohol—which was forbidden even at home—and made sure that there was no mixing of the sexes in public places.

These zealous bullies of Islam, led by a religious leader with the same power as a minister, invoked fear in the population and created a permanent climate of paranoia and apprehension. As the country developed and saw technology improve thanks to oil production, the paradox between the traditions of Wahhabism and the constraints of modern life grew stronger, even in this so-called religious state.

Though the ruling family was represented in all aspects of the regime—from ministerial positions to administration to boards of directors in large corporations—it had nevertheless left all moral magisterium to the descendants of Mohammad bin Abd al-Wahhab, thus creating a quasi-bicephalous system at the highest level. Until his death in 1999, the great mufti Abdel Aziz bin Baz was one of the kingdom's key figures alongside King Fahd. Members of the royal family preferred to leave the clergy to their proselytism, and to fructify the billions of dollars pouring in from the American exploitation of their oil. For Aramco controlled more than 95 percent of the oil flowing from Saudi wells with production increasing from 547,000 barrels per day in 1950 to one million in 1980.[8] Oil represented more than 75 percent of the country's revenue, reaching staggering figures. From $57 million in 1950, the oil returns surpassed $1.2 billion in 1970, exploding after the first oil crisis and reaching the astronomical amount of $119 billion in 1981. On their end, the oil companies dividing the spoils among the Aramco group[9] made staggering profits due to the low royalties they put back, and everyone got shamelessly rich.

As tributaries of American dollars, the emirs prudently adopted a low profile on foreign affairs within the Muslim world. In the 1960s, Saudi Arabia was distrustful of Iraq and Jordan, where the Hashemites—who had been chased out of Hijaz by the Al Saud decades earlier—reigned. Though they followed the issues of the Arab world, Saudi leaders stayed very much in the background on the Israeli-Arab conflict. Most notably, they refused to participate in the military operations of 1967 and 1973.

Saudi Arabia would play a decisive role in the oil embargo in 1973, however, and also within OPEC, the Organization of Petroleum Exporting Countries, created in the 1960s.[10] In 1988, the Americans left Aramco for good. Chevron, Texaco, Exxon, and Mobil, which had already allowed the Saudi state to climb to a 25 percent share in 1972, then to 60 percent in 1974, sold their last shares to Saudi Arabia. The company, which had become the world's leading oil company, was rebaptized Saudi Aramco. At that point, one might have thought American economic imperialism in the Gulf was over. Not exactly.

Several members of Aramco's board of directors were American. Moreover, they were former high-level executives of major oil companies. Because several Americans in management positions continued to work for the company, which was like a state within the state, it kept privileged relationships with North America. But its dependence on the United States was certainly less palpable.

Nonetheless, the damage was done. There was already something rotten in the desert kingdom. The country had not had an easy transition from the time of the Bedouin's camel to the age of the Emir's gleaming Mercedes 600. The ruling family subjected the Saudi kingdom to periodic felling, and power games influenced the revenues as much as government structures served too often to satisfy their pleasures. For quite some time, their economic dependence on large international companies had provoked nationalist reaction in the region. In 1951, the prime minister of Iran nationalized its oil wells. In 1961, it was Iraq that renationalized 99 percent of the surface granted to the Iraq Petroleum Company. Though these defiant movements failed—mostly because the producing countries were unable to keep up the flow of production without the help of the vilified multinationals—the major oil companies understood that the hour of financial arrogance and exclusive monopoly was over.

But it wasn't until after the first oil crisis in 1973 that the trouble brewing in the more traditionalist milieus would explode. A perceived decline in values and the rapid modernization of society increased pressure and renewed Arab nationalism. One of the major turns came in November 1979, when hundreds of rebels, many of them Saudi Arabian, stormed the Great Mosque in Mecca and called on Muslims to overthrow the Al Saud dynasty and condemn all compromise with the West. Three elite French soldiers (who had converted to Islam before entering the holy sites reserved for Muslims), led by the ruthless captain Paul Barril, participated in bringing down the revolt on behalf of the ruling dynasty. The encounter ended with hundreds dead.[11]

Libyan leader Colonel Qaddhafi addressed the Saudi regime on the subject of this tragedy: "How can the prayers rising from these sacred places have significance anymore when Islam has just been humiliated, Muslims degraded, and the house of God occupied?" The same year, Saudi Arabia covertly supported Iraq in its war against Iran, where mullahs had taken power in the maelstrom of the Islamic revolution. After eight years of war, the region found relative peace again from 1987 to 1988. But not for long. In August 1990, Iraq invaded Kuwait. Saudi Arabia, Kuwait's neighbor, as much an ally of the United States as in solidarity with the petro-monarchies, took part in the conflict and opened its territory and its military bases to the international coalition led by the United States. Saudi Arabia would also foot the $55 billion bill for this war waged in the name of liberty, where the price of a barrel of oil was what was really at stake.

Though the future of the petro-monarchies was intact, tension in the Arab world was mounting. Many Muslims were traumatized to see their country "colonized" by the United States, as Saudi Arabia gradually found itself in a state of dependence. The landing of 540,000 non-Muslim soldiers was in complete conflict with the intransigent rules of Wahhabism. Sheikh bin Baz had to be called in for support to find a doctrinal justification for this flagrant infringement against the rules of the *sharia*. Then, in 1991, an unthinkable event occurred. Seven hundred dissidents signed a petition calling for the return to a pure Wahhabism, and openly criticized the regime's conduct. Two sheikhs whose sermons were among the most strident were imprisoned, and the regime appeared more and more divided in the face of this new dissent. In exchange for its support against Iraq, the West demanded that the regime liberalize even more, which only fueled tension among the intransigent imams, who denounced more and more publicly the betrayal of the secular arm of Islam, the royal family, which was supposed to be upholding the standards of Wahhabism in the land. They were even more upset when things started to crumble in the kingdom. In 1993, consequences of the war effort began to show in the form of major budget deficits. One of the richest regimes in the world actually found itself borrowing money to finance economic development.

In 1994, the budget was actually reduced by 20 percent. At the same time, the *New York Times* reported that one of the holes in the budget was the result of loans taken out by the royal family, which never once thought to pay them back.

But the regime did not respond to the crisis until August 3, 1995. For the first time in twenty years, King Fahd went ahead with a major ministerial reorganization that affected more than half of the ruling family's pocketbooks. It was a refreshing change in light of all the criticism, but had little impact. Even though new elite took on important roles, members of the royal family (who were not necessarily competent) still held the most influential positions in the government. The end of an era seemed imminent when King Fahd (age seventy-nine in 2002) suffered a stroke that forced him to hand over power to his half brother, Prince Abdallah.

On November 13, 1995, a car bomb exploded at the U.S. mission to the Saudi National Guard in Riyadh—the first major act of terrorism on Saudi soil. A second act of terrorism followed on June 25, 1996, after the execution of the four Islamists responsible for the first attack.[12] At that point, a nervous Saudi government placated the Islamists by not fully cooperating with the Americans during their investigation of the attack.

The royal family remained split. It was still in a weak position in terms of its relationship with the United States, but at the same time supported certain fundamentalist movements, such as the Taliban, which advocated the practice of a religion similar to the Wahhabi ideal. However, the fundamentalists had long been divided over the regime's ambiguity: several opposition movements were formed in the 1990s, such as the Movement for Islamic Reform in Arabia, founded in London by Saad al-Faqih, and the Committee for Advice and Reform created by Osama bin Laden, a member of one of the most influential families in the kingdom.

Since the attacks of September 11, Saudi Arabia has once again positioned itself behind the star-spangled banner of the United States. Prince Abdallah, who favors a return to a more religious rigor and whom we cannot suppose to have great sympathy for America, still continues to preserve his own interests and that of his country's, whose subsoil contains a quarter of the world's oil reserves. Whatever he does after King Fahd's death will certainly determine the Middle East's future.

9. SAUDI FUNDAMENTALIST NETWORKS

Three key factors explain Saudi Arabia's role in the expansion of a radical form of Islam: religion, the driving force behind the kingdom's proselytism; the banking system as the instrument of the kingdom's religious ambitions; and oil as a deterrent weapon against the West. The Afghan conflict was the catalyst for these different interests, clearing the way for the expansion of a radical Islam and for those thousands of fighters who volunteered to join the rebellion.

With its oil interests in mind, plus the threat of Arab nationalism, and then the Iranian revolution, Saudi Arabia began to lend its support to the Sunni Islamist movements in the 1970s.[1] The search for a central position of influence within the Muslim and Arab world was, as Richard Labévière notes, one of the country's major preoccupations.[2] It needed to dominate the religious front in order to keep the peace and maintain its monopoly on the political front. The backbone of support for the Islamist movements was provided by the organization Muslim World League, founded in 1962 and funded—notably—by Aramco, as well as consortiums of Islamic banks, including Faisal-Finance and Al-Baraka.

Saudi Arabia also took advantage of the rise in the price of hydrocarbons following the war of 1973, when Arab countries and American oil companies increased the flow of crude oil. As a result, Muslim oil-producing countries became considerably richer, particularly Saudi Arabia, whose annual revenues went from $4.3 billion to $34.5 billion between 1973 and 1978. The kingdom, in turn, invested a large part of its profits in the promotion of Islam. Almost all of the Islamist networks in the Near East, Africa, and the West were financed by the Saudi state, or by way of the international Islamic institutions it controlled. These included the Organization of the Islamic Conference (created in 1969), the Muslim World League (an NGO created in 1962 with missionary objectives), and above all Saudi holdings and banks, such as Faisal Islamic Bank (FIS), Dar al-Mal, and Dallah Al-Baraka. At the same time, the Al Saud family and the kingdom's many princes invested in private initiatives that helped form the framework of the country's "Muslim diplomacy."

One result: A radical Islam spread rapidly in Egypt when Anwar al-Sadat took power. The Egyptian Muslim Brotherhood was a group that had taken refuge in Saudi Arabia during the Nasser saga, and returned to Egypt armed with petrodollars in order to establish its influence in Egyptian society.

Though Saudi Arabia had no formal budget devoted to terrorism, its 4,000 princes were financing Islamist movements left, right, and center—the way, in earlier times, indulgences were bought. Take, for example, the wealthy Saudi financier and Sony shareholder Youssef Djamil Abdelatif, who donated $1 million to Ahmed Simozrag, a treasurer at the FIS.[3] As for private funding, Saudi businessmen with colossal fortunes continued to finance various movements, including Osama bin Laden's. Officially disowned by the Saudi kingdom, bin Laden nonetheless kept in close contact with his family, one of the wealthiest in Saudi Arabia, as well as with the ultra-powerful Sudeiri clan, of which Prince Turki Al-Faisal was a member.

Saudi Arabia developed an entire banking web, with the initial function of financing the growth of developing countries on the condition that they be open to the propagation of a Sunni Islam of the "Hanbalite" rite (which had influenced Saudi Wahhabism).[4] The main banking agency was created in 1973, the Islamic Development Bank (IDB), in which the monarchy held 25 percent of the capital. One of the bank's most important recent acts was to compensate Pakistan for the sanctions that had been imposed on it after it conducted nuclear testing in 1998. To do so, the bank increased its lending limit from $150 million to $400 million. Other banking agencies were created to keep the shadowy world of Islamic finance obscured. These included OPEC's "Development Funds for International Affairs" (30 percent Saudi capital), the "Arab Bank for Economic Development in Africa" (24.5 percent Saudi capital), Dar-Al-Mal al Islami, and Al-Baraka.

In order to give a boost to Islamic proselytism, the "Muslim World League" was created in 1962, led by a Saudi Arabian, Abdullah bin Saleh Al Obeïd, with representatives in more than 120 countries. With significant financial backing, the league financed the construction of mosques and Islamic centers around the world. In Europe, it funded the construction of mosques in Madrid, Rome, Mantes-la-Jolie, Evry, and Copenhagen.

Clearly, Saudi Arabia has played a decisive role in the spread of hard-line Islam around the world, notably with the help of petrodollars, cleverly used in the framework of Islamization projects. Perfectly integrated into the capitalist system, Saudi Arabia played the market well—so well that its capital has become indispensable in keeping the world economy working smoothly. Since it had such an important energy reserve, the Saudi kingdom found its proselytizing activities protected by the world's superpower, the United States. There was no stopping Saudi Arabia then, even though such violent groups as Hamas in Palestine, the Taliban in Afghanistan, and the GIA in Algeria depended on it.

Osama bin Laden was a by-product of this. In 1978, at the request of Saudi secret service chief Prince Turki Al-Faisal, bin Laden founded an organization to export this combatant Islam on Afghan soil, called the "Islamic Legion." He went to Peshawar in Pakistan to meet Sheikh Abdullah Azzam, a Palestinian who would become his spiritual guide. Responsible for leading the Arab volunteers in the fight against the Soviets, Azzam created the "Afghan bureau," or the reception center for the Arab volunteers, in the early 1980s. Bin Laden soon became the office's financial manager, and eventually replaced Azzam after his assassination in September 1989.

At that time, the Saudis were backing bin Laden, both financially and logistically. This relationship continued, no matter what the Saudis say, until very recently. It continued after his exile in Sudan, and after the numerous pre–September 11 attacks that have been attributed to him. Several sources, including bin Laden himself during an interview on ABC, reported that until very recently, Turki Al-Faisal and his emissaries made frequent trips to Kandahar in Afghanistan to meet their "protégé," who was gradually becoming something of an undesirable. In an unpublished interview given to a journalist from the French daily *France Soir* in April 1995, bin Laden confirmed this, saying that "the Saudis had chosen [him] to be their representative in Afghanistan."[5]

To support the war effort, Saudi Arabia built a vast network of Islamic charitable and mutual assistance organizations, many of which were, in reality, recruitment and financing centers for bin Laden's activities. These "humanitarian" organizations offered the advantage of being much less controllable from a financial point of view. The largest of these was the International Islamic Relief Organization (IIRO), which financed numerous Islamic "missionaries" and maintained close ties with all of the known Islamic groups. Founded in Jeddah, Saudia Arabia, in 1978, IIRO is based in more than 120 countries. It is an Islamic mutual assistance organization in the health, humanitarian, and agricultural sectors, covering all Islamic fronts, from Bosnia-Herzegovina to Chechnya to Afghanistan.

The association officially admits to being funded by "generous Saudi donors," using the *zakat* system, the religious tax that requires subscribers, whether public or private entities, when purchasing shares to donate a certain amount of their own funds that is separate from the purchase. And so, between

1984 and 1995, a big chunk of the organization's budget was consecrated to "special projects," reaching 34 percent, or $140 million.[6] The major families in the kingdom donated regularly to the organization, following the example of the Saudi defense minister, Prince Sultan bin Aldulaziz, another Sudeiri, who admitted to personally donating 2 million francs to the IIRO each year.[7] In 1999, the organization was even honored as an invited member of the Organization of Islamic Conference (OIC).[8]

The association's European branch was created in London on November 28, 1995,[9] located at 3 Worcester Street in Oxford, and directed by the Saudi Arabian Abdullah Saleh al-Obeïd. The IIRO had several offices in Europe, including France, Switzerland, Germany, and the Netherlands, as well as Sweden.

At first glance, the IIRO appeared to be a well-established Saudi Islamic mutual assistance association benefiting from the kingdom's support. But in reality, it was much more than that. The IIRO was one of the financial and operational vehicles of a militant Islam, largely exploited by the person who became its emblem, Osama bin Laden. The CIA has confirmed that bin Laden "exploited" the IIRO network in his operations.[10]

Several clues support these allegations, and allow a glimpse into the reality of such a powerful organization with ties to terrorist operations. Osama bin Laden's own brother-in-law, Mohammad Jamal Al-Khalifa, formed the IIRO branch in the Philippines in 1992. It was later accused by a former member of the terrorist organization Abu Sayyaf as being a front for terrorist activities, principally for the Moro

Islamic Liberation Front (MILF). According to this source, funds intended for the rebels were channeled through another charity organization in Jeddah—Ikhwan Al Muslimin (or Islamic Brotherhood)—directed by Ustadz Muslimen, who had facilitated a trip to the Philippines in October 1998 for businessman Hussein Mustapha, Al-Khalifa's partner on behalf of Osama bin Laden.[11]

Another troubling clue: The organization's European seat was located at the same address in Oxford as the International Development Foundation (IDF), created by Mohammad Salem bin Mahfouz and Mohammad Saleh Affara. The former belonged to a family of wealthy Saudi bankers who organized the financing of Osama bin Laden's terrorist activities from Saudi Arabia. The latter was a Yemenite intermediary for weapons sales who was implicated in the French armament contract affair, Sawari-2, with Saudi Arabia. Similarly, the London branch of the IIRO had on its board of directors Farid Yaseen Gurashi, whose brother, Ismail Mohammad Gurashi, was the director of the leading Sudanese bank, the Bank of Khartoum. Finally, housed at the same British address was another mutual assistance organization called the Oxford Trust for Islamic Studies,[12] directed by Farhan Ahmad Nizami (an Indian national) and Khalid Alireza (a Saudi Arabian). Khalid Alireza led several construction and transportation companies in Jeddah and Dhahran in Saudi Arabia, including ABT Group, Xenel Industries Ltd., and Saudi Services and Operation Company Ltd.

The IIRO was not the only example, for other Saudi organizations were also at the crossroads of humanitarian financing and Jihad. And so, Prince Abdul Aziz Al Ibrahim, brother of King Fahd's wife, Mounayer, created a foundation in the 1990s whose official aim was humanitarian assistance. And yet the organization's branch in Nairobi, Kenya, called the Ibrahim bin Abdul Aziz Al Ibrahim Foundation,[13] was associated with Osama bin Laden's network in the FBI's investigation into the attacks against the American embassies in Nairobi and Dar es Salaam on August 7, 1998.

The organization's Kenya office was even closed by national authorities in September 1998, after documents seized in its headquarters connected it with Osama bin Laden's operations in the material organization of the attack against the American embassy in Nairobi. At the end of 1998, following an outcry from Muslim representatives in Kenya who denounced the "persecution" to which they were being subjected, and after a general strike in the country, Kenyan authorities ultimately lifted their decision to ban the organization.[14] The foundation was, significantly, financed by the Al Ibrahim family and several Saudi companies.

According to the latest information, Abdul Aziz Al Ibrahim was said to own a portion of the Marina del Rey real estate venture in Los Angeles, acquired through dummy companies.[15] American authorities discovered a loan of $132 million that was granted to Al Ibrahim at the end of 1989 by none other than the fiendish BCCI, the bank at the center of the biggest financial scandal of the century in 1991. In this capacity, he was one of the bank's leading loan beneficiaries.

The backgrounds of these "generous Saudis" are not insignificant. They were generally rich industrialists and financiers with close ties to the royal family. The case of brothers Abdul Aziz and Walid Al Ibrahim was especially revelatory. They made large real estate investments in North Africa, Africa, and the United States. In 1991, along with Saleh Abdullah Kamel, another central figure in Saudi Arabia, and alleged to be in bin Laden's network, they created the leading Arab television satellite service, Middle East Broadcasting Corp (MBC), which purchased the press agency United Press International (UPI) in 1992.

Saudi support for a radical Islam was channeled through a very complex banking system that had at its center two entities created in the early 1980s: Dar-Al-Maal Al Islami (DMI), founded in 1981 by Prince Turki's brother, Mohammad Al-Faisal, and Dallah-Al-Baraka, founded in 1982 by King Fahd's brother-in-law.[16]

Endowed with enormous funding ($1 billion in the case of DMI), these institutions were rooted in both the Saudi kingdom's desire to spread its financial preeminence in the Arab world and in its support for the radical Islamic cause. Add to that the desire, already perceptible during the inception of the BCCI, to create an international financial network capable of sustaining the economic vitality of the Arab countries in the eyes of large Western banks.

DMI SA,[17] also known as Islamic Capital House, is located in the town of Cointrin in Switzerland. It was created on July 29, 1981. Until October 1983, its president was Ibrahim Kamel. He was replaced on October 17, 1983, by Prince Mohammad Al Faisal Al Saud, son of King Al Saud, cousin of King Fahd, and brother of Prince Turki Al-Faisal, former head of the Saudi secret services (who was fired in August 2001). DMI is considered to be the central structure in Saudi Arabia's financing of international Islam. Its main subsidiaries are the Islamic Investment Company of the Gulf, the Saisal Islamic Bank of Bahrain, and Faisal Finance. These high-level establishments enjoy enormous power in the countries where they are established, principally in the Gulf and Sudan.

Functioning on an Islamic method, DMI adheres to the *zakat* system. After the transaction is made, the funds earmarked as *zakat* disappear and are off the books. Later, under no financial regulation, the money may be used to fund Islamist groups such as the IIRO.

Another organization, somewhat more discreet but just as powerful, is Dallah Al-Baraka. Its founder, Saleh Abdullah Kamel, had been adviser to the Saudi minister of finance and the inspector general of finance. In his capacity as a major shareholder in the Albaraka Islamic Investment Bank of Bahrain, Kamel managed several banking entities whose activities were called into question during recent investigations targeting fraudulent and possibly terrorist financing networks.

Kamel was president of the Albaraka Bank-Sudan and shareholder in the Sudanese Islamic Bank,[18] subsidiary of the Faisal Islamic Bank of Egypt SAE,[19] in the Tadamon Islamic Bank and in the Islamic West Sudan Bank. He was also a board member of the National Development Bank in Sudan. Finally, he was one of the founders of the Faisal Islamic Bank-Sudan and of the Arab Investment Co.[20] The Tadamon Islamic Bank was a shareholder since 1991 in Al-Shamal

Islamic Bank in Sudan, considered by American authorities to be one of Osama bin Laden's principal structures of investment and financing after 1991, when the fundamentalist leader moved to Sudan.[21]

Soon after his move to Khartoum in Sudan in 1991, bin Laden helped set up several financial and commercial structures that allowed him to finance his terrorist activities. In addition to the financing from political movements, coordinated by the International Islamic Front for Jihad Against Jews and Crusaders, Osama bin Laden's economic activities were relayed by a holding company named Wadi Al Aqiq.[22] It was run by a Sudanese man in Khartoum named Abu Al-Hasan. According to several corroborating sources, the holding company was composed of nine Sudanese companies as well as an indeterminate number of Yemenese companies in the import-export, publishing, and ceramic sectors, as well as in Kenya in the electrical appliances industry.[23]

But one of bin Laden's principal investments concerned a banking institution, the Al Shamal Islamic Bank,[24] to which he contributed upward of $50 million at that time. This bank allowed him not only to finance his activities but also to move capital to the Jihad's front lines. The recent trials of those responsible for the attacks against American embassies in Africa revealed that Al Shamal's bank accounts also fed the terrorist organization Al Qaeda.

The Al Shamal Islamic Bank's chief executive officer today denies Osama bin Laden's investment in the bank; he recently acknowledged, however, that the fundamentalist leader had two accounts there, opened on March 30, 1992, and inactive since 1997, in the name of Al-Hijrah for Construction and Development Ltd. Even more surprising, he admitted that an account was opened in 1993 in the name of Osama bin Laden's holding company, Wadi Al Aqiq, a law company registered in Saudi Arabia, and that the account had been inactive since 1995.[25] These are troubling revelations considering that Osama bin Laden was stripped of his nationality on April 6, 1994, by the Saudi kingdom,[26] and that all of his assets were supposedly frozen on that date.

One of the bank's noteworthy shareholders was the country's second-largest banking institution, the Tadamon Islamic Bank,[27] established on November 28, 1981. The bank was officially active on March 24, 1983, less than one month before the Al Shamal Islamic Bank obtained banking authorization for its own activities. Led by Sayed Eltigani Hassan Hilal and Salah Ali Abu Elnaja, the bank is active across Sudanese territory, through twenty-one different establishments.[28]

Tadamon had several subsidiaries in Sudan, notably in the agricultural, industrial, and real estate sectors. They included the Islamic Insurance Co., the Islamic Trading and Services Co., and the Real Estate Development Co. Tadamon's shareholders had not really increased since 1991. The only change was in the makeup of its board of directors: The Faisal Islamic Bank of Khartoum[29] was replaced by its subsidiary, the National Co. for Trade and Services, in 1995. The Faisal Islamic Bank, created in 1977, was led by Prince Mohammad Al Faisal Al Saud of Saudi Arabia. It was a subsidiary of the Islamic Investment Company of the Gulf (Bahrain), whose holding is Dar Al Mal Al Islami (DMI). It is very unlikely that executives at DMI ignored the major investment approved by its subsidiary Tadamon, especially since it concerned the creation of a new banking entity.

Another bank believed to have facilitated transfers for Osama bin Laden's networks was the Dubai Islamic Bank,[30] created in 1975, based in the United Arab Emirates, and run by none other than the current minister of finance of the United Arab Emirates.[31] According to the CIA, these transfers fed organizations associated with bin Laden. The Dubai Islamic Bank was also one of the principal shareholders in the BCCI, with more than $80 million in assets there. The bank had been involved in several scandals, most memorably in the laundering of $242 million for the Mali billionaire Foutanga "Babani" Sissoko.[32] Saleh Abdullah Kamel reappeared in the financial dealings of bin Laden's networks in 1999 with Tihama for Advertising, Public Relations and Marketing, a subsidiary of the Dallah Albaraka Group. The company was in fact cited as being one of the Saudi intermediaries in the financial networks for bin Laden's terrorist activities.[33] However, Saleh Kamel was still not worried about the legal developments concerning the companies mentioned above. Only Khalid bin Mahfouz, chief executive officer of Tihama and financial partner of Saleh Kamel, was placed under house arrest and stripped of his functions as president of the National Commercial Bank of Saudi Arabia in 1999.[34]

So, was Saudi Arabia playing with fire in supporting the radical Islamic cause? Was it outdone by its own more or less covert network of support for fundamentalism? The facts collected make us doubt this explanation. There are in fact close ties, often family ties, between the different protagonists of radical Islam, and the connections are not coincidental.

This kind of policy ensures Saudi Arabia's preeminence over Arab nationalism and over Iran in the promotion of Islam. It also keeps the West from entering into conflict with these radicals, who are supported by the leader of the Islamic world. It has been said too often that Osama bin Laden is a "creature" of the CIA, for the simple reason that the United States had contributed, indirectly and temporarily, without a doubt, to his radical cause by financing and supporting the Mujahedeen rebels against the Soviets in Afghanistan in the 1980s. But America's support for bin Laden was in large part the involuntary consequence of its own ambitions in the region. Saudi Arabia's support, on the other hand, was a calculated policy, clear and unambiguous, concerning its brand of Islam in the world. In light of these revelations, Osama bin Laden appears, above all, to be a product of Wahhabism and an instrument of the Saudi kingdom. And both contained converging elements that linked them permanently.

The Saudi attitude toward the American response to the September 11 attacks demonstrates the regime's trouble with regard to Osama bin Laden. The kingdom's refusal to allow American forces to use its air bases in order to attack Afghanistan illustrates the mutual tolerance that exists between Saudi Arabia and bin Laden. Saudi Arabia has yet to cooperate with the United States in its current investigations for fear of provoking fundamentalists in the kingdom. And Osama bin Laden was careful to "spare" the kingdom, even though he attacked its attitude in his early writings.

We speak freely of "state-sponsored terrorism" such as that of Libya and Iran, while Saudi Arabia is spared from the blacklists for the simple reason that it is essential in the international oil scene. Without this stroke of luck, it would probably appear high on the lists.

Osama bin Laden is only an emblematic figure in the major religious and financial issues and interests that underlie the future of even the Saudi regime. The networks that support him are well established—whether the BCCI, the Islamic banks, or the so-called humanitarian organizations—and it is quite unlikely that they will disappear with bin Laden.

The real issue is elsewhere now, and depends on our capacity to call into question Saudi Arabia's political and financial support of the world's fundamentalist movements. It is a heavy burden, but if the West does not step in, such support will continue and take root permanently.

We have long closed our eyes to this situation in order to protect the security of our Saudi ally, allowing the seeds of fundamentalism to grow and become uncontrollable. We refrained from putting any kind of pressure on a power that still today defends the indefensible, and allowed it to exist politically, materially, and financially.

III.
BIN LADEN,
THE MYTH OF A RENEGADE

10. LIBYA 1994:
A TERRORIST IS BORN

He looks much younger in the photograph than in the videos broadcast since September 2001 on the Arab television station Al-Jazeera. This image of Osama bin Laden dates back to 1996, a time when he wasn't hiding as much, and when intelligence agencies were less interested in him. His beard looks thicker, his face and cheeks fuller.

This photograph doesn't come from a family album. It appears at the top left corner of the very first arrest warrant issued against bin Laden, by Interpol. This confidential document, numbered 1998/20232, was intended strictly for police and judicial authorities around the world. But in skimming the page, something about it isn't quite right. It differs in several ways from the version released to the press and displayed on the agency's Web site. In the public version, there is no mention of the summary of charges against the criminal, the date the warrant was filed, or the state requesting the warrant. In other words, the name of the very first country to ask Interpol to use its resources to arrest the person in question is conveniently left out. Strange. But the most surprising omissions can always be explained.

The first Interpol arrest warrant against Osama bin Laden

was actually issued on April 15, 1998, at the request of Libya's Ministry of the Interior. Judicial authorities in Tripoli first filed an international warrant for his arrest, numbered 127288/1998, on March 16, 1998, at Interpol headquarters in Lyon. The international policing organization followed up on the proceedings by issuing its own warrant one month later to police around the world.[1] This official document proves that two years after the attack against American military installations in Dharan, the United States was still not openly pursuing Osama bin Laden, even though he was considered the principal suspect in the attack; had called for a fatwa against the West and America on February 28, 1998; and was involved, according to the United States, in the attack against the World Trade Center in February 1993. The individual identified by the State Department in 1996 as "one of the most significant financial sponsors worldwide of extremist Islamic activity" was not being sought after by American judicial authorities.[2]

According to Libya, the charges justifying this warrant date back to the murder of two German nationals on March 10, 1994—a detail no less surprising than the others, and one that reopened an old case. The victims were Silvan Becker and his wife, Vera, German secret service agents in charge of missions in Africa and of antiterrorism efforts.[3] They were working for the Bundesamt für Verfassungsschutz (Office for Constitutional Protection), one of the three German intelligence agencies. Never before had the names of the Beckers been revealed. Interpol and all Western judicial authorities had known since April 1998 that Osama bin Laden was responsible, however, and theoretically they should have been doing everything in their power to stop him. Even worse, the Interpol document proves that two years after the attack against American military installations in Dhahran, the United States was not the nation that was openly going after Osama bin Laden. Yet he had already issued a fatwa against America and the West.

Why was Colonel Qaddhafi's government the only one tracking down Osama bin Laden? Hadn't the Libyan leader himself supported international terrorism? It's not quite so simple. Answers to all of these questions are closely linked to the history of Libya and Great Britain.

On September 1, 1969, a group of progressive young Libyan officers seized power from King Idriss Senussi while he was enjoying himself at a spa in Turkey. London was immediately enraged, for the Senussi monarchy had been Great Britain's protégé. The world was suddenly introduced to the young but determined face of Muammar el-Qaddhafi, who at the time was twenty-eight years old. Though he would later show a penchant for dictatorial methods, in the first hours of his reign he concentrated on redistributing the country's wealth and following through with the long-overdue economic decolonization. He immediately nationalized the oil industry, first and foremost the sites controlled by British Petroleum, owner of the majority of the country's oil fields.[4] Starting in February 1970, the British Secret Intelligence Service made it a priority to oust Qaddhafi, while the British treasury froze Libyan government assets in London (£32 million were frozen).

Lacking local support and sometimes luck as well, Britain

launched several operations, all of which failed miserably, as former senior SAS officer George Campbell-Johnson would confirm much later.[5] But what did it matter, when a war of attrition had begun between London and Tripoli—one that never really ended. For this reason, in time, Great Britain found friends in Qaddhafi's enemies—especially in the radical religious movements, which saw Qaddhafi as too moderate and adhering to an Islam that was too lax. One of these movements has gotten recent attention: the Libyan Islamic Fighting Group, which appeared on the White House and Justice Department's list of twenty-seven suspect organizations after the September 11 attacks. Jama al-Islamiya al-Muqatila, its Arabic name, is a group of Libyan Islamic combatants, and one of the longest-standing supporters of Osama bin Laden. Its main operational leader, Anas the Libyan, is one of bin Laden's close aides.

From the early 1990s on, al-Muqatila mobilized "Afghani-Libyans," that is to say, former Mujahedeen apprentices who had been recruited by various Muslim Brotherhood offices to fight in Afghanistan with the help of Saudi dollars and American Stinger missiles. After the war, about 2,500 of these religious soldiers from Libya formed a radical movement with the intention of establishing itself in its native country. The group's goal was clear: Members would establish themselves within the Libyan community in order to take control of the government in Tripoli. After the Cold War, as so many others had done, they installed their rear guard in Sudan and pledged allegiance to Osama bin Laden, who seemed from afar to be the most successful of all the fundamentalist leaders.

Bin Laden followed the group's cause with great interest, and also gave them support. Starting in 1993, he even imagined settling down in their country. Located between Algeria, where Islamist forces were growing, and Egypt, where the Jamaa and Islamic Jihad still had strong networks, Libya seemed the most natural place to set up Al Qaeda's central headquarters. Details contained in the Interpol document even prove that the terrorist lived there—in the small city of Jabala-Larde, not far from Banghazi, in the eastern part of the country. There, bin Laden was on Arab soil. Even better, since Qaddhafi was ostracized from other nations, he did not receive foreign aid. On the contrary. Former British secret service agent David Shayler,[6] positioned at the North African branch of the British secret service (MI5), revealed that MI5 had organized an operation to assassinate Qaddhafi, in November 1996—with the support of al-Muqatila combatants.[7] The failed operation was meant to attack Qaddhafi's motorcade during an official trip.

During this period, and at least up until 1996, the British secret service, which depends on the Foreign Office but is supervised by the prime minister, worked in cooperation with Osama bin Laden's main allies. Now it's easy to understand why the Interpol documents remained for so long in the archives, where no one could get at them. And this collaboration was not just occasional, since al-Muqatila's liaison bulletin, *Al-Fajr,* is published in London by an important figure in the radical Sunni community, Saïd Mansour.

Because Osama bin Laden was aggressively targeting Qaddhafi while at the same time his al-Muqatila brothers were receiving support from London, Libyan security authorities were the first to really pursue bin Laden. This was during a period when he was of use to many different states, from the banks of the Tamise to the desert outskirts of Riyadh.

The irony in this game of bluff came in the end of September 2001, when the head of Libya's intelligence agency, Musa Kusa, went to London to share important information with his counterparts at MI6. It was a gift that demanded a return favor: He handed over a list of a dozen names of al-Muqatila members living in London, whom his authorities would very much like to get their hands on.[8]

11. FAMILY SUPPORT

"There's a very interesting thing in the Islamic structure of the family: You are obliged to support your family members. Even if they are distant members. If it's a cousin or a niece or a nephew, especially a brother, you have to support them if you are a capable person. And the people feel sinful if they don't let this money go to its real owner, in this case, Osama bin Laden."

Dr. Saad Al Fagih knows what he's talking about. This Saudi dissident living in London, a former Afghan combatant, kept close company with Osama bin Laden for many years. Is Osama bin Laden really the "black sheep of the family," as one of his brothers called him recently? The same one the family disowned without disinheriting in 1994, after he was expelled from Saudi Arabia in 1991? It was Bakr bin Laden, successor of Salem bin Laden, who died in 1988, who announced to the Saudi press in 1994 that "the entire family regrets, denounces, and condemns all of the acts committed by Osama bin Laden."[1]

Nothing, however, is quite so simple. Osama bin Laden's own sister recently admitted that it was inconceivable that "none of the fifty-four family members kept ties with him." But she also revealed the change in tone that has recently been adopted with regard to her brother. Since the September 11 attacks, Osama bin Laden has become a "half brother" to his siblings. But this word choice is arbitrary; in an Islamic country that practices polygamy, the children born of different wives are simply brothers and sisters.

In an interview with Peter Arnett on CNN, Osama bin Laden asserted that "the Saudi regime was trying to create ill feeling in [his] family," and revealed that on nine different occasions, his mother, uncle, and brothers had visited him in Khartoum in Sudan.

Family hypocrisy, as we have already mentioned, is prevalent in bin Laden's native country: Even though it stripped him of his nationality in 1994, the kingdom was still supporting his cause. Family hypocrisy also had a lot to do with the firm reactions of the bin Laden clan. In reality, their ties with Osama bin Laden had always existed and were never really broken. As one Western intelligence agency noted, the bin Laden family has rigorously followed "the principle of total family solidarity among all its members" since the 1980s.

In this way, two of Osama bin Laden's brothers-in-law, Muhammad Jamal Khalifa and Saad Al Sharif, played a crucial role, according to American authorities, in the financing of Al Qaeda. The first did so through a charity organization based in Jeddah that did work in the Philippines. He also financed bin Laden's activities in Malaysia, Singapore, and Mauritius.[2] Vincent Cannistraro, former counterterrorism coordinator for the CIA, said that Khalifa was suspected of having financed the Islamic Army of Aden, the Yemenite terrorist group close to bin Laden that claimed responsibility for the attack against the USS *Cole*. Khalifa was actually detained for a short time in 1994, after American immigration authorities discovered that he had been sentenced to death in absentia by a Jordanian court for "conspiracy to carry out terrorist acts."[3] After being extradited to Jordan, he was released on a technicality.

One of Osama bin Laden's brothers, Mahrous, followed a path similar to his brother's in the 1970s. Educated in Great Britain in the early 1970s, he made friends with members of the Muslim Brotherhood, a Syrian Islamic group in exile in Saudi Arabia at the time. In 1979, close to five hundred dissidents led by the Muslim Brothers invaded the Great Mosque in Mecca, using trucks belonging to the bin Laden family to transport the weapons. The organization was protesting the Saudi regime's moral breakdown, calling the government "a corrupt, ostentatious, and mindless imitation of the West."

All of the members of the network who participated in the operation were beheaded except for Mahrous bin Laden, who was arrested as an accomplice, then later released from prison. Saudi intelligence services concluded that the bin Laden family, which had participated in the construction of part of the mosque, were the only ones in possession of a site map of the building that could have allowed the group to get by security forces. Mahrous's release was in large part thanks to the bin Ladens' privileged relationship with the Saudi royal family, a relationship dating back several decades. Today, Mahrous bin Laden manages the family group's Medina branch.[4]

The bin Laden family's economic and financial empire was founded in the early part of the twentieth century by its patriarch, Mohammed Awad. Born in Hadramaut in Yemen, he moved to Saudi Arabia in 1928 and settled there. From very early on, the family was closely connected to King Abd al-Aziz, and involved in the emergence and formation of the Wahhabi kingdom. It was the king who helped the bin Ladens start their business by hiring them to do the construction work on part of the royal palace, and later exclusively giving them the job of renovating the holy sites in Mecca and Medina. This mutual trust gave the family hope for success in a kingdom that had yet to be developed. In 1931, Mohammed bin Laden founded the Saudi Binladin Group (SBG), or Binladin Organization,[5] in Jeddah, and it quickly became one of the kingdom's leading companies. Its close ties to the Saudi rulers also explain why the family's business affairs were rarely decided by the ministries or during official meetings. There were no formal offers for the bin Ladens. Instead, contracts were drawn up directly by the king's personal secretary, and authorized by royal decree. For several years, the group had been the official and exclusive contractor for the kingdom's holy sites, as well as for Jerusalem's holy sites until 1967. Mohammed bin Laden was even given the position of minister of public works for several years.[6] The company did many favors in return for such royal treatment, such as training members of the royal family in the basics of business and finance.

The family-held group enjoyed yet another exclusivity, this one financial, which served only to expand its power in the kingdom. It was actually not a company, but an organization, and this status made it exempt from publishing its financial records. Even more important, in a country where treasury bonds are not formally offered—Koranic law is very strict on the notion of interest—the SBG is the only private Saudi institution able to issue bonds. This ability allowed the company to establish itself and still maintain control of its shareholding.

For almost thirty years, the SBG has continued to diversify. Though construction is its main activity, representing more than half its gross revenue, the group has also become a conglomerate in the areas of engineering, real estate, distribution, telecommunications, and publishing. It is one of the kingdom's leading employers, with 35,000 employees in 2001,[7] and with an estimated annual revenue of $3–5 billion.

From its inception, the company received constant support from Saudi authorities, and that support continued even after the death of its founder in 1968. This was one of the reasons why so many international corporations established partnerships with SBG, for it was a way to get established in the Middle East. In the 1980s, the group represented the likes of Audi and Porsche in Saudi Arabia. SBG also developed partnerships with top international groups such as General Electric, Nortel Networks, and Cadbury Schweppes—all of whom, following the example of General Electric, remain convinced that the Saudi group is "completely separate from Osama bin Laden."

New findings show that the family had large investments in some topflight companies, such as Carlyle (see Part IV), whose managers include several former members of George H. W. Bush's administration.[8] According to the *New York Times,* Carlyle waited until October 26, 2001, before breaking ties with the bin Laden family. In 1995, SBG contributed $2 million to

the Carlyle Partners 11 Fund, one of Carlyle's London investment funds.[9] At that time, the fund raised $1.3 billion for the
purchase of several aerospace companies, and the bin Laden
family earned profits of 40 percent on its initial investment.
(Carlyle is a shareholder in several aeronautics and defense
groups in the United States, most notably Lockheed Martin
and General Dynamic.)

At the same time, the *Wall Street Journal* reported, George
W. Bush had had ties in the past with one of Osama bin
Laden's brothers in the oil and construction industries (see
Part IV).

The bin Laden industrial, financial, and political empire
was strengthened even more when the sons of Mohammed bin
Laden (who died in 1968) were old enough to take control of
the company. Most of them were educated in Egypt at the
prestigious Victoria College in Alexandria, one of the last sym-
bols of British hegemony in the region. At the time, the institution counted among its students King Hussein of Jordan;
the Khashoggi brothers; Kamal Adham, future head of Saudi
intelligence; and the actor Omar Sharif.

While his brothers and sisters were studying in the top
American and British schools, Osama bin laden chose to stay
in Saudi Arabia in order to study at King Abd al-Aziz
University.

When Mohammed died in 1968, the family estate was
divided among his twenty-three wives and fifty-four children,
the last one born in 1967. At the time, the children were all
still too young to take over the company, so it became the
responsibility of Mohammed Bahareth, an uncle who had

become the children's tutor. It wasn't until 1972 that bin Laden's eldest son, Salem, took over the empire with the help of several brothers and Mohammed Bahareth.

Rumors circulated about Salem bin Laden's involvement in the Irangate scandal, then later in his support for the Afghan resistance. One of King Fahd's trusted intimates, he died in a plane crash in Texas in 1988. Following Salem's death, the next son in line, Bakr, took control of the company with the help of thirteen other brothers, including Mahrous. Three of those brothers—Hassan, Yeslam, and Yehia—emerged as the main decision-makers in the group.

Mohammed bin Laden's children were born of twenty-three different mothers. This created a kind of clan effect within the family, and also expanded the group's international contacts as a result of each wife's national affiliation. There was a "Syrian group," represented by Bakr and Yehia; a "Lebanese group," represented by Yeslam, and so on. Abdulaziz, one of the youngest sons, was part of the "Egyptian group." Interestingly, Osama bin Laden was the only child whose mother was Saudi Arabian. In the eyes of the authorities, this "Saudi" son would make a trustworthy representative, and would eventually become, as mentioned earlier, a close confidant of Prince Turki, the head of Saudi intelligence.[10]

The bin Laden family interests were so tightly linked with those of the Saudi regime that Osama bin Laden could never have received the family support that he did, whether direct or indirect, without the approval—or at least the benevolent neutrality—of the Saudi regime. Even bin Laden admitted, in 1995, that when the Saudi rulers decided to participate actively in the Islamic resistance in Afghanistan, "they turned to [his] family."[11] In the kingdom, family loyalty also implied an active contribution to its most obscure objectives.

Jean-Charles Brisard's report "The Economic Network of the bin Laden Family"—Appendix VII of this book—shows that, just as the ties between legitimate Saudi Arabian business and commercial interests and Islamic terrorism are extremely porous, so is it with the bin Laden family, its business interests, and its most notorious son, Osama. The complex web of companies in the bin Laden galaxy is meant to hide financial networks, revealing ties between dubious networks and companies with ordinary commercial relations, as well as companies established to permanently mask suspicious financial transfers.

Clearly, the bin Laden family has a taste for secrecy. Perhaps this penchant explains its long and privileged relationships with the highest-level Saudi authorities. For more than seventy years, none of the family "affairs"—whether the arrest of Mahrous bin Laden in the late 1970s, or the involvement in the BCCI scandal, or the terrorism of Osama bin Laden—could shake the family company.

According to one anecdote, when a subcontractor in the bin Laden group gave an interview to a financial journal explaining details of a project in progress, his contract was simply canceled. The Saudi kingdom and the bin Laden family have so many shared interests to protect that their stable relationship will most likely continue forever.

The bin Ladens value their privileges, and the security that

the kingdom gives them, too much to reveal even a tiny frag-
ment of its hidden side. Of course, they share this side with a
kingdom that has tolerated for years the action of one of its
sons in the international promotion of a radical Islam.

In this regard, how can we legitimately accept that there is
no longer any connection between the bin Laden family and
Osama bin Laden, when this same family has had close financial ties with the family of his brother-in-law, Khalid bin Mahfouz, accused of contributing millions of dollars to support
Osama bin Laden's terrorist activities? Members of these families are from the same generation; they sit on the same boards
of directors, share the same investments. How can they ignore
their respective public activities?

There is an even more widespread commodity in the
kingdom where oil is king: Saudi hypocrisy toward the West.

IV.
KHALID BIN MAHFOUZ:
THE LUCRATIVE BUSINESS
OF TERRORISM

12. THE BANKER OF TERROR

Khalid bin Mahfouz is not your typical banker. He's not flashy or audacious. At seventy-three, he prefers to keep a low profile. A diabetic for years, he remains impassive behind his thick glasses and moustache, as if distrustful of anything outside his own world.

In 1950, Khalid bin Mahfouz's father founded Saudi Arabia's first bank, the National Commerical Bank (NCB). As powerful as he is discreet, Khalid bin Mahfouz finances all the kingdom's extravagances, starting with the NCB headquarters in Jeddah. Built in 1983, the twenty-seven-story triangular building overlooking the Red Sea is a monument in itself, dominating the city, the sea, and the desert.

His family is one of the most influential in Saudi Arabia. Like the bin Laden family, the bin Mahfouzes came from the province of Hadramaut in southern Yemen. Having descended from a long line of merchants, they immigrated to Saudi Arabia at the beginning of the last century in order to participate in the building of the kingdom. This initial move would prove advantageous for the family, which, like the bin Laden family, became one of the closest to the Saudi rulers.

Born in 1909, the patriarch, Salim bin Mahfouz, settled in Saudi Arabia in 1922. During World War II, he worked in a foreign exchange office in Jeddah, where he stood out for his strong negotiating skills. Under the patronage of another merchant family, the Kaakis, Salim bin Mahfouz learned quickly, and soon expanded the office's services to form the beginnings of a private banking system. The two families obtained a license in 1950 allowing them to create the NCB. Until 1999, the two families controlled more than 50 percent of the bank.[1]

In 1997, Salim bin Mahfouz was recognized for his banking career by the Arab Bankers Association of North America (ABANA). Former presidents of the association include Talat M. Othman, Camille A. Chebeir, and Ziad K. Abdelnour[2]—figures who played key roles in Khalid bin Mahfouz's career. A half century after the NCB's creation, the bin Mahfouz family is one of the wealthiest in the world, with assets estimated at $1.7 billion.[3]

First Salim, then Khalid bin Mahfouz, knew how to make themselves indispensable in the eyes of the Saudi regime. They increased their investments in countries where the Saudi kingdom wanted to assert its religious influence. The NCB soon became the Saudi royal family's bank, and one of the most successful, with $450 million in profits in 2000.[4] In 1989, Khalid bin Mahfouz was appointed to Aramco's Supreme Council by King Fahd. He went on to become established throughout the world, including in the United States. He owns a luxurious estate in Houston, Texas, which has become the new Mecca for the Saudis, as the *Washington Post* described it in 1981.[5]

When Salim bin Mahfouz died in 1994, Khalid took control of the empire. The bin Mahfouz empire is a vast one, covering the major sectors in Saudi Arabia and abroad, most notably banking, agriculture, pharmaceuticals, and telecommunications. The family's economic activities are rooted in three main holding companies in Jeddah: the NCB,[6] Nimir Petroleum Limited,[7] and the Saudi Economic and Development Company (SEDCO). From this base, the family holds majority shares in close to seventy companies around the world.

Khalid bin Mahfouz was a key figure in the Bank of Credit and Commerce International, or BCCI, affair. Between 1986 and 1990, he was a top executive there, holding the position of operational director.[8] His family held a 20 percent share in the bank at the time.[9] He was charged in the United States in 1992 with tax fraud in the bank's collapse.[10] In 1995, held jointly liable in the BCCI's collapse, he agreed to a $245 million settlement to pay the bank's creditors, allowing them to indemnify a portion of the bank's clients. The specific charges against the bank were embezzlement and violation of American, Luxembourg, and British banking laws.

After dominating the financial news throughout the 1990s, the BCCI is now at the center of the financial network put in place by Osama bin Laden's main supporters.[11]

The Bank of Credit and Commerce International was founded on November 29, 1972, by a Pakistani man, Agha Hasan Abedi, who comes from a family of Shiite Muslims. After getting his law degree, he started a career in banking, notably with the Habib Bank. After the partition of India, Abedi went to Karachi in Pakistan in the late 1940s. There, he met Yusif Saigol, the heir of a wealthy family of merchants, who financed the creation of the United Bank Ltd. Taking advantage of the country's economic crisis, and of the Arab dependence on Pakistani labor, he convinced authorities in Abu Dhabi in 1966 to open a branch for Pakistani workers in the United Arab Emirates, and to allow him to manage the workers' finances.

Agha Hasan Abedi's determination to create an international financial institution capable of embodying and supporting the economic vitality of Arab countries in view of large Western banks would depend on two things: the administrative support of Pakistan and the financial support of the Emirates. In order to ensure the BCCI's independence, Abedi decided to create two holding companies consolidating all of the branches. BCCI Holdings SA was registered in Luxembourg in 1972, while BCCI SA was registered in the Cayman Islands in 1975. At the same time, a fund for employee shareholding called International Credit and Investment Company Holding was created in the Cayman Islands.

In order to improve the BCCI's international standing, the founders got support from the Bank of America. Eager to expand its presence in the Gulf States, the bank took a 25 percent stake in the BCCI, for a total of $2.5 million. The Bank of America became a shareholder alongside Sheikh Zayed bin Sultan Al-Nahayan; Kamal Adham, Saudi Arabia's former head of intelligence; and Faisal Al-Fulaij, president of Kuwait Airways; as well as rulers from the different emirates that make up the United Arab Emirates.

Success came quickly for the BCCI, and the oil crisis played an important part in its expansion. In 1988, the BCCI counted four hundred branches in seventy-three countries. However, from the very beginning, the bank adopted some unusual financing methods, such as allocating large loans without a real guarantee, in return for investments in the company according to the practice of "loan back." This way, the main loan beneficiaries were the shareholders themselves, such as Kamal Adhan ($400 million) and the Gokal family ($80 million).

The BCCI also intended to establish itself in the very heart of Western finance, the United States. In 1976, it tried to purchase the National Bank of Georgia with the cooperation of its president, Thomas Bertram Lance, one of Jimmy Carter's associates, who would become the President's budget director. The BCCI's agreement with the Bank of America did not, however, allow it to have stakes on American soil. Two American lawyers stepped in to handle negotiations. They were Clark M. Clifford and Robert Altman, associates of Thomas Bertram Lance. In 1977, the BCCI and Ghaith Pharaon bought the Bank of America's holding in the BCCI (for $34 million). The same year, the BCCI tried to purchase another American bank, the Chelsea National Bank. The offer was presented by the Gokal family, with the BCCI acting as financial adviser. But American regulators refused the deal because of the ties between the BCCI and the Gokals. The BCCI was subjected to American laws requiring the monitoring of all foreign banks investing in the United States because it was registered in countries without sufficient regulations.

Ghaith Pharaon, who already had investments in several

banks in Detroit and Houston—acquired with the support or in partnership with the former governor of Texas, John Connally—was put in contact with Thomas Bertram Lance.

Ghaith Pharaon made an offer to buy the National Bank of Georgia in 1977 and appointed Roy Carlson—formerly of the Bank of America—its manager. It turned out that the BCCI had granted Ghaith Pharaon a loan for this purchase, and that he was acting as a screen for the bank.

At the end of 1977, Eugene Metzger, and Jackson Stephens, an associate of Thomas Bertram Lance and Jimmy Carter, were looking for a buyer for Financial General Bankshares. Represented by a group of investors, the BCCI decided to buy IDB. The investors included Kamal Adham, Faisal Al-Fallaj, Sheikh Sultan bin Zayed Al-Nahyan, and Abdullah Darwaish. The group attempted to buy the company's stocks without declaring the purchase. Federal authorities, in turn, forced them to sell back the shares. In order to get around this problem, the interested parties created the Credit and Commerce American Holdings (CCAH) in 1978 in the Dutch Antilles, and made Clark Clifford, Robert Altman, Jack W. Beddow, and A. Vincent Scoffone its managers. In 1980, the holding company announced its purchase of Financial General Bankshares. Federal authorities approved the purchase in 1982, deeming that the BCCI was neither financing nor directing the takeover. Managed by Clark Clifford, Robert Altman, and Aijaz Afridi, the bank became the First American Bank. It wasn't until 1991 that federal authorities discovered a loan granted to CCAH by the Banque Arabe et Internationale d' Investissement (BAII), a French institution closely linked to the

BCCI, headed by Yves Lamarches. The guarantor on the $50 million loan was a BCCI subsidiary in the Cayman Islands. In addition, one of the shareholders in the CCAH was Mashriq Corp, also a BCCI subsidiary. Finally, it was discovered that, between 1980 and 1989, the BCCI had granted loans to the CCAH for a total of $856 million.

In 1985, Ghaith Pharaon proceeded with the purchase of the Independence Bank, another American institution, thanks to a loan granted on the basis of a letter of credit from the BAII. In 1986, he sold a part of his stake in the BCCI to Khalid bin Mahfouz and his brothers, who became 20 percent shareholders in the bank. This wouldn't stop the FBI and the IRS from issuing an arrest warrant against Ghaith Pharaon in 1991 for tax fraud in the BCCI affair, as well as extortion in the United States.[12]

Starting in the mid-1980s, the BCCI was accused of other fraudulent activities. In 1985, American authorities fined the bank $4.7 million for fraud and nondisclosure in a $12 million transfer. American authorities uncovered a vast BCCI operation of tax evasion and money laundering, following an undercover investigation by customs authorities that led to the arrest and conviction of Khalid Amjad Awan and Nazir Chinoy. In 1990, two Colombian drug traffickers, Rudolf Armbrecht and Gonzalo Mora, were also arrested and convicted in the case. The BCCI had notably transferred funds to subsidiaries in Panama through company accounts and offered loans through the BCP in Switzerland in exchange for cash deposits made in Miami. These operations took place even though the bank knew of the criminal origins of the money.

In 1988, a BCCI branch in Colombia was accused of granting a loan to drug lord Pablo Escobar that reportedly financed the assassination of a Colombian magistrate.

Following Manuel Noriega's arrest in 1989, American judicial authorities revealed that the BCCI, in particular Amjad Awan, was in charge of managing the former dictator's personal accounts, as well as those of several drug traffickers in Panama. The BCCI participated in the laundering of $25 million from Manuel Noriega's accounts. The BCCI also had ties with several weapons traffickers, as well as with Abu Nidal, whose secret accounts were handled out of a London branch. The BCCI facilitated financial operations for Iraqi arms dealer Samir Najmadeen, as well as for Adnan Kashoggi, one of Kamal Adham's close contacts. Kashoggi was secretly selling arms to Iran, and at the same time was in contact with an Iraqi intermediary, Manucher Ghorbanifar.

In 1987, the BCCI financed the purchase of high-resistance steel for General Inam Ul-Haq, who was in charge of the Pakistani nuclear arms program. The bank also financed the creation of a high-tech research center run by the head of Pakistani nuclear research, A. Qadir Khan.

In Peru, authorities discovered that the BCCI had given the government in power at that time $3 million between 1986 and 1987 in exchange for a deposit of $270 million in an account in Panama in order to mislead international organizations about the country's financial situation.

The BCCI was granted immunity until 1990 because it was registered in accommodating countries, and its financial operations had largely gone unmonitored. But an audit conducted by Price Waterhouse in 1990 showed that loans to share-holders based on the "loan back" policy totaled $2 billion in 1989. The main beneficiaries were the Gokal family, who received a loan of $1.2 billion, against a guarantee of $65 million; Ghaith Pharaon, who received $288 million, against his brother Wabel's 11 percent holding; and Khalid bin Mahfouz, who received $152.5 million, against his $150 million invest-ment in the bank in 1986. Price Waterhouse issued a warning in 1991 citing losses evaluated at $5 to $10 billion.

The Abu Dhabi ruler who always seemed to intervene in time, who had contributed upward of $1 billion in financial aid to the bank, and who had become the leading shareholder, could no longer come to the bank's rescue.

On July 2, 1991, regulators in the United States, Great Britain, France, and Spain—as well as administrative authori-ties in Switzerland and Luxembourg—decided to liquidate the bank, and the ruling took effect July 5. On July 29, the New York district attorney charged the bank's main managers with fraud. The BCCI was fined $200 million.

The U.S. Senate report on the BCCI described Khalid bin Mahfouz as "the most powerful banker in the Middle East."[13] In reality, he is much more than that. At the crossroads of busi-ness affairs and militant Islam, he embodies all of the kingdom's contradictions in regard to Islamic fundamentalism.

Khalid bin Mahfouz's problems began in 1992 with the BCCI scandal, in which he was accused of having precipitated the collapse. At the same time, the Senate report on the BCCI revealed documents implicating the National Commercial

Bank in the delivery of arms between Israel and Iran in the 1980s. The operation was financed by the Saudis in the framework of an agreement to liberate American hostages in Beirut.

In view of these accusations, Khalid bin Mahfouz was forced to step down as CEO of the NCB in 1992. His brother Mohammed took over for him in the interim until his return in 1996, after he agreed to a settlement to pay back BCCI creditors.

His decline continued in 1999, with the American investigations into the U.S. embassy attacks in Africa one year earlier. American authorities discovered suspicious transfers of "tens of millions of dollars" made after April 1999 from the NCB to charity organizations associated with Osama bin Laden, some of which were controlled by Khalid bin Mahfouz's own family.[14]

Normally hesitant to cooperate with American authorities, Saudi Arabia was faced with a moral dilemma, as well as a major attack on its own interests, because the bank was also "its bank." The kingdom finally ordered an audit the same year in order to verify the allegations. The audit uncovered massive transfers made to charity organizations with ties to Osama bin Laden, some of which were controlled by members of the bin Mahfouz family. Shortly thereafter, Saudi authorities placed Khalid bin Mahfouz under house arrest in a hospital in Taif. According to our information, he is still there as of mid-2002.

With Saudi interests at stake, the kingdom needed to safeguard what it could, and to have more control in the bank's management. Starting in July 1999, the Saudi regime decided to dilute the bin Mahfouz holdings by purchasing a major share of their investment and placing it in the Public Investment Fund (40 percent) and the General Organization for Social Insurance (10 percent). At the same time, Abdullah Salim Bahamdan, who had long served as CEO, became the bank's new president.

Furthermore, the Saudis had to handle the bin Mahfouzes carefully, since they knew the family had close ties with Osama bin Laden. As former CIA director James Woolsey confirmed, in addition to the financial support given by the bin Mahfouzes, there are also family ties between them. Khalid bin Mahfouz's own sister is married to Osama bin Laden.[15] The Saudi kingdom was therefore careful not to punish the bin Mahfouz family too much, though Khalid was attracting so much media attention that it was hard to avoid reprimanding him. However, this was not the case for his family or his brother-in-law's family.

The bin Mahfouz sons were allowed to keep a 16 percent share in the bank; Khalid's wife, Naila Kaaki, kept 10 percent; and most surprising, Khalid himself kept a 10 percent share. The bin Mahfouz family would therefore remain an important shareholder in the bank. In addition, with two bin Mahfouz sons (Abdul Rahman and Sultan) and Khalid's brother-in-law, Saleh Hussein Kaaki, on the board of directors, the bin Mahfouz family still represented 30 percent of the nine-member board.[16]

The bin Mahfouz financial and charity network is one of the most active in facilitating Osama bin Laden's activities. We are now discovering the many ramifications and connections between this empire and the Al Qaeda organization.

The two worlds have come in contact many times over the years. While it is sometimes difficult to prove direct financial support, there is, however, enough interconnection between economic structures and Islamic entities to suggest their collusion.

The bin Mahfouz universe offers examples of both cases. Several entities are connected directly or indirectly to Osama bin Laden. These include companies like Al Khaleejia for Export Promotion and Marketing Co., the Saudi Sudanese Bank and SEDCO, as well as charity-focused NGOs like the International Development Foundation in Great Britain, Blessed Relief in Sudan, and the Muwafaq Foundation in Saudi Arabia.

The advertising agency Al Khaleejia for Export, Promotion and Marketing,[17] created in 1977 and run by one of Khalid's brothers, Waleed bin Mahfouz, is suspected by the United States of having made donations to charity organizations tied to Osama bin Laden. Another figure involved in these networks through various Sudanese banks is Saleh Abdullah Kamel, who also has a financial stake in the advertising agency. In 1992, after the BCCI scandal, when Khalid bin Mahfouz was forced to step down, Saleh Kamel declared: "Khalid is known for his honesty and integrity . . . the accusations against him are unfounded and false."[18] The man was nonetheless fined $170 million for his "honesty."

As we indicated above, Khalid bin Mahfouz's brother, Mohammed Salim bin Mahfouz, is the founder with Mohammed Saleh Affara of the International Development Foundation (IDF),[19] which was based until recently in Oxford. Originally from Yemen, Mohammed Saleh

Affara, an intermediary for arms sales, is implicated in the Sawari-2 affair.

It so happens that the IDF was located at the same Oxford address as the International Islamic Relief Organization (IIRO), one of Osama bin Laden's main recruitment centers. Another organization, the Oxford Trust for Islamic Studies, is also located at the same address in England.

Even more troubling, the bin Mahfouz family holding company, SEDCO, has a British subsidiary called SEDCO Services Limited,[20] registered on December 6, 1994, in London. As of September 6, 1999, the company's address was the same as that of the International Development Foundation.

Camille Chebeir the President of SEDCO Services, was vice president and CEO of the Saudi National Commercial Bank, headed by Khalid bin Mahfouz. On December 21, 1999, he was appointed a board member of Hybridon Inc. as a representative of SEDCO, which is a shareholder in the American pharmaceutical group.

Mohammed Salim bin Mahfouz is also the founder of the Saudi Sudanese Bank in Khartoum, Sudan.

One of Khalid bin Mahfouz's sons, Abdul Rahman bin Mahfouz, is a manager of the Sudanese branch of the Saudi charity organization Muwafaq (Blessed Relief), suspected of helping to organize the assassination attempt against Egyptian president Hosni Mubarak in Ethiopia in 1995.[21] This organization, suspected of having ties to Osama bin Laden, is also accused by the CIA of having received funds via the Saudi National Commercial Bank, headed at the time by Khalid bin Mahfouz.

Investigators are also interested in the Saudi-based Muwafaq Foundation, headed by the wealthy Saudi industrialist Yassim Al Qadi, cited by American authorities as one of thirty-nine organizations or individuals suspected of conspiring with the Al Qaeda terrorist organization.

The Saudi branch of Muwafaq includes several executive members from the kingdom's most privileged families. Yet the U.S. Treasury Department claimed that "Muwafaq is a screen for Al Qaeda, and is financed by rich Saudi businessmen." The U.S. Treasury Department added that the foundation agreed to "transfer millions of dollars to Osama bin Laden."[22]

A 1997 report from the UN General Assembly on the human rights situation in Sudan indicated that several members of the foundation were murdered in Malakal, Sudan, in 1996. The report mentions that the foundation sponsors nutritional and educational programs in several regions in Sudan and that it is also active in agriculture and social services.

The Muwafaq Foundation has an offshore holding company whose representatives were identified as a result of legal proceedings in Great Britain. Documents released during the trial revealed that in addition to Yassim Al Qadi, two members of the bin Mahfouz family were involved in the holding company, including Abdul Rahman, who is a director of Blessed Relief in Sudan. He is also a board member of the National Commercial Bank.

Yassim Al Qadi is an important figure in the bin Mahfouz universe. He is a shareholder and a board member of Global Diamond Resources, a California-based company specializing in diamond exploration. He is also active in the real estate, banking, and chemical industries in Saudi Arabia, Turkey, Kazakhstan, Pakistan, and Malaysia.

The CEO of Global Diamond Resources explained that Yassim Al Qadi's decision to invest in the company was made in London in 1998, in the presence of Arab investors, including a member of the bin Laden family. He added that he accepted Al Qadi's investment of close to $3 million on the basis of a guarantee from the bin Laden family.[23]

According to other sources, Yassim Al Qadi had already been named by the United States as a major financial contributor to the terrorist group Hamas. The U.S. Department of Justice had therefore decided to freeze his assets in a Chicago-based foundation called the Quranic Literacy Institute. One of the foundation's leaders, Mohammed Salah, was also suspected of contributing to a financing network for Hamas. American federal agents concluded that in 1991, Yassim Al Qadi had tried to cover up a deposit of $820,000, which came from one of his Swiss bank accounts and was used by Mohammed Salah to buy weapons for Hamas.

According to our findings, Yassim Al Qadi is also a director of the Pakistani company Shifa International Hospitals Ltd, based in Islamabad. Raies bin Mahfouz is on the company's board of directors. Yassim Al Qadi is an example, like so many others, of the shift in Saudi financial networks toward terrorism, and of the close ties uniting the bin Ladens and the bin Mahfouzes at the heart of these networks.

At the same time, other companies reveal the connections between Kamal Adham, former director of Saudi intelligence and key player in the BCCI scandal, and various companies, including the Delta International Bank SAE and the Arabian Shield Development Co., in which Kamal Adham was a shareholder.

The fact that associates of Khalid bin Mahfouz held important management and executive positions in the Al Shifa pharmaceutical factory is another testament to the involvement of powerful Saudi businessmen in Osama bin Laden's networks.

One such Saudi businessman, Saleh Idris, of Sudanese descent, had owned the factory since April 1998, before it was the object of American military strikes on August 20, 1998. The United States estimated that the factory may have been manufacturing chemical weapons. Before this date, the CIA believed that Osama bin Laden was a main shareholder in the factory, investing through dummy companies. An American investigative agency, Kroll Associates, concluded that it was unlikely the factory was developing chemical weapons.

However, Saleh Idris is linked through several investments to Khalid bin Mahfouz and Mohammed Al Amoudi. These ties shed new light on what was at stake in the Al Shifa factory.

Saleh Idris is involved in Al-Majd General Services Ltd, located at the headquarters in Khartoum of Abu Fath Al-Tigani Investment Intena, which is a subsidiary of the Tadamon Islamic Bank, shareholder of the Al Shamal Islamic Bank, one of Osama bin Laden's main financial vehicles (see p. 211).

Saleh Idris is also manager of the Saudi Sudanese Bank, whose president is none other than Khalid bin Mahfouz. Throughout the 1980s, Saleh Idris was even a board member of the Saudi National Commerical Bank. Saleh Idris is also

Mohammed Al Amoudi's partner within the British company M.S. Management Ltd., with Nasrullah Khan.

Khalid bin Mahfouz is one of the leading shareholders (25 percent) in the International Bank of Yemen, of which the Bank of America owns 20 percent. The Yemenite bank is led by Ahmed Kaid Barakat and Ali Lutf Al Thor. The bin Mahfouz family also owns a moving company based in Jeddah called Marei Bin Mahfouz and Ahmad Al Amoudi Co. of which Mohammed Hussein Al Amoudi is a shareholder in the company.

Al Amoudi is also president of Al Amoudi Group Company Ltd of Saudi Arabia, one of the kingdom's leading conglomerates, whose chairman, Sheikh Hamed bin Ali Mussalam, was implicated in the Sawari-2 affair. Mussalam is also an associate of the founder of International Development Foundation in London.

The bin Mahfouz galaxy is not only made up of dubious investments, but its creator gives a new dimension to business relations. He was able to establish such relations in the past, notably with the United States.

A Pakistani bank in which he is the main shareholder is a good example: Prime Commercial Bank is run by Sami Bubarak Baarma, a Saudi Arabian citizen, born in 1955; Saeed Chaudhry; and Abdul Rahman bin Khalid bin Mahfouz, son of Khalid Mahfouz.

Sami Mubarak Baarma is an executive of SNCB Securities Limited in London, another bin Mahfouz financial subsidiary. For the NCB, he manages a financial network called Middle

East Capital Group (MECG), based in Lebanon. One of MECG's directors is Henry Sarkissian, who runs several companies in the Binladin Group. Sami Mubarak Baarma is also in charge of the Saudi National Commercial Bank's international division. As a result of his influence in Pakistan, he became a member of the Carlyle Group's advisory committee.

The Carlyle Group's leading investors include many figures from former U.S. president George H. W. Bush's entourage, as well as that of President George W. Bush. Its board of directors includes important figures from the Bush team: James A. Baker III, former secretary of state under the first President Bush; Frank C. Carlucci, former secretary of defense under Ronald Reagan; Richard G. Darman, former director of the Office of Management and Budget under George H. W. Bush between 1989 and 1993; and John Sununu, former White House chief of staff under George Bush. In addition, Saudi Prince Al-Waleed bin Talal, nephew of King Fahd, owns an indeterminate stake in the group. Even President George W. Bush was a member of the board of directors of one of the Carlyle Group's subsidiaries, Caterair, between 1990 and 1994.

In 1987 an obscure Saudi financier named Adbullah Taha Bakhsh invested in Harken, a Texas oil company of which George W. Bush was a director from 1986 to 1993.

The deal consisted of recapitalizing the company, which was going through difficult times. This Saudi investor is none other than the partner of Khalid bin Mahfouz and Ghaith Pharaon. And so Taha Bakhsh became an 11.5 percent shareholder in Harken Energy Corp.

His representative within Harken Energy is not unknown

either. Talat Othman, is a member alongside Frank Carlucci of one of America's most prestigious think tanks, the Middle East Policy Council as well as being a leading Arab-American supporter of the Republican party.

These investors know each other well. They've been sitting on the same boards for more than ten years, alongside Salem bin Laden, the brother of Osama bin Laden who died in a plane crash in Texas in 1988.

It is therefore not surprising to find James R. Bath on the list of shareholders in two other companies controlled by George W. Bush—Arbusto '79 Ltd. and Arbusto '80 Ltd. In the late 1970s, James R. Bath, a wealthy Texas entrepreneur, invested $50,000 in these companies to get them off the ground. At the time, he was the U.S. business representative for Salem bin Laden according to the terms of a 1976 trust agreement. It came out later, in 1993, in an official U.S. document, that he was also the legal representative of Khalid bin Mahfouz.

The two entities founded by George W. Bush were later merged with Harken Energy; all traces of these transactions have disappeared.

Khalid bin Mahfouz was very active in Texas at the time. During a deposition before the Financial Crimes Enforcement Network (FinCEN), James R. Bath claimed to own Skyway Aircraft Leasing Ltd, which in fact belonged to Khalid bin Mahfouz.

In 1990, Mahfouz procured a loan of $1.4 million for James R. Bath, allowing him to buy a stake in the Houston Airport. Following Salem bin Laden's death in 1988, Khalid bin Mahfouz took back this holding.

But the bin Mahfouz empire also shares common interests with American oil companies, specifically concerning Central Asia in the area around the Caspian Sea, which is coveted by these companies.

In the last few years, Khalid bin Mahfouz's Nimir Petroleum signed exploration and drilling agreements in the major Gulf States, Central Asia, from Oman to Kazakhstan, and even in Venezuela.

In 1994, Nimir Petroleum agreed to partner with the Saudi group Delta Oil Company, which had been trying for years to get a contract in order to build a gas and oil pipeline between Turkmenistan and Pakistan—via Afghanistan. The main partner in the $5 billion project was none other than the American corporate giant Unocal Corp. Negotiations with the Taliban had come to a deadlock, and the Delta Oil–Unocal consortium was undoubtedly counting on Khalid bin Mahfouz's support in the undertaking.

Besides, Khalid bin Mahfouz was not the only Saudi businessman to take a strong interest in Central Asia's oil at the time. Starting in 1991, Dallah Albaraka, a group controlled by Saleh Abdullah Kamel, was also getting involved in the exploitation of several sites in Kazakhstan and Uzbekistan.

In the world of the BCCI, there is another facet of the BCCI that is little known. It involves investments made by the bank's main protagonists in the luxury goods industry, through a financial group in the Gulf controlled by Khalid bin Mahfouz's circle.

In 1982, a group of investors from the Middle East created

a financial company with the goal of building a diversified portfolio, with assets estimated today at more than $5 billion. The group concentrated on reputable and financially stable investments in the areas of publishing, distribution, watchmaking, and luxury goods.

The company, Investcorp, is located in Manama, the capital of Bahrain, and was founded by the region's most elite oilmen and financiers: Nemir Kirdar, an Iraqi businessman and former manager of Chase Manhattan Bank in the Persian Gulf; Ahmed Ali Kanoo, who died in 1997; Ahmed Zaki Yamani, former oil minister of Saudi Arabia; and Abdul Rahman Salim Al Ateeqi, former oil minister of Kuwait. Investcorp's holding company, Investcorp Investment Holdings Corp., is registered in the Cayman Islands, and its main subsidiary overseeing international activities, Investcorp SA, is registered in Luxembourg.

Inspired by the movement toward autonomy and the financial emancipation of the Persian Gulf after the first oil crisis—especially in view of large Western financial institutions—Investcorp was established on similar principles to those that led to the creation of the BCCI in 1972. Though the two entities are not in the same industries—the BCCI is a banking institution, while Investcorp is meant to be an investment company—they were both created with the joint support of the Emirate authorities, Saudi investors, and Western banks (Bank of America in the case of the BCCI, and Chase Manhattan in the case of Investcorp).

In addition, their holding companies were located in the same offshore centers (the Cayman Islands and Luxembourg).

The two entities also have common shareholders. In addition

to its two main executives (Abdul Rahman Salim Al Ateeqi, chairman, and Nemir Kirdar, president and CEO) as well as representatives from the government of the United Arab Emirates, Investcorp also has an executive committee made up of eighteen of the group's main shareholders, many of whom were shareholders in the BCCI.

At least four of these members represent the interests of, or are closely involved with, Saudi businessmen who played a major role in the BCCI affair. They are Abdullah Taha Bakhsh, Mohammed Abdullah Al Zamil, Bakr Mohammed bin Laden, and Omar Al Aggad.

Between 1976 and 1982, Abdullah Taha Bakhsh—an investor in Harkin energy, recall—was the representative for the bin Laden family in the United States. He also represents Khalid bin Mahfouz's financial interests in the Middle East. What's more, several sources emphasize the fact that he represents the interests of Khalid Salim bin Mahfouz on the board of directors of Investcorp. In fact, bin Mahfouz holds a 25 percent stake in Investcorp, thanks to Bakhsh's services.

Mohammed Abdullah Al Zamil is one of the main executives of the Bahrain Islamic Bank BSC. The financial institution has stakes in close to twenty banks around the world, including the Tadamon Islamic Bank, an important shareholder in the Al Shamal Islamic Bank, mentioned earlier in regard to Osama bin Laden's personal investments. In addition, Mohammed Abdullah Al Zamil heads the family-held Al Zamil Company in Saudi Arabia, in which Khalid bin Mahfouz is the main shareholder.

Finally, his son Hamad Al Zamil is a partner with Khalid

bin Mahfouz in the Jeddah-based advertising group Tihama for Advertising, Public Relations and Marketing. Its president, Saleh Abdullah, was president of the Albaraka Bank-Sudan and a shareholder in the Tadamon Islamic Bank.

Bakr Mohammed bin Laden is Osama bin Laden's older brother. He has headed the Binladin Group since 1988, which has several subsidiaries in common with Khalid bin Mahfouz, notably through the Saudi Investment Company (SICO), created in 1980. Throughout the 1980s, the company, which is led by Yeslam bin Laden, another brother of Osama bin Laden, created a network of dummy companies registered in the Cayman Islands, the Bahamas, and Ireland. These companies are generally controlled by SICO, as well as by former BCCI partners.

Omar Al Aggad has large investments in Saudi Arabia. At the same time, he is a shareholder in the Swiss charity organization Welfare Association, which promotes development and social programs in Palestine. It is headed by Abdul Majeed Shoman, former president of Saudfin, a Swiss holding company owned by the Pakistani shipping tycoon Abbas Gokal, who was the cofounder and one of the BCCI's main shareholders. Gokal was sentenced to fourteen years in prison in 1997 for his participation in the liquidation of the bank in Great Britain, in particular for misappropriation of funds and conspiracy to commit fraud. The Court of Appeals in London upheld this verdict in March 1999.

Investcorp's investments have not always been judicious, and the company is caught in several litigations, notably in the United States, Great Britain, and France for fraud and breaking accounting laws. The context of Investcorp's creation, as we explained, is similar to that of the BCCI in the early 1980s, especially in the discovery of fraudulent practices. Its shareholders would have liked to diversify their assets in creating a financially and politically sound group.

The ties between the bin Mahfouz family and various figures in the BCCI scandal on the one hand, and Osama bin Laden's networks on the other, are proof of the porousness of the Saudi financial milieu. The possibility that a banker, through lack of vigilance, allowed funds to be transferred to such organizations is not unimaginable. But the bin Mahfouz case goes beyond the classic scenarios, which at the time saved numerous BCCI executives, who found themselves implicated—sometimes unknowingly—in dubious transactions.

Khalid bin Mahfouz personifies Saudi Arabia's vitality and banking might. He is also personifies his ruler, who is also his best customer. In this multifaceted kingdom, he played the role of conniver, while the kingdom, for several years, played the role of accommodator, if not collaborator. His reach was vast, was his ruses. A telling anecdote: In 1990 he purchased eleven Irish passports for him and his family in a million-dollar deal secretly handled by the Irish prime minister Charles Haughey. Haughey—the subject of several corruption scandals in his long political career—apparently handed the documents over at a special lunch at Dublin's Shelborne Hotel. The exposure of this deal caused a scandal in 1994 and much embarrassment in late 2001 and when it was reported that Haughey had done business with a bin Laden associate.

(The passports are now out of date and the Irish authorities have been told, if approached, not to renew them.)

Khalid bin Mahfouz, then, temporarily personified for the kingdom the official instrument of its own contradictions in regard to world and in special regard to Osama bin Laden, who became the terrorist it should have disowned.

AFTERWORD

A 1998 memo written by Al Qaeda military chief Mohammed Atef reveals that Osama bin Laden's group had detailed knowledge of negotiations that were taking place between Afghanistan's ruling Taliban and American government and business leaders over plans for a U.S. oil and gas pipeline across that Central Asian country.

The e-mail memo was found in 1998 on a computer seized by the FBI during its investigation into the 1998 African embassy bombings, which were sponsored by Al Qaeda. Atef's memo was discovered by FBI counterterrorism expert John O'Neill, who left the bureau in 2001, complaining that U.S. oil interests were hindering his investigation into Al Qaeda. O'Neill, who became security chief at the World Trade Center, died in the September 11 attack.

Atef's memo shines new light on what Al Qaeda knew about U.S. efforts to normalize relations with the Taliban in exchange for the fundamentalist government's supporting the construction of an oil and gas pipeline across Afghanistan. As we document in the book, the Clinton and Bush administrations negotiated with the Taliban, both to get the repressive regime to widen its government as well as look favorably on U.S. companies' attempts to construct an oil pipeline.

The seven-page memo was signed "Abu Hafs," which is the military name of Atef, who was the military chief of Al Qaeda and is believed to have been killed in November 2001 during U.S. operations in Afghanistan. It shows Al Qaeda's keen interest in the U.S.-Taliban negotiations and raises more questions as to whether the U.S. military threat to the Taliban in July 2001 could have triggered Al Qaeda's September 11 attack.

Atef's memo is not about the pipeline alone, though it mentions the project several times. It is an analysis of the political situation facing the Taliban. It documents the movement's rise, its leadership, the geopolitical importance of Afghanistan, the Taliban's relationship with Pakistan, as well as the movement's relationship with the Arab Mujahedeen. The document's intended readership is unclear. But it reveals that the pipeline was seen as a strategic offering toward the West, in order to make the Taliban government acceptable to the United States and Pakistan, as well as to reduce military and investigative pressure on the country to rein in or even extradite bin Laden.

Atef explains that the United States wants "to take control of any region which has huge quantities of oil reserves," and "the American government is keen on laying the oil and gas pipelines from Turkmenistan through Afghanistan to Pakistan." Atef concludes that Al Qaeda's "duty toward the movement [Taliban] is to stand behind it, support it materially and morally, especially because its regional and international enemies are working night and day to put an end to it and make it fail."

It seems clear the military chief didn't expect the pipeline negotiations to bear fruit. Referring to the Pakistani government as "nonbelievers," and noting that the pipeline "will be under American control . . . and it also goes through the territories of Pakistan which are allied to America," Atef implies that the Taliban has no intention of ultimately cooperating with the project, but is trying to string along the Americans and Pakistanis to win some breathing space for its unpopular government.

The Atef memo is the latest piece of evidence documenting a murky chapter in recent American history—the overtures of the last two American administrations to the repressive Taliban regime. The newly discovered Atef memo makes clear that in 1998, at least, Al Qaeda was well informed about negotiations between the Taliban and the U.S. on the oil pipeline and other American concerns. The memo also shows that those negotiations were the Taliban's gambit to extend its power; Mullah Omar's government never had any intention of allowing U.S. firms to construct an oil pipeline, or letting the U.S. dictate the members of its ruling body. Given the inside knowledge Al Qaeda had about U.S.-Taliban negotiations, it's reasonable to suspect bin Laden's group also received and understood the U.S. threat of military action delivered in late July as a threat of war. It is also worth asking whether, had this threat of July 2001 been widely known, U.S. intelligence agencies might have analyzed the information they were receiving about bin Laden's plots against the U.S. differently.

Still, *plus ça change*. The Saudi royal family has refused to share information about the fifteen Saudi citizens who took part in the September 11 hijackings. And yet the White

House chief of staff describes the Saudi Arabians as "wonderful allies" in the war on terrorism.[1] Whatever tensions exist between the two allies, the ties that bind them are far stronger than what separates them. The U.S. is the largest buyer of Saudi oil—about 1.7 million barrels a day, more than twice the consumption fifteen years ago. Saudi Arabia is also the largest purchaser of American weapons, having bought $39 billion of U.S. arms in the 1990s. Saudi Arabia is also a major investor in the U.S. In 2001, trade reached almost $20 billion, according to U.S. figures.[2]

The key to this relationship is what Ali al-Naimi, the Saudi minister of petroleum and mineral resources, told a recent conference sponsored by the Council on Foreign Relations, Petroleum Industry Research Foundation, and the U.S. Saudi Business Council: "As the world's dominant oil producer and supplier, Saudi Arabia has been committed to ensuring the stability of the international oil market and the reliability of supplies to customers...[and]...has consistently championed the cause of price moderation."[3]

During Saudi Crown Prince Abdullah's visit to the George W. Bush ranch in Texas—ostensibly to discuss the Middle East crisis—the crown prince was joined by al-Naimi, who is officially supervising the kingdom's $25 billion gas initiative plan, which is designed to to give foreign investors—including the oil and gas companies based in Texas—a stake in natural water, gas, and electricity projects. Al-Naimi was there to assure investors that that rising violence in the Middle East would derail these deals.[4]

And over in Afghanistan, interim Afghan leader Hamid Karzai—a former consultant on Unocal's payroll—decided on May 30, 2002, to revive the pipeline project with Pakistan and Turkmenistan, signing an agreement under which the three governments agree to implement a pipeline from Turkmenistan to Pakistan through Afghanistan. Thus the hunt for foreign investment, the new Great Game—to borrow Ahmed Rashid's phrase—is on again. Mohammed Ebrahim Adel, Afghanistan's new deputy minister of mines and industries, says: "Naturally, Unocal is economically and technically stronger . . . we are sure Unocal will win."[5] Would that U.S. intelligence agencies' investigations into Al Qaeda activities in the months before September 11 had such a productive ending.

Those of us living in wealthy countries, however, can no longer avoid criticism of the last fifty years of foreign policy, especially oil policy. Our economic development has depended on alliances with oil dictators and has encouraged them in their promotion of the most reactionary beliefs.

Sooner or later the terrorists and their commanders and supporters will stand trial, maybe even the states that harbored and objectively supported them. What remains uncertain is the fate of those who inspire and finance them, through action, negligence, or self-interest.

Yes, on September 11, Osama bin Laden turned the page on a long chapter of misunderstandings and unlikely alliances that shaped, sometimes reinforced, but always upheld the tenets of a radical Islam. These alliances include some of the most respectable financiers in the world; a family who helped build the Saudi kingdom; Afghan friendships based on opportunism rather than clever stratagem; secret misdeeds in Libya, accomplished with the help of Great Britain's friends; a man sought by the FBI but saved by the State Department, singled out by Western political leaders, but actually pursued by Colonel Qaddhafi; and Taliban friends, with whom American diplomats continued to reconcile before finally bombing them.

Osama bin Laden encompasses some of all these things. Yet contrary to what some claim (often in order to preserve the petro-monarchies that are so generous toward their obligers), Osama bin Laden does not have the qualities of a hard-line terrorist leader blinded by fanaticism, which would have alienated him during the war against the Soviets.

In looking at his past and retracing his journey, we must realize to what extent the attacks he commanded are not the work of an unstable mind. He comes from a good family, and wants to play a part in his country's destiny—to defend it with the weapons we originally provided.

APPENDICES

APPENDICES

APPENDIX I

CHRONOLOGY

1957   Osama bin Laden is born in Riyadh, Saudi Arabia. He is the seventeenth child of a family of fifty-four, whose father, Mohammed bin Laden, was born in Yemen.

1979   Osama bin Laden graduates with a degree in civil engineering from King Abdul Aziz University in Jeddah.

1979   December 26: the Soviet army invades Afghanistan. Osama bin Laden leaves Saudi Arabia to join the Afghan resistance.

1980–1986 Osama bin Laden helps organize the Muslim resistance in Afghanistan.

1988   Osama bin Laden founds the Al Qaeda organization for the recruitment and financing of the Afghan resistance.

1989   June 30: the Islamic National Front takes power in Sudan.

1989   After the Soviets retreat from Afghanistan, Osama bin Laden returns to Saudi Arabia, where he supports the antiestablishment movements and works for the family business, the Saudi Binladin Group.

1990   August 2: Iraq invades Kuwait.

1991   In April, Osama bin Laden leaves Saudi Arabia after opposing the kingdom's alliance with the United States. He goes to Afghanistan, then to Khartoum in Sudan, where Muslims are welcome without visas.

1991   The United States installs its military bases in Saudi Arabia.

1992   Osama bin Laden defines Al Qaeda's foundations: they should put aside opposition to Shiite terrorist groups, and cooperate with the opposition to American presence on Saudi soil, and the confrontation with American forces in the horn of Africa, notably Somalia. At the same time, he sets up several companies in Khartoum in order to finance his political activities. He is joined by 480 Afghan combatants.

1992   December 29: a bomb explodes in a hotel in Aden, where American troops are en route to the humanitarian operation in Somalia.

1993   Sudan is officially considered by the West to be a state that sponsors terrorism. Bin Laden's militants try to obtain nuclear weapons components.

1994   In January, information is released citing Osama bin Laden's financing of at least three training camps in northern Sudan, where militants from several countries are receiving military training.

1994   March 10: Osama bin Laden and three accomplices murder two German nationals in Surt, Libya, one of whom is a counterintelligence agent.

1994   April 9: the Saudi government decides to revoke Osama bin Laden's Saudi nationality and freeze his assets in light of his support for radical movements.

1995   Osama bin Laden sets up several training camps in northern Yemen, near the Saudi border.

1995   In February, Ramzi Yousef, who instigated the attack on the World Trade Center, is arrested in Pakistan and extradited to the United States. Details from the investigation establish several links with Osama bin Laden.

1995   In June, an assassination attempt targets President Hosni Mubarak in Addis Ababa. Osama bin Laden is suspected of financing the operation.

1995   In August, Osama bin Laden calls for a guerrilla

campaign targeting American forces stationed in Saudi Arabia in an open letter to King Fahd.

1995 November 13: five Americans and two Indians are killed in an attack on a Saudi National Guard building in Riyadh. Osama bin Laden denies involvement but applauds the operation.

1996 In May, Sudan expels Osama bin Laden, who then returns to Afghanistan.

1996 May 31: four Saudis accused in the attack against installations in Riyadh are executed.

1996 In the spring, President Clinton signs a top-secret order authorizing the CIA to use all means necessary to crush the Al Qaeda network.

1996 June 25: a truck filled with explosives destroys a military installation in Dhahran, killing nineteen American servicemen. American investigators point to Osama bin Laden.

1996 August 23: Osama bin Laden launches a declaration of war against the United States, demanding that American troops leave the Arabian peninsula, that the holy sites be liberated, and that the Saudi regime be overthrown, and calls on fundamentalist groups to join his battle.

1998   In February, Osama bin Laden and several Islamic groups call for the killing of all Americans, including civilians, throughout the world.

1998   March 16: Libya issues the first international arrest warrant against Osama bin Laden and three accomplices for murder.

1998   June 8: the New York Grand Jury issues charges against Osama bin Laden for "conspiring to attack American military installations."

1998   August 6: the Egyptian Jihad issues a warning to the United States declaring that America will receive "a message written in a language they understood."

1998   August 7: two explosions hit the American embassies in Nairobi, Kenya, killing 213 people, and Dar es Salaam, Tanzania, killing eleven.

1998   August 20: the American army retaliates by destroying several training camps in Afghanistan and the Al Shifa pharmaceutical factory in Sudan, suspected of producing weapons. The Sudanese government contests the allegations. Osama bin Laden is included on the U.S. Treasury Department's list of individuals suspected of terrorist activities and whose funds may be seized.

1998   November 4: Osama bin Laden is charged again in

the United States, this time for the attacks against American embassies in Africa.

1999   January 16: the U.S. Department of Justice charges Osama bin Laden again, along with eleven other accomplices, in the attacks against American embassies.

2001   May 29: four members of Osama bin Laden's networks are found guilty in the attacks against American embassies. Two of the suspects are sentenced to life in prison, two get the death penalty.

2001   September 11: two hijacked civilian planes crash into the World Trade Center, while another hits the Pentagon and a fourth crashes in Pennsylvania. The largest-scale attacks ever carried out by a terrorist organization leave more than 3,000 people dead.

APPENDIX II

INTERPOL ARREST WARRANT
FOR BIN LADEN

The following document has never before been published. It is the first international arrest warrant made by a state against Osama bin Laden. Dated March 16, 1998, it was issued by Libya for murder and illegal possession of firearms. Osama bin Laden is cited as the perpetrator of the murder committed on March 10, 1994, in Libya. The arrest warrant was released by Interpol on April 15, 1998.

BIN LADEN Usama
A-268/5-1998

PRESENT FAMILY NAME: BIN LADEN

FORENAME: Usama   SEX: M

DATE AND PLACE OF BIRTH: 1957 - Jeddah, Saudi Arabia

FATHER'S FORENAMES: Abdulrahamn 'Awadh

<u>IDENTITY CONFIRMED - NATIONALITY: SAUDI ARABIAN (CONFIRMED)</u>

<u>LANGUAGE SPOKEN</u>: Arabic.

<u>ACCOMPLICES</u>:

AL-'ALWAN Faraj Mikhaïl Abdul-Fadeel Jibril, born in 1969, subject of red notice File No. 1998/20220, Control No. A-270/5-1998;

AL-WARFALI Faez Abu Zeid Muftah, born in 1968, subject of red notice File No. 1998/20223, Control No. A-271/5-1998;

AL-CHALABI Faraj, born in 1966, subject of red notice File No. 1998/20230, Control No. A-269/5-1998.

<u>SUMMARY OF FACTS OF THE CASE</u>: LIBYA: On 10th March 1994, BIN LADEN, AL-CHALABI, AL-'ALWAN and AL-WARFALI killed two German nationals near Surt.

<u>REASON FOR NOTICE</u>: Wanted on arrest warrant No. 1.27.288/1998, issued on 16th March 1998 by the judicial authorities in Tripoli, Libya, for murder and illegal possession of firearms.

EXTRADITION WILL BE REQUESTED FROM ANY COUNTRY EXCEPT ISRAEL.

If found in a country from which extradition will be requested, please detain; if found elsewhere, please keep a watch on his movements and activities. In either case, immediately inform INTERPOL TRIPOLI (Reference 6.27.8497.352 of 15th April 1998) and the ICPO-Interpol General Secretariat.

File No. 1998/20232   **Control No. A-268/5-1998**

BIN LADEN Usama
A-268/5-1998

NOM DE FAMILLE ACTUEL : BIN LADEN

PRENOM : Usama   Sexe : M

DATE ET LIEU DE NAISSANCE : 1957 - DJEDDAH (Arabie saoudite)

PRENOMS DU PERE : Abdulrahamn 'Awadh

IDENTITE EXACTE - NATIONALITE SAOUDIENNE (EXACTE)

LANGUE PARLEE : Arabe.

COMPLICES :

- AL-'ALWAN Faraj Mikhaïl Abdul-Fadeel Jibril, né en 1969, objet de la notice rouge N° de dossier 1998/20220, N° de contrôle A-270/5-1998.
- AL-WARFALI Faez Abu Zeid Muftah, né en 1968, objet de la notice rouge N° de dossier 1998/20223, N° de contrôle A-271/5-1998.
- AL-CHALABI Faraj, né en 1966, objet de la notice rouge N° de dossier 1998/20230, N° de contrôle A-269/5-1998.

EXPOSE DES FAITS :

LIBYE : Le 10 mars 1994, près de Syrte, les nommés AL-CHALABI, AL-'ALWAN, AL-WARFALI et BIN LADEN ont tué deux ressortissants allemands.

MOTIF DE LA DIFFUSION :

Fait l'objet du mandat d'arrêt N° 1.27.288/1998, délivré le 16 mars 1998 par les autorités judiciaires de TRIPOLI (Libye) pour meurtre et détention illégale d'armes à feu.

L'EXTRADITION SERA DEMANDEE EN TOUT PAYS SAUF EN ISRAEL.

En cas de découverte dans un pays auquel l'extradition sera demandée, procéder à sa détention provisoire ; en cas de découverte dans tout autre pays, surveiller ses déplacements et ses activités. Dans tous les cas, aviser immédiatement INTERPOL TRIPOLI (Référence N° 6.27.8497.352 du 15 avril 1998), ainsi que le Secrétariat général de l'O.I.P.C.-Interpol.

   N° de dossier : 1998/20232   N° de contrôle : A-268/5-1998

BIN LADEN Usama
A-268/5-1998

الاسم العلني الحالي: بن لادن

الاسم الشخصي: أسامة

الجنس: ذكر

تاريخ ومكان الولادة: 1957 ــ جدة/المملكة العربية السعودية

اسما الأب الشخصيان: عبدالرحمن عوض

الهوية مؤكدة ــ الجنسية سعودية (مؤكدة)

يتكلم العربية

شركاؤه:

فرج ميكائيل عبدالفضيل جبريل العلوان المولود عام 1969 ، الـذي صدرت بشأنه النشـرة الحمـراء ذات رقـم الملف 1998/20220 ورقم المراقبة A-270/5-1998 ؛
فائز ابو زيد مفتاح الورفلي المولود عام 1968 ، الذي صـدرت بشأنـه النشـرة الحمـراء ذات رقـم الملـف 1998/20223 ورقم المراقبة A-271/5-1998 ؛
فرج الشلبي المولود عام 1966 ، الذي صدرت بشأنه النشرة الحمراء ذات رقم الملف 1998/20230 ورقم المراقبة A-269/5-1998 .

ملخص وقائع القضية: ليبيا: بتاريخ 1994/3/10 ، بالقرب من مدينة سرت، قام الشلبي والعلوان والورفلي وبـن لادن بقتل مواطنين ألمانيين.

سبب اصدار النشرة: مطلوب بموجب مذكرة توقيف رقمها 1998/288.27.1 وتاريخها 1998/3/16 صـادرة عـن السلطات القضائية في طرابلس/ليبيا لقتل وحيازة اسلحة نارية بدون ترخيص.

سيُطلب تسليمه من أي بلد من بلدان العالم عدا اسرائيل.

اذا عُثر عليه في بلد من البلدان التي سيُطلب منها تسليمه فيُرجى توقيفه، واذا عُثر عليه في غيرها فيُرجى مراقبة تنقلاته ونشاطاته. وفي الحالتين يُسارع الـى إعـلام انـتربول طرابلـس (المرجـع 352.8497.27.6 المـؤرخ 1998/4/15) والأمانة العامة لـ م د ش ج ــ انتربول.

رقم المراقبة A-268/5-1998   رقم الملف 1998/20232
وثيقـة سرية استعمالهـا مقصـور علـى الشرطـة والسلطـة القضائيـة

BIN LADEN Usama
A-268/5-1998

APELLIDO ACTUAL: BIN LADEN

NOMBRE: Usama

SEXO: M

FECHA Y LUGAR DE NACIMIENTO: 1957 en JEDDA (ARABIA SAUDI)

NOMBRES DEL PADRE: Abdulrahamn 'Awadh

IDENTIDAD COMPROBADA - NACIONALIDAD SAUDI COMPROBADA

IDIOMA QUE HABLA: Arabe.

COMPLICES: AL-'ALWAN Faraj Mikhaïl Abdul-Fadeel Jibril, nacido en 1969, objeto de la difusión roja nº de expediente 1998/20220, nº de control A-270/5-1998. AL-WARFALI Faez Abu Zeid Muftah, nacido en 1968, objeto de la difusión roja nº de expediente 1998/20223, nº de control A-271/5-1998. AL-CHALABI Faraj, nacido en 1966, objeto de la difusión roja nº de expediente 1998/20230, nº de control A-269/5-1998.

EXPOSICION DE LOS HECHOS: Libia: el 10 de marzo de 1994, AL-CHALABI, AL-'ALWAN, AL-WARFALI y BIN LADEN mataron a dos alemanes en un lugar cerca de Syrte.

MOTIVO DE LA DIFUSION: Objeto orden de detención nº 1.27.288/1998 expedida el 16 de marzo de 1998 por las autoridades judiciales de TRIPOLI (LIBIA) por asesinato y tenencia ilícita de arma de fuego.

SE SOLICITARA SU EXTRADICION A CUALQUIER PAIS, SALVO A ISRAEL.

De encontrarlo en alguno de los países a los que se pide la extradición, procédase a su detención; de encontrarlo en algún otro país vigílense sus desplazamientos y actividades. En todos los casos, avísese inmediatamente a INTERPOL TRIPOLI (Ref. 6.27.8497.352 del 15 de abril de 1998), así como a la Secretaría General de la OIPC-INTERPOL.

N° de Expediente 1998/20232   N° de Control A-268/5-1998

APPENDIX III

INTERPOL "RED NOTICE" ON BIN LADEN

The following document is Interpol's "Red Notice," Osama bin Laden's specification sheet as it appears in the organization's files. Updated regularly, it provides international police with basic identification information, as well as the charges against Osama bin Laden.

162

GE 1216/99

- PRIORITY: Normal

- DATE: 6 March 2000

- FROM: Interpol Washington

- OUR REF: 19980909401/SPC

- SUBJECT: BIN LADEN, f/n Usama; born in 1957

- RedHead   PERSON WANTED FOR PROSECUTION

- 1.   IDENTITY PARTICULARS

*IPCE Usa 4-12-98

- WARNING: THIS PERSON MAY BE: *red A-266/5-1998 Libye
-    Armed
-    Dangerous   EP 20232/98

OK GE 20215/98 → R258/5-98 (LIBYE)
- 1.1   PRESENT FAMILY NAME:
-    Bin Laden   GE 30253/98 TANZANIE
            GE 30272/98 → KENYA
- 1.2   FAMILY NAME AT BIRTH / PREVIOUS FAMILY NAMES:
-    Bin Laden   GE 1216/99 USA (NOTICES)

- 1.3   FORENAMES:
-    Usama,

- 1.4   SEX:
-    M   MRRB 4

        - 5 AVR. 2000
- 1.5   DATE AND PLACE OF BIRTH: QUALITY CONTROL
-    Date Unknown, 1957
-    Jeddah,
-    Saudi Arabia

- 1.6   FATHER'S FAMILY NAME AND FORENAMES:
-    Bin Laden,   Abdul Rahamn Awadh

- 1.7   MOTHER'S MAIDEN NAME AND FORENAMES:
-    not known

ypol le 5/4 B/G

1.8   RESULT OF IDENTITY CHECK:
      IDENTITY CONFIRMED

1.9   NATIONALITY(IES):
      Saudi Arabia ...   (CONFIRMED)

1.10 IDENTITY DOCUMENTS:
      Passport Number: not known
      Other Identification Information:
      none known

1.11 ALSO KNOWN AS:
      Usamah Bin Muhammad Bin Laden; Shaykh Usamah Bin Ladin; Abu Abdullah; Mujahid
Shaykh; Hajj; al Qaqa; "the Director."

1.12 DESCRIPTION:
      Height: 195.6 cm
      Weight: 67.5 kg
      Hair Color: Black
      Eye Color: Brown
      Complexion: Medium

1.13 DISTINQUISHING MARKS AND CHARACTERISTICS:
      Usually wears full beard and mustache, may walk with a cane.

1.14 OCCUPATION:
      Religious Cleric; Arms Dealer

1.15 LANGUAGES SPOKEN:
      Arabic

1.16 REGIONS/COUNTRIES LIKELY TO BE VISITED:
      Middle East; Southwest Asia

1.17 ADDITIONAL INFORMATION:
      Also the subject of Red Notice Control Number A-268/5-1998, File Number 1998/20232
issued at the request of IP Libya for killing two German nationals in 1994.

2.   JUDICIAL INFORMATION

2.1   SUMMARY OF FACTS OF THE CASE:
      BIN LADEN is wanted for his role in the bombing of United States Embassies in Kenya
and Tanzania on 7th August 1998. BIN LADEN was a leader of "al Qaeda," a group that
conspired to commit violent acts against the United States. Specifically, on 23 August 1996, BIN
LADEN signed and issued a declaration of jihad against Americans in the Arabian peninsula,

164

authorizing his followers to commit violent acts against the U.S. In February, 1998 BIN LADEN endorsed a fatwah authorizing the killing of American civilians anywhere in the world where they can be found. The substance of these were repeated by Bin Laden during a press conference in May, 1998. During July and August, 1998 members of "al Qaeda" made preparations to detonate explosives near the U.S. embassies in Kenya and Tanzania. The embassies were actually bombed on 7 August 1998. More than 216 lives were lost in the Kenya explosion and more than 10 lives were lost in the explosion in Tanzania.

2.2   ACCOMPLICES:
Muhammad Atef; Wadih El Hage; Mohamed Sadeek Odeh; Mohamed Rashed Daoud Al-Owhali; Mustafa Mohamed Fadhil; Khalfan Khamis Mohamed; Ahmed Khalfan Ghailani; Sheikh Ahmed Salim Swedan;Msalam, f/n Fahid, Mohammed Ally

2.3   CHARGE:
Murder; Murder Conspiracy; Attack on a United States Facility

2.4   LAW COVERING THE OFFENCE:
Title 18 United States Code Sections 2332(b), 844(f) and 930(a)

2.5   MAXIMUM PENALTY POSSIBLE:
Life in prison

2.6   TIME-LIMIT FOR ENFORCEMENT: None

2.7   ARREST WARRANT: *PK*   S   ER: 04/11/98
No. S(2) 98 CR. 1023 issued on 16 December 1998
by the judicial authorities in United States District Court, Southern District of New York; New York, New York (USA)
Name of signatory: Theodore Katz, United States Magistrate Judge

2.8   RECORD OF CONVICTION / SENTENCE AVAILABLE AT THE GENERAL SECRETARIAT IN THE LANGUAGE USED BY THE REQUESTING COUNTRY: NO

3 - ACTION TO BE TAKEN IF FUGITIVE IS FOUND
PROVISIONAL ARREST

It is understood that:
- the NCB of the country where the wanted person is found should immediately inform the requesting NCB (quoting reference and date) and the General Secretariat;
- if that country considers red notices to be valid requests for provisional arrest, the fugitive should be provisionally arrested.

EXTRADITION

Please tick the wording required (before asking for publication of a red notice, the requesting

NCB should obtain an assurance from its competent judicial authorities that extradition will be requested):

(X) EXTRADITION WILL BE REQUESTED FROM ANY COUNTRY WITH WHICH THE REQUESTING COUNTRY IS LINKED BY A BILATERAL EXTRADITION TREATY, AN EXTRADITION CONVENTION OR BY ANY OTHER CONVENTION OR TREATY CONTAINING PROVISIONS ON EXTRADITION THAT COVER THE OFFENSE(S) IN QUESTION,

or

() EXTRADITION WILL BE REQUESTED FROM ANY COUNTRY WITH WHICH THE REQUESTING COUNTRY IS LINKED BY A BILATERAL EXTRADITION TREATY, AN EXTRADITION CONVENTION OR BY ANY OTHER CONVENTION OR TREATY CONTAINING PROVISIONS ON EXTRADITION THAT COVER THE OFFENSE(S) IN QUESTION, WITH THE EXCEPTION OF THE FOLLOWING COUNTRIES:

or

() EXTRADITION WILL BE REQUESTED FROM ANY COUNTRY WITH WHICH THE REQUESTING COUNTRY IS LINKED BY A BILATERAL EXTRADITION TREATY, AN EXTRADITION CONVENTION OR BY ANY OTHER CONVENTION OR TREATY CONTAINING PROVISIONS ON EXTRADITION THAT COVER THE OFFENSE(S) IN QUESTION AND ALSO FROM THE FOLLOWING COUNTRIES: ANY COUNTRY THAT CAN EXTRADITE FOR THE OFFENSE(S) UNDER ITS DOMESTIC LAW.

or

() EXTRADITION WILL BE REQUESTED FROM ANY COUNTRY WITH WHICH THE REQUESTING COUNTRY IS LINKED BY A BILATERAL EXTRADITION TREATY, AN EXTRADITION CONVENTION OR BY ANY OTHER CONVENTION OR TREATY CONTAINING PROVISIONS ON EXTRADITION THAT COVER THE OFFENSE(S) IN QUESTION AND ALSO FROM ANY COUNTRY THAT CAN EXTRADITE FOR THE OFFENSE(S) UNDER ITS DOMESTIC LAW, EXCEPT FOR THE FOLLOWING COUNTRIES.

Requesting National Central Bureau:

Interpol Washington
U. S. Department of Justice
Washington, DC 20530
Phone #:   202 - 616 - 9000

166

CF : 98/20215

> ### ADDITIFS ET RECTIFICATIFS
> ### AUX NOTICES INTERNATIONALES DEJA PARUES

ADDITIF

Rédacteur : CC	Groupe NOTICES	Date : 04.04.2000

NOM(S) :   **BIN LADEN**
PRENOM(S) :   Usama
NE(E) :   10.03.1957

N° DE DOSSIER :   1998/20232
N° DE CONTROLE : A-268/5-1998

MRRB 3

1 1 AVR. 2000

QUALITY CONTROL

From INTERPOL WASHINGTON:

BIN LADEN Usama is now subject of a red notice File N° 1998/20232,
Control N° A-326/4-2000 issued at request of IP WASHINGTON for conspiracy to kill
United States nationals by bombing U.S. embassies in Tanzania (Dar Es Salaam) and Kenya
(Nairobi) on 7th August 1998.

ACCOMPLICES:
GHAILANI Ahmed Khalfan born on 14th March 1974, subject of red notice File N°
1999/4424,
Control N° A-329/4-2000
SWEDAN Sheikh Ahmed Salim born on 9th April 1969, subject of red notice File N°
1999/4408,
Control N° A-327/4-2000
MSALAM Fahid Mohammed Ally born on 19th February 1976, subject of red notice
File N° 1999/4393, Control N° A-330/4-2000
FADHIL Mustafa Mohamed born c. 1st January 1976, subject of red notice File N°
1999/4418, Control N° A-328/4-2000

Paid UPD
JGIG3

6.4.2000

APPENDIX IV

STATE DEPARTMENT FACT SHEET
ON BIN LADEN

The following fact sheet on Osama bin Laden was issued by the U.S. State Department in 1996. It mentions for the first time several of bin Laden's financial investments in Sudan, specifically in the Al Shamal Islamic Bank.

TEXT: STATE DEPARTMENT ISSUES FACTSHEET ON BIN LADIN
(Sponsor of Islamic extremist activities described)

August 14, 1996

Washington -- The State Department issued the following factsheet on Usama bin Muhammad bin Awad Bin Ladin on August 14, calling him a financier of Islamic extremist activities.

(begin text)

Usama Bin Ladin: Islamic Extremist Financier

Usama bin Muhammad bin Awad Bin Ladin is one of the most significant financial sponsors of Islamic extremist activities in the world today. One of some 20 sons of wealthy Saudi construction magnate Muhammad Bin Ladin -- founder of the Kingdom's Bin Ladin Group business empire -- Usama joined the Afghan resistance movement following the 26 December 1979 Soviet invasion of Afghanistan. "I was enraged and went there at once," he claimed in a 1993 interview. "I arrived within days, before the end of 1979."

Bin Ladin gained prominence during the Afghan war for his role in financing the recruitment, transportation, and training of Arab nationals who volunteered to fight alongside the Afghan mujahedin. By 1985, Bin Ladin had drawn on his family's wealth, plus donations received from sympathetic merchant families in the Gulf region, to organize the Islamic Salvation Foundation, or al-Qaida, for this purpose.

-- A network of al-Qaida recruitment centers and guesthouses in Egypt, Saudi Arabia, and Pakistan has enlisted and sheltered thousands of Arab recruits. This network remains active.

-- Working in conjunction with extremist groups like the Egyptian al-Gama'at al-Islamiyyah, also know as the Islamic Group, al-Qaida organized and funded camps in Afghanistan and Pakistan that provided new recruits paramilitary training in preparation for the fighting in Afghanistan.

-- Under al-Qaida auspices, Bin Ladin imported bulldozers and other heavy equipment to cut roads, tunnels, hospitals, and storage depots through Afghanistan's~~mountainous terrain to move and shelter fighters and supplies.

After the Soviets withdrew from Afghanistan in 1989, Bin Ladin returned to work in the family's Jeddah-based construction business. However, he continued to support militant Islamic groups that had begun targeting moderate Islamic governments in the region. Saudi officials held Bin Ladin's passport during 1989-1991 in a bid to prevent him from solidifying contacts with extremists whom he had befriended during the Afghan war.

Bin Ladin relocated to Sudan in 1991, where he was welcomed by National Islamic Front (NIF) leader Hasan al-Turabi. In a 1994 interview, Bin Ladin claimed to have surveyed business and agricultural investment opportunities in Sudan as early as 1983. He embarked on several business ventures in Sudan in 1990, which began to thrive following his move to Kh~artoum. Bin Ladin also formed symbiotic business relationships with wealthy NIF members by undertaking civil infrastructure development projects on the re~gime's behalf:

-- Bin Ladin's company, Al-Hijrah for Construction and Development, Ltd., built the Tahaddi (challenge) road linking Khartoum with Port Sudan, as well as a modern international airport near Port Sudan.

-- Bin Ladin's import-export firm, Wadi al-Aqiq Company, Ltd., in conjunction with his Taba Investment Company, Ltd., secured a near monopoly over Sudan's major agricultural exports of gum, corn, sunflower, and sesame products in cooperation with prominent NIF members. At the same time, Bin Ladin's Al-Themar al-Mubarak-ah Agriculture Company, Ltd. grew to encompass large tracts of land near Khartoum and in eastern Sudan.

-- Bin Ladin and wealthy NIF members capitalized Al-Shamal Islamic Bank in Khartoum. Bin Ladin invested $50 million in the bank.

Bin Ladin's work force grew to include militant Afghan war veterans seeking to avoid a return to their own countries, where many stood accused of subversive and terrorist activities. In May 1993, for example, Bin Ladin financed the travel of 300 to 480 Afghan war veterans to Sudan after Islamabad launched a crackdown against extremists lingering in Pakistan. In addition to safehaven in Sudan, Bin Ladin has provided financial support to militants actively opposed to moderate Islamic governments and the West:

-- Islamic extremists who perpetrated the December 1992 attempted bombings against some 100 U.S. servicemen in Aden (billeted there to support U.N. relief operations in Somalia) claimed that Bin Ladin financed their group.

-- A joint Egyptian-Saudi investigation revealed in May 1993 that Bin Ladin business interests helped funnel money to Egyptian extremists, who used the cash to buy unspecified equipment, printing presses, and weapons.

-- By January 1994, Bin Ladin had begun financing at least three terrorist training camps in northern Sudan (camp residents included Egyptian, Algerian, Tunisian and Palestinian extremists) in cooperation with the NIF. Bin Ladin's Al-Hijrah for Construction and Development works directly with Sudanese military officials to transport and provision terrorists training in such camps.

-- Pakistani investigators have said that Ramzi Ahmed Yousef, the alleged mastermind of the February 1993 World Trade Center bombing, resided at the Bin Ladin-funded Bayt Ashuhada (house of martyrs) guesthouse in Peshawar during most of the three years before his apprehension in February 1995.

-- A leading member of the Egyptian extremist group al-Jihad claimed in a July 1995 interview that Bin Ladin helped fund the group and was at times witting of specific terrorist operations mounted by the group against Egyptian interests.

-- Bin Ladin remains the key financier behind the "Kunar' camp in Afghanistan, which provides terrorist training to al-Jihad and al-Gama'at al-Islamiyyah members, according to suspect terrorists captured recently by Egyptian authorities.

Bin Ladin's support for extremist causes continues despite criticisms from regional governments and his family. Algeria, Egypt, and Yemen have accused Bin Ladin of financing militant Islamic groups on their soil (Yemen reportedly sought INTERPOL's assistance to apprehend Bin Ladin during 1994). In February 1994, Riyadh revoked Bin Ladin's Saudi citizenship for behavior that "contradicts the Kingdom's interests and risks harming its relations with fraternal countries." The move prompted Bin Ladin to form the Advisory and Reformation Committee, a London-based dissident organization that by July 1995 had issued over 350 pamphlets critical of the Saudi Government. Bin Ladin has not responded to condemnation leveled against him in March 1994 by his eldest brother, Bakr Bin Ladin, who expressed, through the Saudi media, his family's "regret, denunciation, and condemnation" of Bin Ladin's extremist activities.

(end text)

NNNN

APPENDIX V

CIA MEMO ON BIN LADEN

The following is an unclassified memo from the CIA on Osama bin Laden. The document is not dated.

Factsheet: Usama Bin Ladin

Usama Bin Ladin was born around 1955 in Jeddah, Saudi Arabia. He is the youngest son of Muhammad Bin Ladin, a wealthy Saudi of Yemeni origin and founder of the Bin Ladin Group, a construction firm heavily involved with Saudi Government contracts. Usama Bin Ladin left Saudi Arabia to fight against the Soviets in Afghanistan in 1979. In the mid-1980s he co-founded the Maktab al-Khidamat (MAK) or Services Office, to help funnel fighters and money to the Afghan resistance, in Peshawar with a Palestinian Muslim Brotherhood member named 'Abdallah 'Azzam. The MAK ultimately established recruitment centers around the world—including in the US, Egypt, Saudi Arabia, and Pakistan—that enlisted, sheltered and transported thousands of individuals from over 50 countries to Afghanistan to fight the Soviets. It also organized and funded paramilitary training camps in Afghanistan and Pakistan. Bin Ladin imported heavy equipment to cut roads and tunnels and to build hospitals and storage depots in Afghanistan.

Bin Ladin split from 'Azzam in the late 1980s to extend his campaign to all corners of the globe; 'Azzam remained focused only on support to Muslims waging military campaigns. Bin Ladin formed a new organization in 1988 called Al-Qa'ida—the military "base." After 'Azzam was killed by a carbomb in late 1989, the MAK split, with the extremist faction joining Bin Ladin's organization.

Bin Ladin returned to work in his family's Jeddah-based construction business after the Soviets withdrew from Afghanistan in 1989, but he continued his organization to support opposition movements in Saudi Arabia and Yemen.

Bin Ladin's anti-government activities prompted the Saudi government to expel him in 1991, after which he relocated to Sudan. Although the Afghan war had ended, al-Qa'ida has remained a formidable organization, consisting of mujahedin of many nationalities who had previously fought with Bin Ladin. Many of these have remained loyal to and continue working with him today.

In May 1996, Sudan expelled Bin Ladin, largely in response to US insistence and to the threat of UN sanctions following Sudan's alleged complicity in the attempted assassination of Egyptian President Hosni Mubarak in Ethiopia in 1995. Within a month, Bin Ladin took refuge in Afghanistan, where his support for and participation in Islamic extremist activities continued.

Bin Ladin's Organization

Al-Qa'ida's goal, in Bin Ladin's words, is to "unite all Muslims and establish a government which follows the rule of the Caliphs." Bin Ladin has stated that the only way to establish the Caliphate is by force. Al-Qa'ida's goal, therefore, is to overthrow nearly all Muslim governments, which Bin Ladin views as "corrupt," to drive Western influence from those countries, and eventually to abolish state boundaries.

Al-Qa'ida is multi-national, with members from numerous countries and with a worldwide presence. Senior leaders in the organization are also senior leaders in other Islamic terrorist organizations, including those designated by the Department of State as foreign terrorist organizations, such as the Egyptian al-Gama'at al-Islamiyya and the Egyptian al-Jihad. Al-Qa'ida seeks a global radicalization of existing Islamic groups and the creation of radical Islamic groups where none exist.

Al-Qa'ida supports Muslim fighters in Afghanistan, Bosnia, Chechnya, Tajikistan, Somalia, Yemen, and now Kosovo. It also trains members of terrorist organizations from such diverse countries as the Philippines, Algeria, and Eritrea.

Anti-US Agenda

Bin Ladin advocates the destruction of the United States, which he sees as the chief obstacle to reform in Muslim societies. Since 1996, his anti-US rhetoric has escalated to the point of calling for worldwide attacks on Americans and our allies, including civilians.

-- Bin Ladin publicly issued his "Declaration of War" against the United States in August 1996.

--When anti-US attacks did not materialize immediately, he explained the delay: "If we wanted to carry out small operations, it would have been easy to do so immediately after the statements. Even the nature of the battle requires qualitative operations that affect the adversary, which obviously requires good preparation."

--In November 1996 he pronounced as "praiseworthy terrorism" the bombings in Riyadh and at Khubar in Saudi Arabia, promising that other attacks would follow. He admitted carrying out attacks on US military personnel in Somalia and Yemen, declaring that "we used to hunt them down in Mogadishu."

--He stated in an interview broadcast in February 1997 that "If someone can kill an American soldier, it is better than wasting time on other matters."

--In February 1998, Bin Ladin announced the creation of a new alliance of terrorist organizations, the "International Islamic Front for Jihad Against the Jews and Crusaders." The Front included the Egyptian al-Gama'at al-Islamiyya, the Egyptian Islamic Jihad, the Harakat ul-Ansar, and two other groups. The Front declared its intention to attack Americans and our allies, including civilians, anywhere in the world.

--In May 1998, he stated at a press conference in Afghanistan that we would see the results of his threats "in a few weeks."

Use of Terrorism

Terrorism is a key component of Al-Qa'ida's strategy, and Bin Ladin cites Koranic references in an effort to justify it. He also quotes as authorities prominent past and present Muslim figures who advocate violence, including 'Umar 'Abd al-Rahman, (the "Blind Shaykh") who is serving a life sentence in a US prison for conspiracy to commit terrorism.

Al-Qa'ida has assisted in numerous terrorist operations around the world. It aided al-Gama'at al-Islamiyya's 1995 attempt to assassinate Egyptian President Mubarak, provided a safehouse to World Trade Center bomber Ramzi Yousef, and attacked US soldiers in Yemen and Somalia during Operation Restore Hope—a humanitarian mission to provide relief to starving Somalis.

APPENDIX VI

FBI FILE ON OMAR AND ABDULLAH BIN LADEN

View Document Text
SECRET

ECFVT1:
More : -

Case ID . : 1991-WF-213589   Serial : 39
Responses :

02/23/1996 and closed on 09/11/1996 on ABL because of his
relationship with the WORLD ASSEMBLY OF MUSLIM YOUTH (WAMY), a
suspected terrorist organization.

          (S) Investigation do date has determined the following
information: The captioned subject has lived at 850 North
Randolph Street, #1230, Arlington, Virginia 22203 since
08/29/1997. He has been receiving mail at P.O. Box 8671, Falls
Church, Virginia 22041 since 03/11/1996 and may also receive
mail at 10310 Main Street, Fairfax, Virginia 22030. From June
1994 to August 1997, the captioned subject is believed to have
lived with ABL at 3411 Silver Maple Place, Falls Church, Virginia
22042.

                            SECRET
ommand . . . > .... +
l=Help F3=Exit F4=Prompt F7=Bkwd F8=Fwd F12=Cancel F13=Attrib F14=List
.5=PrevDoc F16=NextDoc F17=PrevWd F18=NextWd

* * * THIS DATA IS FOR INFORMATIONAL PURPOSES ONLY * * *

PERSON LOCATOR: P-FIND

Resident(s)   Approximate Birth Date

BINLADIN, OMAR A (MALE)

Address: 3411 SILVER MAPLE PL, FALLS CHURCH, VA 22042-3545

Telephone Number: 703-205-0995

Dwelling-Type: SINGLE FAMILY

Homeowner Probability: CONFIRMED

On File Since: 9/30/1996

Date Vendor Record Last Updated: 12/9/2000

178

PERSON LOCATOR: P-FIND

Resident(s)   Approximate Birth Date

BINLADIN, OMAR A (MALE)

Address: 3411 SILVER MAPLE PL, FALLS CHURCH, VA 22042-3545

Telephone Number: 703-641-0279

Dwelling-Type: SINGLE FAMILY

Homeowner Probability: CONFIRMED

On File Since: 7/29/1999

Date Vendor Record Last Updated: 12/9/2000

179

███████████████████████████████████████

*** THIS DATA IS FOR INFORMATION PURPOSES ONLY ***

PROPERTY TRANSFER RECORD FOR FAIRFAX COUNTY, VA

Buyer: BINLADIN, ABDULLA M — *Omar's Brother — Store's mother w/ UBL*

Seller: SHIMONKEVITZ, WILLIAM F   *— Abdullah — Bank refs, ZMA — david filyar*

Property Address: 3411 SILVER MAPLE PL, FALLS CHURCH, VA 22042-3545

**************************** SALES INFORMATION ***************************

Recorded Date: 5/22/1995

Sale Price: $ 380,000 (Full Amount Computed From Transfer Tax)

Book/Page: 9412/1779

Assessor's Parcel Number: 0601 36 0053

Legal Description: LOT: 53; SUBDIVISION: WALNUT HILL ESTATES; RECORDER'S MAP
REFERENCE: MAP 0601 36 0053

Ex. 10

180

Agent Status: ACTIVE

Additional Information: INDUSTRY: GENERAL

Number: 388361

Officers/Directors/Partners/Members:

ABDULLAH, IBRAHIM S
VICE PRESIDENT

LADIN, ABDULLAH BIN
PRESIDENT/TREASURER
MOABBIR, SAMEER
VICE PRESIDENT

CALL LEXIS DOCUMENT SERVICES FOR ALL YOUR CORPORATE NEEDS. 800-634-9738

3

APPENDIX VII

THE ECONOMIC NETWORK OF THE BIN LADEN FAMILY
BY JEAN-CHARLES BRISARD

The following report was written by Jean-Charles Brisard in 1996, and updated periodically until July 2001. The study was conducted at the request of a French intelligence agency.

Note: This report examines "companies and organizations likely to have facilitated, through their complexity and obscurity, direct or indirect ties with Osama bin Laden's economic, financial, or terrorist networks." None of the groups or individuals cited in this report should be associated *a priori* and generally to Osama bin Laden's suspected terrorist activities, contrary to what has been reported in the media. The report is careful to distinguish between entities having normal business relations with the bin Laden family and those that have, or had, direct ties with Osama bin Laden.

OUTLINE

I. The Saudi Binladin Group and Its Subsidiaries
   A. Saudi Binladin Group
   B. SICO (Switzerland)
   C. SICO (Offshore and London Companies)

II. Osama bin Laden and Islamic Financial Institutions
   A. Osama bin Laden's Known Investments
   B. Al Shamal Islamic Bank
   C. Gum Arabic Company Ltd.
   D. The Al Shifa Chemical Factory
   E. Dubai Islamic Bank

III. Osama bin Laden and Islamic Charitable and Humanitarian Organizations

Charts

SUMMARY

Note: This study examines companies and organizations likely to have facilitated, through their complexity and obscurity, direct or indirect ties with the economic, financial, or terrorist networks of Osama bin Laden, born July 30, 1957, in Riyadh (Saudi Arabia). It covers more than 500 companies involving close to 400 individuals. It does not include terrorist networks or political organizations that do not correspond to this subject.

Several financial ties were found between Osama bin Laden and the family company, Saudi Binladin Group, as well as relatives, and even members of the Saudi royal family.

These ties are most apparent in the group's financial networks in Europe, as well as in foreign operations and investments led by Saudi financial and humanitarian networks abroad. The connections often involve important figures in well-known fraudulent financial networks (notably the BCCI).

Though the participants who forged these ties may have done so out of benevolence or complacency, it is hard to believe that they could have been so duped in the different situations studied here. The main elements of focus are:

- *The Saudi Binladin Group* (primarily through its subsidiary SICO):
  Connections between certain European representatives and Azzam Publications, a company with close ties to Osama bin Laden; a link with a member of the Palestinian Islamic Jihad; relationships between fraudulent French and international financial networks (BCCI, the Sawari-2 armament contract affair); and indirect

links with shareholders of the Al Shifa pharmaceutical factory in Sudan.

- *The Islamic banking system:* Links with Faisal Islamic Bank and Osama bin Laden's financial setups in Sudan through Al Shamal Bank; support given to shareholders in the Al Shifa factory; support allowing members of Osama bin Laden's networks to stay active; connections with the fraudulent BCCI network.
- *Official Islamic charity and humanitarian organizations:* Connections between the International Islamic Relief Organization and Sudanese financial networks; support given to Osama bin Laden by a humanitarian organization run by King Fahd's brother-in-law.

The study reveals several interconnected structures:

- *Osama bin Laden's family structure*
- *The BCCI's fraudulent network,* whose main protagonists reappear several times and revolve around Ghaith Pharaon (Khalid bin Mahfouz, Adnan Al Fulaij, Kamal Adham, Roger Tamraz).
- *Oil and weapons networks,* primarily Egyptian and Saudi businessmen (Ghaith Pharaon, Mounir and Fakhry Abdelnour, Saffir and Joseph Iskander, Mohammed Saleh Affara).
- *The Saudi financial network,* developed from the holding company Dar Al Maal Al Islami (DMI).

The financial network surrounding Osama bin Laden and his

investments is similar in structure to the fraudulent network put in place in the 1980s by the BCCI. They even share some of the same personalities (former BCCI executives and directors, oil and arms dealers, Saudi investors) and, sometimes, the same companies (NCB, Attock Oil, BAII).

The study points out the fact that BCCI financing networks have survived, even though Osama bin Laden receives parallel support from political or terrorist movements from the Islamist sphere of influence.

The convergence of financial interests and terrorist activities, especially in Great Britain and Sudan, does not seem to have been an obstacle to each group's desired objectives.

A terrorist network backed by a vast financing system is the trademark of Osama bin Laden's operations.

I. THE SAUDI BINLADIN GROUP AND ITS SUBSIDIARIES

A. Saudi Binladin Group (SBG), or Binladin Organization

Saudi Binladin Group (SBG), or Binladin Organization,[1] (P.O. Box 958, Jeddah, Saudi Arabia, 21421), was founded in 1931 by Osama bin Laden's father, Mohammed Awad bin Laden.

The conglomerate is active in the areas of construction, engineering, real estate, distribution, telecommunications, and publishing. Construction accounts for more than half of SBG's gross revenue.

SBG was the first private contractor in Saudi Arabia. Its status as an organization makes it exempt from publishing its financial records. In 1991, its gross revenue was estimated at $5 billion. In 1999, SBG had 37,000 employees. Its share-holding is family held.

Since its creation, the group has received constant support from the Saudi government, even after the death of its founder in 1968. For several years, it was the official and exclusive contractor of the country's holy sites.[2] Several international groups have established partnerships with SBG as a way to become established in the Middle East.

Officially, SBG has broken all ties with Osama bin Laden,[3] ever since the kingdom revoked his Saudi nationality in April 1994. Osama bin Laden would have been entitled to a $300 million inheritance at that time.

Today the group is run by Bakr M. bin Laden, son of Mohammed bin Laden. The eldest son, Salem bin Laden, ran the group until his accidental death in 1988. SBG's board of directors is comprised of Saleh Gazaz, Mohammed Bahareth, Abdullah bin Said, Mohammed Nur Rahimi, Tarek M. bin Laden, and Omar M. bin Laden.

In addition to the activities handled directly by its divisions, the group's main holding companies are as follows (foreign subsidiaries indicated):

- Construction: Binladin Group International (Egypt, Jordan, Lebanon, Malaysia, United Arab Emirates)
- Electrical engineering: Binladen-Bemco
- Infrastructure: Mohammed Bin Laden Organization
- Real estate: Project Management & Development Co. Real Estate Ltd.
- Industry: Al Salem Group
- Textiles: Mimar Industrial Group (Lebanon, Great Britain, Spain)
- Clothing distribution: Casareen Contract Manufacturing (Great Britain)
- Crystal: Palwa Beleuchtungs Gmbh and Palwa Iberica (Germany, Spain)
- Publishing: Hazar Media Group (Lebanon, France, Great Britain, United Arab Emirates, Egypt)
- Maintenance: United Saudi Maintenance & Services Co.
- Distribution: GFC and Casareen Retail International (Great Britain, Malaysia, Singapore, Egypt, Lebanon, France, the United States)

- Freight/shipping: Forship Ltd. (Great Britain, France, Egypt, Canada)
- Telecommunications: Binladin Telecommunications Co.
- Public relations: Middle East International Group—MEIG AG (Switzerland)

SBG's European office is located at 19 Berkeley Street in London. It is run by Thomas Leonard Cowking, a British citizen born March 24, 1947, and Bakr bin Laden, a Saudi Arabian citizen born February 14, 1947.[4] Leonard Cowking is also an executive, alongside Mohammed Ali Moawalla, of Turkey Rock UK Ltd.[5] (see Part IC). Until 1991, SBG UK was named Tyrolese 199 Limited (60 Goswell Road, London). (See Part IC.)

SBG's international subsidiary, Binladin Group International (BGI)—P.O. Box 41008, Jeddah, Saudi Arabia, 21521—is run by Bakr bin Laden (CEO), Yahia bin Laden (managing director), Omar bin Laden (president), and Hasan bin Laden (vice president). Abu Baker S. Al Hamed is the managing director for Public Works and Airports; Ahmed M. bin Laden is the general manager of the Constructions Division; Henry M. Sarkissian is director of Industrial and Energy projects; Mu'taz Sawwaf is director of the Architecture and Interior Design Division; Abu Bakr bin Ali Al Akhdar is director of the Petroleum and Mining Division; and Shafiq M. bin Laden is a member of the board of directors.

Binladen-Bemco and Mechanical Industrial and Power Contracting[6] (P.O. Box 3143, Jeddah, Saudi Arabia, 21471) is in the electrical engineering sector. It is run by Henry Cabrera and Bakr bin Laden. Members of its board of directors include Souren M. Sarkissian, Henry M. Sarkissian, and Greg M. Sarkissian. One of the company's shareholders is Binladen Bros. for Contracting and Industry[7] (P.O. Box 2734, Jeddah, Saudi Arabia, 21461), run by Bakr M. bin Laden, a shareholder in Saudi Traffic Safety Ltd.[8] (P.O. Box 4445, Jeddah, Saudi Arabia, 21491), and Arabian Aerosurvey Company Ltd.[9] (P.O. Box 6079, Riyadh, Saudi Arabia, 11442).

In Europe, the subsidiary Casareen Retail International Ltd.[10] (20 Upper Ground, London), is in the distribution sector. It is run by three Britons: Mark Adams, born November 15, 1966; Thomas Payne, born May 1, 1957; and Nabella Khan, born February 3, 1970. Nabella Khan also has executive responsibilities within Capex Ltd.[11] She is on the board of directors of Hazar Licensing & Marketing Ltd.[12] as well as Casareen Ltd.[13] (12 York Gate, London), run by Sadek Sawwaf.

The organization Casareen France[14] was created on October 6, 1992. Located in Courbevoie in Hauts-de-Seine, France, it was led by Charles Nakhle, born March 10, 1959, in Lebanon, then by Mohamad Kammourieh.

SBG is also active in Europe through Hazar Publishing Ltd.[15] (12 York Gate, London, Great Britain). The publishing house is headed by Basim Nicolas Ziadeh, a Lebanese citizen born November 8, 1950. In France, Éditions Hazar,[16] also located in Courbevoie, is run by Charles Nakhle.

Basim Nicolas Ziadeh is a member of the Arab Nationalist Conference, made up mostly of Egyptian Islamists. Within the organization, he is closely connected to Mona Al-Solh, who is related to Hisham Al-Solh, founder with Dalia Salaam Rhishani of the British Lebanese Association in London, which works in collaboration with the Azzam family (Azzam Publications), who openly supports Osama bin Laden[17] (see Part III). Within the organization, Basim Nicolas Ziadeh also works with Diaedin Daoud, Secretary General of the Nasserist Party in Egypt. Ziadeh attends the Al-Azhar Sunni mosque in Cairo (to be compared with the name of the publishing company he heads). He notably attended the mosque in December 1998 when the organization initiated a call for Jihad against the United States. Diaeddin Daoud was arrested on two occasions with members of the Muslim Brotherhood (1977 and 1981). Osama bin Laden himself adheres to the Sunni sect of Islam.[18]

BGI executive Mu'taz Sawwaf, a Lebanese citizen, born June 12, 1950, also has management duties alongside Mustafa Kamal Kassas, born October 23, 1940, at Dar Al Reisha for Publishing and Distribution Ltd., located at the same London address as Hazar Publishing.

Forship Ltd.[19] (12 York Gate, London) is a shipping/freight company created in 1989. It is headed by Adnan Kronfol, an American born March 1, 1947, and Omar Youssef Salhab (who is also active in several French subsidiaries). In France, Forship[20] (31, rue Chaptal, Paris 75009) is run by Nou had Gholam, a Lebanese citizen.

SBG also has a European subsidiary specializing in public relations: Middle East International Group (MEIG AG)[21] in Zurich, Switzerland. Created in 1998, the company is represented by Hasan bin Laden, Elisabeth Guggenheim, and Pierre Guggenheim.

The German subsidiary in the textile industry is Mimar

Trading Im Und Export Gmbh[22] (Steinschoenauer Str. 4, Gross-Umstadt, Germany). Created in 1994, the company is headed by Mohammed Ghazi Ragheb. Its Dutch subsidiary is Mimar Trading[23] (W Prinzenstraat 134, BL Helmond), headed by U. Ozdemir, born September 1, 1970.

Finally, the group's crystal treatment is handled in Germany by the direct subsidiary Palwa Beleuchtungsgesellschaft Mit Beschraenkter Haftung[24] (Steinschoenauer Str. 2, Gross-Umstadt, Germany). Created on March 30, 1987, the company is headed by Mohammed Ghazi Ragheb (Mimar Gmbh executive) and Ahmed Farid Al Azem. One of its shareholders is Basim Nicolas Ziadeh (head of Hazar Publishing in London and of Multimedia Ventures Ltd.[25] in London with Namir Michel Cortas, who is also active in Hazar Publishing).

Palwa executive Farid Al Azem is also an executive at Egyptian Finance Co.[26] (4, Hasan Sabri Street, P.O. Box 1824, Zamalek, Cairo, Egypt). This finance and investment company was created in 1974, and its leading shareholders include American Express and the Saudi group Olayan. Its board of directors includes Farid W. Saad, Mounir F. Abdelnour, Jamil W. Saad, Gilbert N. Gargour, Akram Abdul Hijazi, and Elie Baroudi.

Olayan is headed by Suliman Saleh Olayan, born November 5, 1918, in Onaira, Saudi Arabia. The group has ties to Akram Ojjeh, Kamal Adham, and Ghaith Pharaon.

Akram Abdul Hijazi, born September 14, 1939, a Greek citizen, manages the British company Worldmass Ltd.[27]

Elie Baroudi is on the board of directors of International Corporate Bank Inc.[28] (111 Paseo de Roxas, Manila, Philippines), in which American Express is a shareholder.

Mounir Abdelnour and his brother, Fakhry Abdelnour, ran Middle East Petroleum and Interstate, registered in Panama. In the early 1980s, it supplied Egyptian oil to South Africa in violation of the UN embargo.[29] It was South African Strategic Fuel Fund that coordinated the operations to bypass the embargo. During this time, Fakhry Abdelnour was in contact with Emmanuel Shaw, the former Liberian minister of economy. Shaw was also involved in these operations through Tiger Oil. His partner was Marc Rich, who was implicated for weapons sales in Irangate and sought by the FBI.[30] Emmanuel Shaw manages an offshore company called First Liberian Holdings, and one of its partners is Mazen Rashad Pharaon, brother of Ghaith Pharaon, born September 7, 1940, in Saudi Arabia. Ghaith Pharaon was also one of the leading figures in the BCCI affair (see parts IC & IID). Mazen Rashad Pharaon has close ties with Libyan chief of state Muammar al-Qaddhafi, to whom he supplied arms.[31] The Pharaon brothers' financial success was essentially due to family fortune, passed down from their father, Rashid, who was an adviser to Saudi Arabia's founder, King Abd al-Aziz. Rashid Pharaon held several diplomatic posts in Europe between 1948 and 1954. Ghaith Pharaon was educated in Paris, Lebanon, Syria, Switzerland, and the United States, where he studied petroleum engineering. In the 1960s, he was introduced to the head of Saudi intelligence, Kamal Adham, who in turn introduced him to BCCI founder Agha Hasan Abedi, with whom he made several business investments. Ghaith Pharaon served as a screen in the bank's fraudulent operations, notably in the purchase of the National Bank of

Georgia (NBG) and of Financial General Bankshares (FGB), before the collapse of the BCCI in 1991. Kamal Adham ran one of Ghaith Pharaon's companies, Attock Oil (see Part 2d). In 1996, Ghaith Pharaon sold a part of his shares in the BCCI to Khalid Salim bin Mahfouz and his brother, who became 20 percent shareholders (see Part IB). Ghaith Pharaon is wanted by the FBI for fraud in the BCCI affair and for extortion. He is the object of warrants issued by several courts in New York, Washington, Georgia, and Florida.[32]

Run by Bruce Rappaport, the Bank of New York-Inter Maritime Bank[33] (5 Quai du Mont-Blanc, Geneva, Switzerland) was implicated in BCCI affairs, and in American arms sales to Iran (Irangate). The bank's president partnered with Oliver North, who was in charge of arms trade for the National Security Council at the time. Inter Maritime Bank's vice president at the time was Alfred Hartmann, a Swiss citizen born February 21, 1923. He was also former director of the Banque de Commerce et de Placements SA (BCP)—a subsidiary of the BCCI—and board member of the BCCI. The BCP participated in several of the BCCI's fraudulent operations. The bank has several specialized subsidiaries, including the British company Inter Maritime Securities Underwriters Ltd.[34] (renamed Inter Maritime Management SA), located at the same address as the bank.

The bank is affiliated with the Lebanese branch of the Saudi-based National Commercial Bank,[35] located in Beirut. The Saudi bank is run by Khalid bin Mahfouz, former director and shareholder of the BCCI, suspected of having financed Osama bin Laden's operations.

B. SICO (SWITZERLAND)

On May 19, 1980, SBG formed an investment subsidiary in Switzerland called Cygnet SA, which became Saudi Investment Company (SICO)[36]—2 rue François-Le-Fort, Geneva—with 1 million Swiss francs. SICO is run by Yeslam bin Laden, brother of Osama bin Laden. Its directors are Baudoin Dunand, born December 5, 1954, in Saint-Germain-en-Laye (France). Kjell Carlsson, born March 7, 1951, in Ludvikh (Sweden); Franck Warren; Bruno Wyss; Charles Rochat; El Hanafi Tiliouine; and Béatrice Dufour. Bruno Wyss heads the import-export automobile company Sport-Garage Bruno Wyss (Untere Bruehlstrasse 31, Zofingen, Switzerland, 4800).

SICO was registered by Magnin, Dunand & Associés,[37] a law office created in 1972 (2 rue Charles Bonnet, in Geneva), made up of Baudoin Dunand; Jean-Jacques Magnin, born December 5, 1940, in Geneva; Otto-Robert Guth, born November 22, 1950, in Budapest; and Mohammed Mardam Bey, born October 19, 1962, in Damascus, Syria.

Saudi Investment Company (SICO) has stakes in the following companies:

- Metal manufacturing: CI Group PLC [38]
- Financial services: Johnsons Fry Holdings PLC [39]
- Construction: Starmin PLC, with Talal y Zahid & Bros. and Ahmed Abdullah.[40]
- Construction: Water Hall Group PLC, with El-Khereili Trading & Electronic and Goldenash Ltd.[41]

• • •

In addition to these operations, SICO made other investments through Nicris Ltd., located at 2 rue Charles Bonnet in Geneva, the same address as the law office Magnin, Dunand & Associés. The company is run by Yahi bin Laden, vice president of the Saudi Binladin Group, based in Jeddah. Nicris is in fact an 18 percent shareholder in the American pharmaceutical company Hybridon Inc.[42] (155 Fortune Blvd., Milford, Massachusetts), headed by Eugene Andrews Grinstead, Sudhir Agrawal, and Robert Andersen. In March 1998, Yahia bin Laden controlled a 7.5 percent stake in the American group.

In addition to Nicris Ltd., the following also have investments in the company:

- Intercity Holdings Ltd. (14 percent), located at Cuson Milner House, 18 Parliament Streeet, Hamilton, Bermuda
- SEDCO (14 percent), P.O. Box 4384, Jeddah, Saudi Arabia, 21491
- Pillar SA (26 percent), located at 28 avenue de Messine, Paris, France[43]
- Faisal Finance Switzerland SA (7 percent), located at 84 avenue Louis Casai, Geneva

In 1997, Hybridon Inc. deposited $1.034 billion in an account in the Bank Fur Vermogensanlagen Und Handel (BVH BANK), registered in Düsseldorf, a few months before it went bankrupt in November 1997—and before the public prosecutor's office in Düsseldorf opened a judicial inquiry for bankruptcy, laundering, and fraud against its president, Dominique Santini, brother of the former vice-president of the French national assembley André Santini. The inquiry gave rise to an international letters rogatory. Dominique Santini is also a director at BAII Gestion (12 Place Vendôme, Paris, France), a securities investment organization created in 1984, and a subsidiary of the Banque Arabe et Internationale d'Investissement (BAII), located at the same address. The BAII had close ties with the BCCI, as one of its shareholders was the First Arabian Corp., implicated by American federal authorities in 1991 as a screen for the BCCI in the attempted fraudulent purchase of the American bank Financial General Bankshare, by a group of investors including Kamal Adham, Faisal Al-Fulaij, and Abdullah Darwaish. Similarly, American authorities found that, in 1985, Ghaith Pharaon was able to proceed with the purchase of the Independence Bank thanks to a loan granted on the basis of a letter of credit from the BAII. What's more, the president of the BAII, Christian Lamarche, was a director and board member of the BCCI.[44]

Faisal Finance Switzerland SA (84 avenue Louis Casai, Cointrin, 1216) is run by Iqbal El Fallouji. It is a branch of the Islamic holding company Dar Al Maal Al Islami (DMI) SA, located at the same address in Switzerland. DMI is run by Prince Muhammad Al Faisal Al Saud (see Part 2b).

Saudi Economic and Development Company Ltd. (SEDCO)[45]—P.O. Box 4384, Jeddah, Saudi Arabia, 21491— created in 1976, is a distributor of electrical and electronic equipment. Its president is Mohammed bin Mahfouz, born June 24, 1944, in Saudi Arabia. Its board of directors is made up of family members, including Khalid Salim bin Mahfouz, Saleh Salim bin Mahfouz, Abdullah Salim bin Mahfouz, and Ahmed Salim bin Mahfouz.

Its main subsidiary, Al Khaleejia for Export, Promotion and Marketing Co., or Al Maddah Corp.[46] (P.O. Box 1892, Jeddah, Saudi Arabia), is run by Waleed bin Mahfouz. This advertising company was created in 1977 and is suspected by the United States of having donated funds to Osama bin Laden. In addition, SEDCO is a leading shareholder in Bin-laden Telecommunications Company Ltd.[47] (P.O. Box 6045, Jeddah, Saudi Arabia), run by Saleh M. bin Laden.

Mohammed Salim bin Mahfouz is the founder, with Mohammed Saleh Affara, born July 21, 1934, a British cit-izen, of International Development Foundation (IDF),[48] located at 3 Worcester Street in Oxford, England. Originally from Yemen, Mohammed Saleh Affara, an intermediary for arms sales, is implicated in the Sawari-2 affair with Saudi Arabia. He is one of Ali bin Mussalam's associates. Mohammed Saleh Affara notably created Arab Investment Ltd., located on Gloucester Road in London, in 1982, as well as Moco Invest-ments Pond Bridge Ltd. (London), and Tekem International Ltd. (Hong Kong). Finally, Mohammed Salim bin Mahfouz is the founder of Saudi Sudanese Bank[49] in Khartoum, Sudan (see Part 2d). IDF is located at the same address as the Inter-national Islamic Relief Organization, one of Osama bin Laden's recruitment centers (see Part 3).

Khalid bin Mahfouz was a central figure in the BCCI affair. Cheikh Khalid Salim bin Mahfouz was born December 9, 1928. Like the bin Laden family, the bin Mahfouzes came from the province of Hadramaut in Yemen.[50] His father, Salim bin Mahfouz, was born in 1909 and died in 1994. Married to Naila Abdulaziz Kaaki, Khalid bin Mafhouz has three children: Abdulrahman, Iman, and Sultan bin Mahfouz, born March 2, 1973. His brother is Mohammed bin Salim bin Mahfouz, born June 24, 1944.[51] His daughter-in-law is Umayya Yassen Kaaki.

The bin Mahfouz family is one of the wealthiest in the world, with assets estimated at $2.4 billion in 1999.[52] Khalid bin Mahfouz was a key figure in the BCCI affair. Between 1986 and 1990, he was a top executive there, holding the position of operational director.[53] His family held a 20 percent share in the bank at the time.[54] He was charged in the United States in 1992 with tax fraud in the bank's collapse. In 1995, held jointly liable in the BCCI's collapse, with Haroon Kahlon,[55] he agreed to a $245 million settlement to pay the bank's creditors, allowing them to indemnify a portion of the bank's clients.

His father Salim opened the first banking establishment in Saudi Arabia in 1950, the National Commercial Bank, in which the Bin Mahfouz family controlled 52 percent until 1999.[56] In June, the Saudi regime decided to purchase a 50 percent share in the bank. The family nonetheless still controls the most important executive positions within the NCB.[57] His father, Salim Ahmed bin Mahfouz, was recognized in 1997 for his banking career by the Arab Bankers Association of North America (ABANA). Former presidents of the New York-based association include Talat M. Othman (1985 to 1986), Camille A. Chebeir (1992), and Ziad K. Abdelnour (1995).[58]

The bin Mahfouz empire covers the major sectors in Saudi Arabia and abroad, most notably banking, agriculture, pharmaceuticals, and telecommunications.

The family's economic activities are rooted in three main holding companies in Jeddah: the National Commercial Bank[59] (P.O. Box 3555, King Abdul Aziz Street), Nimir Petroleum Limited[60] (Almahmal Centre, 18th floor), and Saudi Economic and Development Company (SEDCO) (P.O. Box 4384). From this base, the family holds majority shares in close to seventy companies around the world.

These financial establishments include:

National Commercial Bank (Saudi Arabia)
SNCB Corporate Finance Limited (Great Britain)[61]
Jordan International Bank (Great Britain)
SNCB Securitiers Limited (Great Britain and the United States)[62]
Langdon P. Cook (United States)[63]
Eastbrook (United States)[64]
Arab Asian Bank (Bahrain)[65]
Arab Financial Services Company (Bahrain)[66]
Trans Arabian Investment Bank (Bahrain)[67]
Taib Bank EC, Taib Investment Management Co., Taib Securities WLL (Bahrain)
Yatrim Bank AS (Turkey)
Middle East Capital Group SAL (Lebanon)[68]
Crédit Libanais SAL (Lebanon)[69]
United Bank of Saudi and Lebanon SAL (Lebanon)[70]
First Phoenician Bank SAL (Lebanon)

Prime Commercial Bank Ltd. (Pakistan)[71]

Middle East Financial Group (Luxembourg)

International Trade and Investment Bank (Luxembourg)

Housing Bank and Housing Bank Jordan Fund (Jordan)[72]

Industrial Development Bank (Jordan)

Capital Investment Holding Co. EC (Bahrain)

Jordan International Bank Plc (Great Britain)

International Development Foundation (Great Britain)

International Bank of Yemen[73]

Yemen Holdings[74]

Al Murjan Company, Al Murjan Minerals Co., Al Murjan Trading & Industrial Co., Al Murjan Environmental Management & Technologies (Saudi Arabia)

Al Zamil Company (Saudi Arabia)[75]

Red Sea Insurance EC, Red Sea Paint Factory (Saudi Arabia)[76]

Saudi Davy Company Limited (Saudi Arabia)[77]

Saudi International Group Limited (Saudi Arabia)[78]

Saudi Tarmac Company Limited (Saudi Arabia)[79]

Saudi Industry and Development Co. Limited (Saudi Arabia)

Health Care Technologies International Limited (Saudi Arabia)

Al Hikma Medical Supplies and Services Co. Limited (Saudi Arabia)

Binladin Telecommunications Company (Saudi Arabia)[80]

Saif Noman Said and Partners

Marei bin Mahfouz & Ahmad Al Amoudi Co. (Saudi Arabia)[81]

Al Khaleejia for Export Promotion and Marketing or Al Maddah Corp. (Saudi Arabia)[82]

Saudi Sudanese Bank (Sudan)[83]

Saudi Sudanese Commercial Co. (Sudan)

Saudi Sudanese Solidarity Investment Co. Limited (Sudan)

Nimir Petroleum Corp., Nimir Petroleum Operating Limited, Nimir Petroleum Overseas Limited (Saudi Arabia and Great Britain)[84]

Arabian Shield Development Co. (United States)[85]

Intercity Holdings Limited (Bermuda)

Hybridon Inc. (United States)

Metrowest (United States)

Isolyser Co. Inc. (United States)

HTI Investment Limited NV (Dutch Antilles)

AAK Properties Limited (Great Britain)[86]

Delta International Bank SAE (Egypt)[87]

Several of these companies have come in contact with Osama bin Laden's networks, in particular the International Development Foundation (see point B), Al Khaleejia for Export Promotion and Marketing Co. (see point B), Saudi Sudanese Bank (see Part IID), and SEDCO. In addition, according to former CIA director James Woolsey, Khalid bin Mahfouz's sister is married to Osama bin Laden.[88]

At the same time, other companies reveal ties with Kamal Adham (see Part IA). These include Delta International Bank

SAE and Arabian Shield Development Co., in which Kamal Adham is a shareholder.

Prime Commercial Bank is run by Sami Bubarak Baarma, a Saudi Arabian citizen born February 23, 1955; Saeed Chaudhry; and Abdul Rahman bin Khalid bin Mahfouz, son of Khalid Mahfouz. The bank's main office is in Lahore, Pakistan. Sami Mubarak Baarma is an executive of SNCB Securities Limited in London. He is also in charge of the Saudi National Commercial Bank's international division. He is a member of the advisory committee for the Carlyle Group, an American company.

Carlyle Group's leading investors include many figures from George H.W. Bush's entourage, as well as that of President George W. Bush.[89] Its board of directors includes important figures from the Bush team: James A. Baker III, former secretary of state under George Bush; Frank C. Carlucci, former secretary of defense under Ronald Reagan; Richard G. Darman, former director of the Office of Management and Budget under George Bush between 1989 and 1993; and John Sununu, former White House chief of staff under George Bush. In addition, Saudi Prince Al-Waleed bin Talal, nephew of King Fahd, owns an indeterminate stake in the group. Even President George W. Bush was a member of the board of directors of one of Carlyle Group's subsidiaries, Caterair, between 1990 and 1994. Khalid bin Mahfouz is indirectly linked to George W. Bush through Abdullah Taha Bakhsh, a Saudi investor and partner of Khalid bin Mahfouz and Ghaith Pharaon. Bakhsh became an 11.5 percent shareholder in Harken Energy Corp in 1987.[90] Talat Othman, born April 27, 1936, in Betunia, Palestine, is a member of the board of directors of the oil company, which George W. Bush was a director of from 1986 to 1993.[91] Othman is a member alongside Frank Carlucci of one of America's most prestigious think tanks, the Middle East Policy Council.[92] Finally, James R. Bath is on the list of shareholders in two other companies controlled by George W. Bush—Arbusto 79 Ltd. and Arbusto 80 Ltd. In the late 1970s, James R. Bath, a wealthy Texas financier, invested $50,000 in these companies to get them off the ground. At the time, he was the U.S. business representative for Salem bin Laden according to the terms of a 1976 trust agreement. It came out later, in 1993, in an official U.S. document, that he was also the legal representative of Khalid bin Mahfouz.[93] The two entities founded by George W. Bush were later merged with Harken Energy. In addition, during a deposition before the Financial Crimes Enforcement Network (FinCEN), James R. Bath claimed to own Skyway Aircraft Leasing Ltd, which in fact belonged to Khalid bin Mahfouz. In 1990, Mahfouz procured a loan of $1.4 million for James R. Bath, allowing him to buy a stake in the Houston Airport. Following Salem bin Laden's death in 1988, Khalid bin Mahfouz took back this holding.[94]

Saeed Chaudhry is on the board of directors of the National Commercial Bank and the International Bank of Yemen.

The bin Mahfouz family holding company, SEDCO, has a British subsidiary called SEDCO Services Limited[95] (9 Curzon Street, London), registered on December 6, 1994. As of September 14, 1999, International Development Foundation's new office is located at this same address (see above).

SEDCO's British subsidiary has two directors: Adnan Soufi, a Saudi Arabian citizen born September 23, 1953, who lives in Jeddah (P.O. Box 5486, Saudi Arabia, 21422); and Dr. Ahmed Nashar, born February 1, 1957, who also lives in Jeddah (P.O. Box 5485, Saudi Arabia, 21422). Adnan Soufi is also a manager at Bidenden Golf Club,[96] located at Weeks Lane in Bidenden, Great Britain, along with Camille Abbas Chebeir, an American citizen living at 155 Monterey Ave., Pelham, New York. Camille Chebeir was vice president and CEO of the Saudi National Commercial Bank, headed by Khalid bin Mahfouz. On December 21, 1999, he was appointed board member of Hybridon Inc., as a representative of SEDCO, which is a shareholder in the American pharmaceutical group.[97]

Ahmed Nashar is the former manager of the BCCI's Pakistani branch.

On July 7, 1998, Yeslam bin Laden created an airline in Geneva called Avcon Business Jets Geneva SA[98] with 100,000 Swiss francs, located at the same address as SICO headquarters. The company is a subsidiary of AVCON AG,[99] created in 1988, and located in Kloten, Switzerland. AVCON AG is headed by watchmaker Sandro Arabian, born March 3, 1941, in Geneva, who lives in Monaco. The following are Avcon Business Jets' directors: Juerg Edgar Brand-Jud, a Swiss citizen; Alfred Muggli, a Swiss citizen; and the company Unitreva[100] in Zurich. Juerg Edgar Brand-Jud is on the boards of several airlines alongside Alfred Muggli. Unitreva AG, which is also a shareholder in Avcon AG, is headed by Rolf Peter Fuchs.

Juerg Edgar Brand-Jud heads several companies, most notably Eunet AG[101] in Zurich, as well as several companies based in Zug: Eurofloats AG,[102] G5 Executive Holding AG,[103] Heliz Air Services AG,[104] Poseidon Derivatives AG,[105] Premiere Beteiligunden Gmbh,[106] Facto Treuhand AG,[107] Grocor Group AG,[108] and Sky Unlimited AG.[109]

Sandro Arabian controls several investment and real estate companies in Switzerland and France. The most active is Sogespa Finance SA[110] in Neuchâtel, Switzerland. Its president is Pierre-Alain Blum, born July 31, 1945, in Neuchâtel. The company has ties to Claude-André Weber, as well as Agenda Holding and Look Holding SA. In France, Sandro Arabian heads the Parlook holding company in Nevers, whose board of directors includes Michel Vauclair, born May 29, 1947 in Rocourt, Switzerland, and Bruno Finaz, born February 7, 1951, in Lyon, France. The company controls Look Cycle SA[111] in Nevers, whose directors include Pierre-Alain Blum (president of Sogespa Finance); John Jellinek, born May 30, 1945, in Chicago; and Bruno Finaz. Sandro Arabian also has investments in film and television production. He owns SPAD[112] (with Pierre-Alain Blum) and Simar Films,[113] both in Paris. Several of these companies have since disappeared.

Sandro Arabian is also president of LK Holding[114] in Nevers, which has been in compulsory liquidation since 1998. The company was headed by James Hamlin Mac Gee, born September 20, 1940, in Salem, South Dakota. From 1984 to 1986, he was the foreign manager of the First Arabian Management Co. Ltd. (FAMCO)[115] in Boulogne-Billancourt, controlling a British subsidiary. The investment company was headed by Pierre Levine, a French citizen, born December 27, 1951, in Plessis-Robinson, France. First Arabian Co.—whose shareholders include Prince Abdullah bin Musaid of Saudi Arabia and Salem bin Laden—was at the heart of the BCCI scandal. After 1974, the company was led by Roger Tamraz, who notably had investment deals with Kamal Adham, one of Ghaith Pharaon and Khalid bin Mahfouz's partners.[116]

James Hamlin Mac Gee is also a director of the Société Occidentale pour la Finance et l'Investissement (SOFIC) in Neuilly-sur-Seine. A securities investment company, it is headed by Jean-Pierre Calzaroni, born August 29, 1940, in Cambodia; and Peter Bunger, born October 25, 1940, in Magdebourg, Switzerland.

C. SICO (Offshore and London Companies)

At the time SICO was created, SBG was also setting up offshore companies in the Cayman Islands, the Dutch Antilles, and the British Virgin Islands. The same law office in Geneva created these companies, which include SICO Curaçao (Dutch Antilles), whose president is Yeslam bin Laden and whose directors are Saleh bin Laden, Béatrice Dufour, and Charles Tickle; Falken Ltd. (Cayman Islands); Tropiville Corp. NV (Dutch Antilles); and Islay Holdings (Islay Island). Charles Tickle is the CEO of Daniel Corp., an American real estate company (P.O. Box 385001, Birmingham, Alabama).

These intermediary corporate structures facilitated the creation of UK subsidiaries in the 1980s: SICO (London) Ltd., located at Kennet House, Kennet Wharf Lane, Upper Thames Street in London, created November 15, 1984, and closed December 15, 1992; SICO (UK) Ltd., located at 21 St. Thomas Street in Bristol, registered on August 2, 1985, and closed May 15, 1990; SICO Services Ltd., located at the same address as the first, registered on September 27, 1985, and closed December 19, 1989.

These companies were gradually replaced by the investment company Russell Wood Holdings Ltd.,[117] joint subsidiary of Tropiville Corp. and Falken Ltd. Located at 30 Great Guildford Street in London, the company was created on February 17, 1987. Its executives include Hanafi Tiliouine (who is on the board of directors of SICO in Geneva) and Akderali Mohammed Ali Moawalla, born April 9, 1949, in Tanzania.

On June 9, 1987, Russell Wood Holdings Ltd. created a subsidiary called Russell Wood Ltd.,[118] whose executives include Akderali Mohammed Ali Moawalla (executive of Russell Wood Holdings Ltd.); John Cyril Dorland Pilley, born January 25, 1935, in Great Britain; and Seng Hock Yeoh, born May 2, 1951, in Malaysia.

On May 8, 1984, Akberali Mohammed Ali Moawalla created Teqny Ltd.[119] with Sajjad Jiwaji, a British citizen, born September 25, 1956. Then on April 30, 1985, he created the investment company Lonshare Nominees Ltd.,[120] located at 30 Great Guildford Street in London. Akberali Mohammed Ali Moawalla is also a director in Saudi Binladin International Sdn Bhd, the Malaysian subsidiary of Saudi Binladin Group, and whose president is Omar bin Laden.[121]

Starting in 1987, Russell Wood Ltd. created a tangled network of investment companies:

- Globe Administration Ltd.,[122] located at Devonshire House, 60 Goswell Road in London. Created on October 29, 1987, it is a subsidiary of Islay Holdings, whose director is Akberali Mohammed Ali Moawalla.[123]
- Falcon Capital Management Ltd.,[124] located at 30 Guilford Street in London (at Russell Wood headquarters). It was created on May 9, 1988, and is headed by Akberali Mohammed Ali Moawalla.
- Falcon Capital Nominees Ltd.,[125] located at 30 Guilford Street in London. Created on May 9, 1988, it is headed by Akberali Mohammed Ali Moawalla.
- Falcon Properties Ltd., located in the Bahamas (see Part IID).
- Turkey Rock UK Ltd.[126] (formerly Tyrolese 350 Limited), located at 66 Lincoln's Inn Fields in London, and created on February 20, 1996. One of its directors is Leonard Cowking (a representative for the Saudi Binladin Group in Europe).
- Saffron Advisors UK Ltd.[127] (formerly Tyrolese 359 Limited), located at 19 Berkeley Street in London. Created on May 17, 1996, it is headed by Akberali Mohammed Ali Moawalla, and Basil Mehdi Al Rahim, an American citizen born June 14, 1953.

The main shareholder in the Tyrolese investment funds is First

Arabian Management Holding Ltd., registered in the Dutch Antilles. Its British subsidiary, First Arabian Management Co. (UK) Ltd., located at Lynton House, 7-12 Tavistock Square in London, is headed by Colin Granville Murray. The registration also mentions as its holding companies FAMCO SA (Saudi Arabia) and FAMCO Panama. FAMCO's shareholders included Salem bin Laden and Prince Abdullah bin Musaid of Saudi Arabia (see Part IIB).

II. OSAMA BIN LADEN AND ISLAMIC FINANCIAL INSTITUTIONS

A. Osama bin Laden's Known Investments

Throughout the 1990s, Osama bin Laden set up a financial network allowing him to finance his terrorist activities. In addition to the financing from political movements, coordinated by the World Islamic Front for Jihad Against Jews and Crusaders, based in Kandahar, Afghanistan, Osama bin Laden's economic activities were relayed by a Khartoum-based holding company named Wadi Al Aqiq,[128] run by a Sudanese man named Abu Al-Hasan.

According to several corroborating sources, the holding company is composed of seven Sudanese companies as well as an indeterminate number of companies in Yemen in the import-export, publishing, and ceramic sectors, as well as in Kenya in the electricity industry.[129] Officially, Osama bin

Laden froze his assets in Sudan after he left the country in 1996. However, it is unclear whether the ties, direct or indirect, between these groups and Osama bin Laden continued.

The main companies involved, and identified by the FBI,[130] are the following:

- Al-Hijrah for Construction and Development Ltd., or Hijrah Contracting Company, based in Khartoum, which notably built the new Khartoum airport as well as 1,200 kilometers of highway connecting Khartoum to Port Sudan.
- Taba Investment Company Ltd., an agricultural investment company based in Sudan that controls the majority of the country's corn, sunflower, and sesame crops.
- Al Shamal Islamic Bank, a Sudanese bank established jointly with the Sudanese National Islamic Front (see point B).
- Gum Arabic Company Ltd., a Sudanese company specializing in the processing and marketing of gum arabic (see point C).
- Ladin International, an investment company in Khartoum.
- Al-Themar Al-Mubaraka, an agricultural production company based in Sudan.
- Al Qudarat, a transport company.

Other findings cite interests in the chemicals industry.

• • •

B. Al Shamal Islamic Bank

Soon after moving to Khartoum in 1991, Osama bin Laden set up several financial and commercial structures that allowed him to finance his terrorist activities. One of his main investments concerned a banking institution, Al Shamal Islamic Bank[131] (P.O. Box 10036, Khartoum, Sudan), to which he contributed at least $50 million at that time.[132]

One of the bank's noteworthy shareholders is the country's second-largest banking institution, Tadamon Islamic Bank[133] (P.O. Box 3154, Baladia Avenue, Khartoum, Sudan), established on November 28, 1981. The bank officially started doing business on March 24, 1983, less than one month before Al Shamal Islamic Bank obtained banking authorization for its own activities. Led by Sayed Altigani Hassan Hilal and Sayed Salah Ali Abu Alnaja, the bank is active throughout Sudan, through twenty-one different establishments.

Its main shareholders in 1998 were: National Co. for Development and Trade (15 percent) in Khartoum; Kuwait Finance House KSC; the Dubai Islamic Bank PLC (see point E); Yasien Leather Co.; and Bahrain Islamic Bank BSC;[134] as well as numerous individual shareholders, including Abdel Rahim Makawi, Al-Sheikh Abdalla Al-kamil, Abdel Basit Ali, Mohammad Ibrahim Mohammad Alsubaie, Abdalla Ibrahim Mohammad Alsubaie, and Mohammad Hussein Alamoudie (Al Amoudi). The minister of social affairs in the United Arab Emirates was also among those with financial stakes in the bank.

Tadamon has several subsidiaries in Sudan, primarily in the agricultural, industrial, and real estate sectors. They include Islamic Insurance Co., Islamic Trading and Services Co., and Real Estate Development Co.

Tadamon Islamic Bank's shareholders have not really evolved since 1991. The only change was in the board of directors representation: Faisal Islamic Bank of Khartoum[135] (P.O. Box 2415, Khartoum, Sudan) was replaced by its subsidiary, National Co. for Development and Trade, in 1995. Faisal Islamic Bank, created in 1977, was led by Prince Muhammad Al Faisal Al Saud of Saudi Arabia.

It is a subsidiary of the Islamic Investment Company of the Gulf (Bahrain), whose holding is Dar Al Mal Al Islami SA (DMI)[136] (84 avenue Louis-Casal, Cointrin, Switzerland). DMI was created on July 29, 1981. Until October 1983, its president was Ibrahim Kamel. He was replaced on October 17, 1983, by Prince Muhammad Al Faisal Al Saud, son of King Al Saud, cousin of King Fahd. DMI is considered to be the central structure in Saudi Arabia's financing of international Islam.

C. Gum Arabic Company Ltd.

Soon after settling in Sudan, Osama bin Laden became a majority shareholder in Gum Arabic Company Ltd.[137] (P.O. Box 857, Khartoum, Sudan). Founded in 1969, the company is said to control almost all of the country's production, marketing, and exporting of gum arabic. Together with its subsidiary in Port Sudan, the company employs 120 workers.

After Osama bin Laden left Sudan in 1996, the company's management was restructured, and Omer El Mubarak became its new president.

In 1995, the government of Sudan held a 30 percent share in the company, while the rest was divided among private investors. At the time, it was headed by Fouad Mustafa Abu El Elia, and its main staff consisted of Mubarak Mirghami, M. Hag-Ali, Makawi S. Akrat, Mubarak M. Logman, Mahmoud A. Hafiz, Mustafa Daoud, Salih M. Salih, Abdallah Mohamed El Hassan, and Osman Mohamed El Hassan.

The management at the time developed family activities in Europe starting in 1995.

Members of M. Hag-Ali's family went to Great Britain to create, in 1995, KHTM Company Limited, located at 73 First Avenue, Acton, London, specializing in the distribution of pharmaceutical products. The company is run by Khalid Ibrahim Hag-Ali, born September 22, 1963, in Sudan, and Hala Mohamed Hamad.

J. H. Akrat runs Semperit Benelux[138] (Ambachtsstraat 13d, 3861 RH Nijkerk in the Netherlands), specializing in rubber importing. It is a subsidiary of Semperit Technische Produktc Gmbh[139] (P.O. Box 201, Vienna, Austria, 1031), specializing in pharmaceutical and cosmetic production, run by Rainer Zellner and Helmut Rauch. The two companies belong to the group Semperit Aktiengesellschaft Holding[140] (Modecenterstrasse 22, Vienna, Austria, 1031), controlled by the same people.

D. THE AL SHIFA CHEMICAL FACTORY

Saudi businessman Saleh Idris, of Sudanese descent, had owned the Al Shifa pharmaceutical factory since April 1998, before it was the object of American military strikes on August 20, 1998. The United States estimated that the factory could have been manufacturing chemical weapons. Before this date, the CIA believed that Osama bin Laden was a main shareholder in the factory, investing through dummy companies.

An American investigative agency, Kroll Associates, concluded that it was unlikely the factory was developing chemical weapons.

Nevertheless, Saleh Idris is linked through several investments to Khalid bin Mahfouz and Mohammed Al Amoudi.

Saleh Idris is involved in Al-Majd General Services Ltd.,[141] located at the headquarters of Abu Fath Al-Tigani Investment Intena (15 Alemarat, Khartoum, Sudan), which is a subsidiary of Tadamon Islamic Bank, shareholder of Al Shamal Islamic Bank (see point B).

Saleh Idris is also manager of Saudi Sudanese Bank[142] (P.O. Box 1773, Kh Baladia Street, Khartoum, Sudan), whose president is Khalid bin Mahfouz, leading shareholder of the National Commercial Bank in Saudi Arabia[143] (P.O. Box 3555, King Abdul Aziz Street, Jeddah, 21481). Throughout the 1980s, Saleh Idris was a board member of the Saudi bank. Saleh Idris is also Mohammed Al Amoudi's partner within the British company M.S. Management Ltd., with Nasrullah Khan (who is related to Nabella Khan, executive of Casareen Retail International Ltd., one of SBG's subsidiaries).

In addition, Khalid bin Mahfouz is one of the leading shareholders in the International Bank of Yemen (25 percent), located at 106 Zubeiry Street, Sana'a. The Yemenite bank is led by Ahmed Kaid Barakat and Ali Lutf Al Thour. The bin Mahfouz family also owns a moving company in Saudi Arabia called Marei Bin Mahfouz and Ahmad Al Amoudi Co.[144] (P.O. Box 1642, Jeddah). Mohammed Hussein Al Amoudi is a shareholder in the company. Finally, members of the bin Mahfouz family and Ahmed Kaid Barakat (president of the International Bank of Yemen) are involved in the insurance company Red Sea Insurance EC[145] (P.O. Box 5627, Jeddah, Saudi Arabia, 21432).

Mohammed Hussein Al Amoudi is an executive of Al Amoudi Group Company Ltd. (P.O. Box 13271, Jeddah, Saudi Arabia, 21493), one of the kingdom's leading conglomerates. Its chairman is Ali bin Mussalam, implicated in the Sawari-2 armament contract affair (see Part IB). Mohammed Hussein Al Amoudi and Khalid bin Mahfouz are both shareholders in World Space, a consortium of telephone operators aiming to develop communications by satellite.[146]

In 1998, Mohammed Hussein Al Amoudi created the pharmaceutical company Pharmacure.[147]

Before it was taken over by Saleh Idris, the Al Shifa factory was controlled by Bashir Hassan Bashir and Salim Baabood.[148] Since 1995, Bashir Hassan Bashir has been a manager of Faisal Islamic Bank in Khartoum, whose president is Prince Mohammad Al Faisal Al Saud. Faisal Islamic Bank is an indirect shareholder of Al Shamal Bank (see point B).

Faisal Islamic Bank is also managed by Dafae Allah Al Haj

Yousif, president of Rainbow Factories Ltd.[149] (P.O. Box 1768, Khartoum, Sudan), whose main shareholders are Aziz Kfouri Sons Ltd. and Gabir Abuelizz. The company specializes in construction equipment. He also runs, with Khalil Osman Mahmoud, Gulf International[150] (P.O. Box 2316 and 1377, Khartoum, Sudan), a company specializing in textile, chemical, and agricultural products. The company has offices in France and Great Britain. Its board of directors includes Mohmoud Sid Ahmed Swar El Dahab, who heads World Prime Trading Ltd.[151] (Woodham Road, Horsell Woking, Surrey, Great Britain). Gabir Abuelizz, shareholder in Rainbow Factories Ltd., runs Gabir Abuelizz Contracting and Trading Company Ltd.[152] (P.O Box 706, Khartoum, Sudan).

Gulf International has a pharmaceutical subsidiary, Sudanese Chemical Industries Ltd.[153] (P.O. Box 2178, Khartoum, Sudan), whose president and leading shareholder is Joseph Iskander, brother of Safir Iskander, an arms dealer and associate of Ghaith Pharaon. The company's bank is Al Shamal Islamic Bank (see Part B). Joseph Iskander is the CEO of the engineering and construction company Al Hamra Engineering Company WLL[154] (P.O. Box 769, Sharjah), whose president is Hanna Nicola Ayoub, and whose director is Yacoub Yousuf Al Hamad. The company is a subsidiary of Al Hamra Group of Companies (Hameng Holdings Ltd.),[155] P.O. Box 2048 Safat, Kuwait, 13021. Its main shareholders are Hanna Nicola Ayoub, Elias Shalhoub, and Adnan Al Fulaij, who is Ghaith Pharaon's partner in Attock Oil Company Ltd.[156] (38 Grosvenor Gardens, London). Faisal Al Fulaij, brother of Adnan Al Fulaij, was Ghaith Pharaon's partner in the BCCI's fraudulent purchase of

Financial General Bankshare. Khalid bin Mahfouz was also convicted in the United States in the BCCI scandal.[157]

Another director of Faisal Islamic Bank, Salah Ahmed Omer Kambal, is president of Norsud Services SA,[158] a financial services and pharmaceutical company created on March 2, 1994, located at 8 rue de l'Arquebuse in Geneva. Its vice president is Jost Vencenz Steinbruchel, a Swiss national, who also runs the trust company Granite Trust SA,[159] located at the same address. In addition, Steinbruchel is vice president of Eclodec Ltd.,[160] a British real estate company located at 43 London Road, Kingston Upon Thames, in Surrey.

Salim Baabood has several investments in Oman controlled by Said bin Salem Al Wahaibi. He is a shareholder in the following companies: Al Haq Trading and Contracting Company LLC[161] (P.O. Box 647, Salalah 211, Oman), and Assarain International Construction Company LLC[162] (P.O. Box 5910, Ruwi, Oman).

E. DUBAI ISLAMIC BANK

According to several sources, the CIA has found that Dubai Islamic Bank[163] (P.O. Box 1080, Dubai City, UAE) helped finance some of Osama bin Laden's activities.

Created in 1975, the Islamic banking establishment is run by Mohamed Khalfan bin Kharbash, the current UAE minister of finance.

The bank is a shareholder of Bahrain Islamic, Islami Bank Bangladesh Ltd.,[164] and Tadamon Islamic Bank,[165] which is a shareholder of Al Shamal Islamic Bank (see Part IIB).

Dubai Islamic Bank's shareholders include the government of Dubai (10 percent) as well as the government of Kuwait (10 percent).

Dubai Islamic Bank was one of the BCCI's main shareholders, with $80 million invested. The bank was caught in a number of scandals, including the $242 million money-laundering operation involving Foutanga (Babani) Sissoko, the billionaire from Mali.[166]

III. OSAMA BIN LADEN AND ISLAMIC CHARITABLE AND HUMANITARIAN ORGANIZATIONS

Saudi Arabia has built a vast network of Islamic charitable and humanitarian organizations, one of which is the International Islamic Relief Organization (IIRO), [167] located at 3 Worcester Street in Oxford, and run by Abdullah Saleh Al Obeid. Its address is the same as that of another organization, the International Development Foundation (IDF), created by Mohammed Salem bin Mahfouz and Mohammed Saleh Affara (see Part IB).

Finally, at the same British address is another mutual assistance organization, Oxford Trust for Islamic Studies, [168] directed by Farhan Ahmad Nizami, an Indian citizen, and Khalid Alireza, a Saudi Arabian citizen. Khalid Alireza is an executive of ABT Group (P.O. Box 2824, Jeddah, Saudi Arabia), a construction and transportation company; Xenel

Industries Ltd. (P.O. Box 2824, Jeddah, Saudi Arabia); and Saudi Services and Operation Company Ltd. (P.O. Box 753, Dhahran Airport, Saudi Arabia, 31932).

Islamic Relief has several branches in Europe, primarily in France, Switzerland, Germany, the Netherlands, and Sweden. According to the CIA, Osama bin Laden "exploited" the IIRO network in his operations.

Prince Abdul Aziz Al Ibrahim, brother of King Fahd's wife Mounayer, created a foundation in the 1990s whose official objective was humanitarian assistance. And yet the organization's branch in Nairobi in Kenya, called Ibrahim bin Abdul Aziz Al Ibrahim Foundation[169] (P.O. Box 742499, Eldama Ravine Garden), was associated with Osama bin Laden's network in the FBI's investigation into the attacks against the American embassies in Nairobi and Dar es Salaam on August 7, 1998.

The organization's Kenya office was even closed by national authorities in September 1998, after documents seized in its headquarters connected it with Osama bin Laden's operations in the material organization of the attack against the American embassy in Nairobi. The foundation was primarily financed by the Al Ibrahim family and several Saudi companies.

Brothers Abdul Aziz and Walid Al Ibrahim have large real estate investments in North Africa, Sub-Saharan Africa, and the United States. In 1993, they bought the leading Arab television satellite service, Middle East Broadcasting Corp. (MBC), created in 1988 by Saleh Abdullah Kamel. MBC owns the press agency United Press International (UPI).

Saleh Abdullah Kamel was born in 1941 in Makkah, Saudi Arabia. He is the son of Abdullah Kamel and Fatma Nagro,

and the husband of Mayda M. Nazer. He has a business degree
from King Saud University in Riyadh, and is the former
adviser to the Saudi minister of finance. He is also an executive and shareholder of Albaraka Islamic Investment Bank
BSC (P.O. Box 1882, Al Hedaya Building 1, Government
Road, Manama, Bahrain), which also has offices in Pakistan
(Faisalabad, Islamabad, Karachi, and Lahore).

In addition, Saleh Kamel has been president since 1986 of
Albaraka Bank-Sudan and shareholder in the Sudanese Islamic
Bank,[170] subsidiary of Faisal Islamic Bank of Egypt SAE;[171]
Tadamon Islamic Bank (see Part IIB); and Islamic West Sudan
Bank. He was also a board member of the National Develop-
ment Bank in Sudan. Finally, he was one of the founders of
Faisal Islamic Bank-Sudan (see Part IIB) and of Arab Invest-
ment Co.[172]

In 1969, Saleh Abdullah Kamel founded Dallah Albaraka
Group, quickly establishing himself as one of the leading pro-
moters of an Islamic financial and banking system capable of
rivaling large Western institutions, and of supporting the
kingdom's religious and political ambitions around the world.
He has also founded several Islamic charitable organizations
that promote cultural and social programs. Saleh Abdullah
Kamel's personal fortune was estimated at $3.5 billion in 1999.

In his capacity as a major shareholder in Albaraka Islamic
Investment Bank of Bahrain, Saleh Abdullah Kamel manages
several banking entities whose activities have been called into
question during recent investigations targeting fraudulent or
terrorist financing networks.

Saleh Kamel has been president since 1986 of Albaraka

Bank-Sudan and shareholder in the Sudanese Islamic Bank, subsidiary of Faisal Islamic Bank of Egypt SAE, in Tadamon Islamic
Bank, and in Islamic West Sudan Bank. He is also a board
member of the National Development Bank in Sudan. Finally,
he was one of the founders of Faisal Islamic Bank-Sudan.

Tadamon Islamic Bank has been a shareholder since 1991
in Al Shamal Islamic Bank in Sudan, considered by American
authorities as one of Osama bin Laden's main structures of
investment and financing after 1991—when the fundamentalist leader moved to Sudan[173] (see Part IIB).

In early 1999, several sources revealed that Osama bin
Laden was receiving financial and logistical support from the
terrorist organization Moro Islamic Liberation Front (MILF),
in the Philippines. According to these sources, MILF's
financing was channeled through another charity organization
in Saudi Arabia called Ikhwan Al Islimin, directed by Ustadz
Muslimen. Muslimen had facilitated a trip to the Philippines
in October 1998 for businessman Hussein Mustapha, partner
of Mohammad Jamal Al-Khalifa, who is Osama bin Laden's
brother-in-law.

Osama bin Laden had for years been a follower of Cheikh
Abdullah Azzam,[174] who was murdered in September 1989.
Azzam had been running a publishing company in London
called Azzam Publications (BCM Uhud, 27 Old Gloucester
Street), which published a biography of Osama bin Laden as
well as several other works that openly justify armed violence.
Azzam Publications has a Web site justifying armed violence.
It was registered by Karim D.

After his death, Cheikh Azzam's relatives created similar

companies in Great Britain: Islamic World Report Ltd. (Salisbury House, Station Road, Cambridge), London International Islamic and Middle Eastern Book (same address), and Hood Hood Books Ltd. (29 Bolingbroke Grove, London). The companies are run by Abd Al Rahman Azzam, a British citizen, born April 20, 1963; Mona Azzam, a British citizen, born November 13, 1964; and Dalia Salaam Rishani, a Lebanese citizen, born April 14, 1967.

CHARTS

Chart 1: Saudi Binladin Group

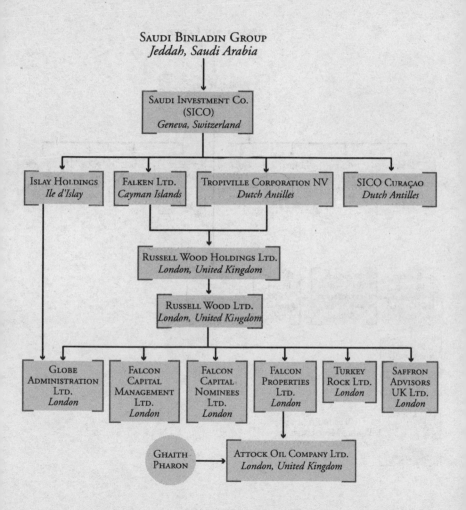

SAUDI BINLADIN GROUP
Jeddah, Saudi Arabia

SAUDI INVESTMENT CO. (SICO)
Geneva, Switzerland

ISLAY HOLDINGS
Ile d'Islay

FALKEN LTD.
Cayman Islands

TROPIVILLE CORPORATION NV
Dutch Antilles

SICO CURAÇAO
Dutch Antilles

RUSSELL WOOD HOLDINGS LTD.
London, United Kingdom

RUSSELL WOOD LTD.
London, United Kingdom

GLOBE ADMINISTRATION LTD.
London

FALCON CAPITAL MANAGEMENT LTD.
London

FALCON CAPITAL NOMINEES LTD.
London

FALCON PROPERTIES LTD.
London

TURKEY ROCK LTD.
London

SAFFRON ADVISORS UK LTD.
London

GHAITH PHARON

ATTOCK OIL COMPANY LTD.
London, United Kingdom

Chart 2: Investments of bin Laden

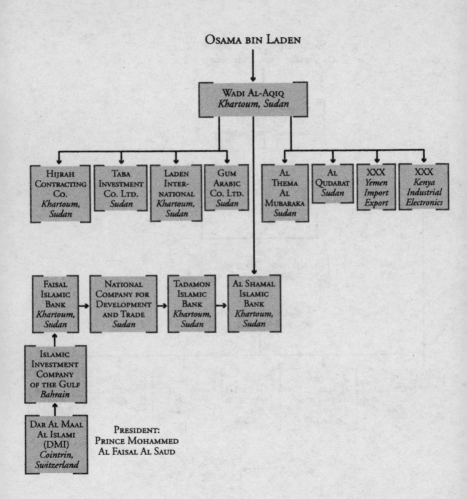

Chart 3: Bin Laden Family

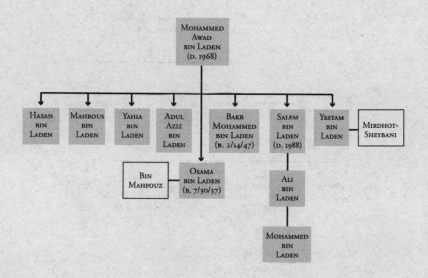

Chart 4: Bin Mahfouz Family

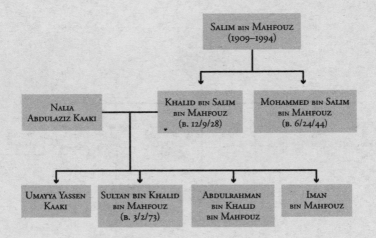

Chart 5: Bin Laden and Mahfouz

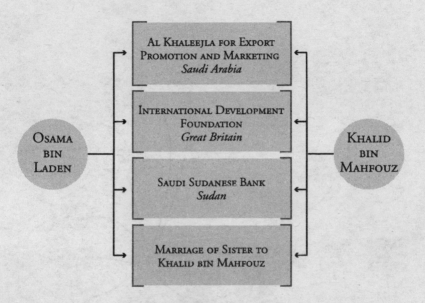

Chart 6: BCCI

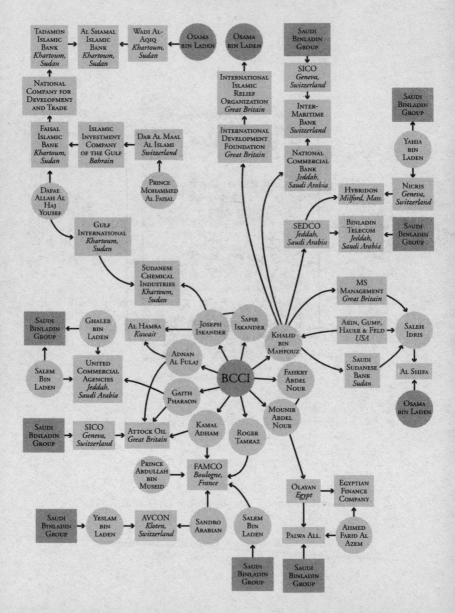

NOTES

PREFACE
1. Meeting with Guillaume Dasquié.
2. www.intelligenceonline.com.
3. *Agence France Presse*, March 27, 2001.

PROLOGUE
1. Meetings between Jean-Charles Brisard and John O'Neill, July 2001.
2. See Appendix VII, p. 181.
3. Interviews with Jean-Charles Brisard, July 22 and 23, 2001.
4. See Appendix VII.

FOREWORD
1. Interview on WHDH-TV, November 3, 1999.
2. George Bush was the director of the CIA from 1976 to 1977, before becoming vice president under Ronald Reagan, then president from 1989 to 1993.
3. *Guardian*, November 6, 2000; *Newsday*, April 2, 1991.
4. *San Francisco Chronicle*, April 5, 2001, and *Independent*, January 10, 2002.
5. Located North of Afghanistan, Kazakhstan (a former Soviet republic) has been nicknamed "New Kuwait" by experts in oil procuring. The Kazakh subsoil has 15 million proven barrels of oil, and 65 million estimated. Chevron is a major player in this market, by way of the Tengizchevroil consortium it controls.
6. Taliban is the plural of Talib, which means "student" in Arabic.
7. *Times* (London), February 5, 2001.
8. "The resolution aims to force the Taliban to close 'terrorist' training camps within 30 days and hand over bin Laden, who is accused by the US of plotting bombings of two US embassies in Kenya and Tanzania in August 1998, in which 225 people died and more than 4,000 were wounded. The measure also tightened an existing flight embargo and a freeze on the Taliban's assets abroad. It bans the sale of chemicals used to convert opium to heroin." *Guardian*, December 20, 2000.
9. "Well-oiled relationships: Pipeline diplomacy greases new U.S.—Russian harmony," *Daily Telegraph*, October 24, 2001.
10. *Ottawa Citizen*, February 5, 2001.
11. For a complete history of the Taliban's rise to power, see Ahmed Rashid's *Taliban: Militant Islam, Oil and Fundamentalism in Central Asia* (New Haven: Yale University Press, 2000).

1. LAILI HELMS: LOBBYIST FOR THE TALIBAN

1. "The Liaison; She Spoke for Taliban and Now Pays a Price," *New York Times,* November 27, 2001; also: "The Accidental Operative," *Village Voice* June 6, 2001.
2. Archives from the Committee for a Free Afghanistan and from the organization Friends of Afghanistan. For background on these organizations see also *Christian Science Monitor,* April 11, 1986.
3. Statement by Deonna Kelli, a former researcher at East Carolina University and coordinator of the Association of Muslim Social Scientists. Corroborated by Ms. Laili Helms to this book's fact-checker.
4. The DCI includes the CIA director as well as a cabinet in charge of coordinating all the agency's activities. The DCI also handles all sensitive contact with foreigners.
5. The Bureau of Intelligence and Research provides diplomats with political analyses and strategic research.
6. On March 21, 2001, at 2 P.M., Sayed Rahmatullah Hashimi was interviewed by Juan Williams on National Public Radio. On March 23, 2001, at 6.30 P.M., he was questioned by Bill Redeker on ABC News.
7. NPR, March 21, 2001.
8. ABC *World News Tonight,* March 23, 2001
9. *New York Times,* March 19, 2001
10. *Washington Post,* March 23, 2001
11. Ibid.
12. *Wall Street Journal,* March 27, 2001
13. Ibid.
14. Ibid.
15. "U.S. Strategy on Saudi Exile Shifts to 'Speak No Evil,'" *Wall Street Journal,* April 3, 2001
16. Principally Saudi Arabia, the United Arab Emirates, and Pakistan. On foreign issues, these countries follow the guidelines set by Saudi Arabia, the leading financial supporter of radical Sunnism and the number-one ally of the United States in the Arab world.
17. According to archives from the U.S. Embassy in Islamabad. See also the *Atlanta Constitution,* January 21, 2000.

2. THE STATE DEPARTMENT: SPONSOR OF THE TALIBAN

1. Rashid, *Taliban,* p. 6.
2. Chardzhu is a city in Turkmenistan, and Gwadar a city in Pakistan on the Persian Gulf. See Rashid, *Taliban,* pp. 157-169.
3. See Chapter 3.
4. *CIA Country Handbook 2001,* www.cia.gov.
5. Modern Afghan society is still dominated by the clan system. It is the result of an agrarian economy in a mountainous zone, and rein-

forced by a sparse population and a high level of illiteracy (more than 80 percent in the 1990s). *CIA Country Handbook 2001*, www.cia.gov.

6. Afghanistan's 15 million inhabitants are divided among four principal ethnic groups: Pashtuns (40 percent), Tajiks (30 percent), Turkmens (Uzbeks and Kazakhs, 15 percent), and Hazaras (Mongolian origin, 12 percent). *CIA Country Handbook 2001*, www.cia.gov.

7. Rashid, *Taliban*, p. 88.

8. Rashid, *Taliban*, pp. 24-25.

9. If the comparison seems exaggerated, it has nonetheless been confirmed that Mohammad Omar took up arms against the tyrants of the valley as much out of the goodness of his heart as to eliminate his rivals. Rashid, ibid.

10. *Washington Post*, July 19, 1992; *Christian Science Monitor*, October 14, 1999.

11. Theological movement founded in the 18th century, and very expansionist by nature.

12. Fundamental opposition exists between Sunni and Shiite Islam, originating from a schism concerning the recognition of the Prophet's descendants. The Arabic Peninsula, which espouses a radical Sunnism, is deeply opposed to the Persian Shiites.

13. Dilip Hiro, "Oil, the Gulf and the Iranians," *Nation*, September 19, 1987.

14. See Chapter 3.

3. A Pipeline for the Taliban

1. *Oil and Gas Journal*, February 23, 1981.

2. *Washington Post*, October 5, 1998.

3. FT Energy Newsletters, "East European Energy Report," March 27, 1995.

4. www.unocal.com/aboutucl/history/index.htm.

5. This was a cavalier move that pushed Bridas to take legal action against Unocal. After several years of proceedings, the Argentinean company won the case.

6. *Oil & Gas Journal*, October 30, 1995.

7. *Houston Chronicle*, October 21, 1995.

8. Rashid, *Taliban*, p. 45.

9. "State Department becomes cooler to the new rules of Kabul," *New York Times*, October 23, 1996.

10. *Washington Post*, June 19, 1989.

11. Rashid, *Taliban*, p. 178.

12. "Afghani Factions Say They Want Peace," *Washington Post*, July 1, 1996.

13. "U.S. wakes up to Afghanistan's Strategic role," *AFP*, April 23, 1996.

14. "U.S. interest in Afghanistan growing as tensions mount,", *AFP*, April 20, 1996.

15. "Afghan Factions Say They Want Peace," ibid.
16. "Afghan President slams US attitude to Taliban," *AFP*, March 18, 1996.
17. "When America Liked the Taliban," *New Republic*, October 22, 2001.
18. *Washington Post*, October 6, 1996.
19. "Good News /Bad News in the Great Game," *Time*, October 14, 1996.
20. Zalmay Khalilzad, "Afghanistan: Time to Reengage," *Washington Post*, October 7, 1996. Khalilzad is currently George Bush's special envoy to Afghanistan; he was a former consultant to Unocal, as was Hamid Karzai, Afghanistan's interim president. *Independent*, January 10, 2002.
21. *Nation*, November 8, 2001.
22. *Omaha World Herald*, July 27, 1997.
23. Rashid, *Taliban*, p.171.
24. On Boardman and Oakley, see Rashid, ibid, p. 171-172.
25. CentGas's funds were divided as follows: 70 percent for Unocal, 15 percent for Delta Oil, 10 percent for the Russian company Gazprom, and 5 percent for Turkmenrosgas, a state-owned Turkmen company.
26. *Journal of Commerce*, November 3, 1997.

4. MULLAH OMAR: A TROUBLESOME ALLY

1. For the full account see Rashid, *Taliban*. pp. 55-66.
2. "Poppy harvest is blooming under the Taliban's rule," *Daily Telegraph*, April 3, 1997.
3 "Walk softly, Taliban tell Afghan women," *Daily Telegraph*, July 23, 1997.
4. Photography was forbidden by the Taliban. "Taliban hold Bonino in hospital ward," *Daily Telegraph*, September 30, 1997.
5. *Washington Post*, April, 11, 1997.
6, Laurence Wrighte, "The Counter-Terrorist," *New Yorker*, January 14, 2002.
7. On October 10, 2001, about a month after the September 11 attacks, the White House called on General Downing to lead investigations of the Al Qaeda organization. He works directly with President Bush's security adviser, Condoleezza Rice. See www.whitehouse.gov/news/release/2001/10./2001.
8. *New York Times*, April 15, 1997.
9. *Washington Post*, November 19, 1997.
10. *Guardian*, December 12, 1997.
11. *Guardian*, July 24, 1998.
12. *Financial Times*, August 10, 1998.
13. *Independent*, September 4, 1998.
14. *Seattle Times*, August 21, 1998.
15. During Senate hearings on March 9, 1999, Mavis Leno, one of the leaders of the Feminist Majority, formally accused Unocal of having supported the Taliban.

5. NEGOTIATING AT ALL COSTS

1. *Guardian,* February 4, 1999; *New York Times,* February 4, 1999; *Washington Post,* October 29, 2001.
2. *AFP,* February 17, 1999.
3. It is now proven that Prince Turki Al-Faisal, son of former King Faisal, actually tried to obtain the extradition of Osama bin Laden for him to be judged by Saudi authorities. His first appeals to the Taliban were made in the second half of 1999. Director of Saudi secret services of the GID since 1977, Turki Al-Faisal was let go on August 30, 2001. On October 10, 2001, in an open letter published by the Arab newspaper *Al-Sharq Al-Aswat,* he proclaimed Osama bin Laden responsible for the attacks in Nairobi, Dar es Salaam, and on the World Trade Center and Pentagon on September 11.
4. Reports from UN Security Council hearings on August 31, 1999, on the situation in Afghanistan.
5. *AFP,* October 20, 1998.
6. *Washington Post,* July 7, 1999.
7. *New York Times,* July 5, 1999.
8. *AFP,* July 5, 1999.
9. *Daily Telegraph,* October 9, 1999.
10. *AFP,* October 11, 1999.
11. *Press Trust of India,* December 8, 2001.
12. *AFP,* October 7, 1998.
13. See Musharraf's Web site: www.pak.gov.pk.
14. *Observer,* October 17, 1999.
15. *Press Trust of India,* December 8, 2001.
16. Archives from the U.S. Embassy in Islamabad.
17. United Nations archives, January 17, 2000.
18. *Boston Globe,* November 18, 2000.
19. "Remarks by Abdur Rahman Zahid," Federal News Service, September 27, 2000.
20. This recognition was made by Thomas Pickering, Undersecretary of State for Political Affairs, during a visit to Moscow. During a press conference at the Spaso House on October 18, he detailed the content of his discussions with Vyacheslav Trubnikov, the Russian deputy foreign minister, regarding the work being done by the 6+2 group. Federal News Service, October 18, 2000.
21. AP, November 3, 2000.
22. *Press Trust of India,* November 13, 2000.
23. *Deutsche Presse Agentur,* November 23, 2000.
24. *AFP,* November 28, 2000.
25. *Washington Post,* November 29, 2000.

26. Federal News Service, December 13, 2000.
27. *Guardian,* December 20, 2000.

6. CHRONICLE OF A FORBIDDEN NEGOTIATION

1. *Times* (London), February 5, 2001.
2. The Campaign for Responsive Politics estimates conservatively that the oil and gas industry donated $1,889,206 to Bush. www.opensecrets.org.
3. *Christian Science Monitor,* April 29, 2001.
4. *San Francisco Chronicle,* April 5, 2001.
5. See www.whitehouse.gov/government/evans.bio.htm.
6. See www.esa.doc.gov/508/esa/biography.htm.
7. *Financial Times,* February 9, 2001.
8. The General Accounting Office publishes reports and leads investigations for various congressional commissions.
9. *Washington Post,* January 24, 2002.
10. Stratfor Report, July 2001.
11. *Intelligence Online,* September 6, 2001: *In These Times,* October 15, 2001.
12. *Hindu Times,* June 2, 2001.
13. *In These Times,* October 15, 2001.
14. Statement of the U.S. goals with the UN, February 12, 2001. Nancy Soderberg: "We were asked by Mr. Vendrell to try and find a way to have a continuing dialogue on humanitarian issues with the Taliban." www.un.it/usa/99_040.htm.
15. Report from UN Secretary General, August 17, 2001. See above. www.un.org/docs/sc/reports/2001/789e.pdf.
16. *Le Monde Diplomatique,* January 2002.
17. *Guardian,* September 26, 2001.
18. *Le Monde Diplomatique,* ibid.
19. Testimony of Niaz Naik, former foreign minister of Pakistan, obtained by Pierre Abramovici for a television program on the French channel France 3. Naiz also repeated these allegations to the *Guardian* newspaper in London. See "Threat of US strikes passed to Taliban weeks before NY attack," *Guardian,* September 22, 2001. See also David Leigh's op-ed "Attack and Counter-attack: Evidence suggests that Washington had planned to move against Bin Laden in the sumnmer. Was the attack on America a pre-emptive strike?" *Guardian,* September 26, 2001.
20. *Le Monde Diplomatique,* November 19, 2001.
21. *Guardian,* September 18, 2001.
22. BBC News, September 18, 2001.
23. *Le Monde Diplomatique,* January 2002.

24. Statement by the spokesperson for the French minister of foreign affairs, July 17, 2001.
25. Report from UN Secretary General, August 17, 2001. See above.
26. *AFP,* August 2, 2001.

7. THE IMPOSSIBLE INVESTIGATION

1. *Washington Post,* April, 18, 1996.
2. Interview in the *New York Times,* December 10, 2001.
3. Christopher Whitcomb, interviews at the Massachusetts College of Liberal Arts, October 24, 2001.
4. "Has someone been sitting on the FBI?" *BBC Newsnight,* November 6, 2001.
5. "FBI claims bin Laden enquiry was frustrated; officials told to back off on Saudis before September 11," *Guardian,* November 7, 2001.
6. Ibid. Palast was told by these intelligence sources that the constraints became worse after the Bush administration took over in 2001. Intelligence agencies were told to "back off" from investigations involving "other members of the bin Laden family, the Saudi royals, and possible links to the acquisition of nuclear weapons by Pakistan. 'There were investigations that were effectively killed.'"
7. *BBC Newsnight,* November 6, 2001.
8. FBI documents obtained from the National Security News Service (NSNS).
9. *BBC Newsnight,* November 6, 2001.
10. Mansoor Ijaz, "Clinton let bin Laden slip away and metastasize," *Los Angeles Times,* December 5, 2001.
11. George Tenet, CIA director, Hearings on worldwide threats to US national security, Senate Armed Services Committee, March 19, 2002, FDCH Political Transcripts.
12. Grand Jury Indictment, USA v. Zacarias Moussaoui, December 11, 2001.
13. "American chaotic road to war," Dan Balz and Bob Woodward, *Washington Post,* January 27, 2002.
14. Testimony of a CBS news journalist recounted to Jean-Charles Brisard on May 5, 2002.
15. Since the writing of this chapter, a political firestorm has erupted in the United States concerning intelligence failures and what George Bush might or might not have known before September 11. See *Nation,* June 10, 2002, for comprehensive analysis. See also Salon.com, May 23, 2002, for a lengthy interview with Jean-Charles Brisard on this chapter's revelations but also his thoughts on the general intelligence failure. Furthermore, on May 27, 2002, *Time* published FBI Special Agent and Minneapolis Chief Division Counsel Coleen M. Rowley's whistle-blowing memo, dated May 21, 2001, to FBI director Robert Mueller. Its second section corroborates Brisard's revelation: "As the Minneapolis

agent's reasonable suspicions quickly ripened into probable cause, which, at the latest, occurred within days of Moussaoui's arrest when the French intelligence service confirmed his affiliations with radical fundamentalist Islamic groups and activities connected to Osama bin Laden . . . While reasonable minds may differ as to whether probable cause existed prior to the receipt of the French intelligence information, it was certainly established after that point and became even greater with successive, more detailed information from the French and other intelligence sources." p. 70.

16. Department of the Treasury, Shutting down the terrorist financial Network, December 5, 2001.

17. "Israël tells Citibank of Hamas funding fears," *Jerusalem Post,* January 23, 2001.

18. "Raids seek evidence of money laundering," *New York Times,* March 21, 2002.

19. Virginia secretary of state, corporate record; *US Business Directory,* 2001.

20. *Who's Who* biography, 2001.

21. *Bankers Almanack,* 2000.

22. *Major Companies Database,* 2001.

23. *Major Companies Database,* 2001.

24. Department of Consumer and Regulatory Affairs, Corporate Record; Virginia secretary of state, corporate record.

25. Virginia secretary of state, corporate record.

26. Virginia secretary of state, corporate record.

27. *US Business Directory,* 2002.

28. Criminal Complaint, USA v. Benevolence International Foundation, April 29, 2002.

29. "Islamic charity, leader charged; Palos Hills group linked to Al Qaeda," *Chicago Tribune,* May 1, 2002.

30. Florida Department of State, corporate record.

31. *Major Companies Database,* 2000.

32. Creditreform German Companies, 2002.

33. *New York Times,* December 5, 1992, about the war in Bosnia.

8. OF OIL AND KORAN

1. In the sixth and seventh centuries, Mecca was an important cultural and commercial center. The sanctuary Al Kaaba (the "Sacred House of Allah," first built by Adam) is a commonly visited place of pilgrimage. From 632 to 634, the region was ruled by the Caliphs. In 660, the Omayyids moved the center of power to Damas (Syria).

2. Wahhab also attacked the philosophers, Sufis and Shiites (who disagreed with the order of the Caliphs who succeeded Muhammed).

3. Standard Oil Company of California, the first oil company, was created in 1870 by John D. Rockefeller in Cleveland.

4. Today Standard Oil Company of California is known as Chevron, which merged with Gulf. Standard Oil Company of New Jersey became Exxon and Socony-Vacuum became Mobil. All of these are major companies in the oil industry.

5. Crowned king in November 1953, Saud was more interested in his sports cars than he was in governing his country. He was repudiated by the family and forced to relinquish power in 1964.

6. In his book *Arabie Saoudite, la dictature protégée* (Paris: Albin Michel, 1995), Jean-Michel Foulquier reports that when the Syrian expert handling the kingdom's budget asked King Abdul Aziz to include oil exports as receipts, he responded, outraged: "This oil is mine. It belongs to me. Just tell me how much you need and I'll give it to you."

7. The Sunna: a collection of the Prophet Muhammad's comments and the decisions he made in interpreting the verses of the Koran. Al Ijmaa: the position of the ulama when an exegesis is necessary. Al Ijtihad: the consultation of jurists in very particular cases.

8. In 1946, Saudi Arabia produced 8 million tons of oil per year. In 1994, annual production approached 390 million tons of crude oil.

9. The capital was initially held at 30 percent by Socal (which later became Chevron), 30 percent Texaco, 30 percent Esso, and 10 percent Mobil.

10. OPEC set three goals for itself: to increase member countries' revenues to insure their development; to insure the granting of national production in place of the major oil companies; to unify production policies.

11. *Le Monde,* August 23, 1994.

12. The 1995 attack left six dead, including five Americans. The 1996 attack, which also involved a car bomb, killed nineteen at the America air base in Khobar.

9. SAUDI FUNDAMENTALIST NETWORKS

1. "The Genesis and Reality of the Pro-Islamic Strategy of the United States," Alexandre Del Valle Strategic Review No. 70-71, April 1999.

2. Richard Labévière, *Les Dollars de la terreur,* (Paris: Cerasset, 1999).

3. Del Valle, ibid.

4. Ninth-century classical Islamic law school founded by Ahmad ibn Hanbal in Baghdad that inspired Muhammad ibn Abd al-Wahhab. Hanbalites are traditionalists who base their legal rulings on the Koran and the words and actions of the Prophet.

5. Cited in "Bin Laden, le milliardaire diabolique," *Le Point,* no. 1513, September 14, 2001.

6. International Islamic Relief Organization, 2001.

7. *Ain Al Yaqeen,* January 21, 1999.

8. OIC statement, July 1, 1999.

9. ICC Financial Analysis Reports, 2001; ICC Directors, 2001; ICC Directory of UK Companies, 2001.

10. Vincent Cannistraro, former director of antiterrorism for the CIA, quoted in *USA Today,* October 1, 1998.

11. *Deutsche Presse Agentur,* February 13, 1999; Japan Economic Newswire, February 13, 1999.

12. ICC directors, 1998.

13. Africa Online, 1998.

14. *AFP,* December 17, 1998.

15. "County Authorizes Talks on Marina del Rey Hotel Plan," *Los Angeles Times,* August 1, 2001.

16. "Blowback," *Jane's Intelligence Review,* August 1, 2001.

17. Creditreform Swiss Companies, 1999.

18. *Bankers Almanack,* 1999.

19. *Bankers Almanack,* 1999.

20. *Complete Marquis Who's Who,* 1986.

21. U.S. State Department Factsheet 08/96; Congressional Research Service Issue Brief 08/27/98; U.S. v. Usama Bin Laden trial transcript, U.S. District Court, Southern District of New York 05/01.

22. U.S. Grand Jury Indictment (USA v. Usama bin Laden), S2 98 Cr. 1023, point 10d, 05/11/98; "Bin Laden reportedly severed financial ties with Sudan, Saudi Arabia," BBC Summary of World Broadcast, August 25, 1998.

23. *African Economic Digest,* August 29, 1994. The principal companies involved and identified by the FBI were the following: Al-Hijrah for Construction and Development Ltd., or Hijrah Contracting Company, based in Khartoum, which built the new Khartoum airport as well as 1,200 kilometers of highway connecting Khartoum to Port Sudan; Taba Investment Company Ltd., an agricultural investment company based in Sudan that controls the majority of the country's corn, sunflower, and sesame crops; Gum Arabic Company Ltd., a Sudanese company specializing in the processing and marketing of gum arabic; Ladin International, an investment company in Khartoum, Sudan; Al-Themar Al-Mubaraka, an agricultural production company based in Sudan; and Al Qudarat, a transport company.

24. *Bankers Almanack,* 1998.

25. Al Shamal Islamic Bank, statement by chief executive officer Mohammad S. Mohammad, September 2001.

26. *Moneyclips,* April 7, 1994.

27. IAC Company Intelligence, 2001; *Bankers Almanack,* 2000.

28. Its principal shareholders in 1998 were: National Co. for Development and Trade in Khartoum; Kuwait Finance House KSC; the Dubai Islamic Bank PLC; Yasien Leather Trade Co; and Bahrain Islamic Bank BSC, as well as numerous individual shareholders, including Abdel Rahim Makawi, Al-Sheikh Abdalla Al-Kamil, Abdel Basit Ali, Mohammad Ibrahim Mohammad Alsubaie, Abdalla Ibrahim Mohammad Alsubaie, and Mohammad Hussein Alamoodie (Al Amoudi). The minister of social affairs in the United Arab Emirates was also among those with financial stakes in the bank.

29. IAC Company Intelligence, 1997.

30. *Bankers Almanack,* 2000; IAC Company Intelligence, 2001.

31. Among its shareholders are the governments of Dubai and Kuwait (which account for 10 percent of the capital). The bank is a shareholder in Bahrain Islamic Bank, Islami Bank Bangladesh Ltd., and Tadamon, and also has investments in Al Shamal Islamic Bank.

32. "Dubai bank withstands BCCI collapse," UPI, June 3, 1996; "Closing in on Baba," *Miami New Times,* April 8, 1999; "Islamic bank rocked by allegations of massive fraud," *AFP,* March 30, 1998; "BCCI payout, Islamic bank dividend tied," UPI, May 19, 1996; "BCCI deal buoys UAE stocks," Inter Press Service, February 6, 1995; "Arab bank's objections may put BCCI deal in jeopardy," *Financial Times,* May 6, 1992; "Baba's big bucks," *Miami New Times,* July 30, 1998; "Nouvelle affaire de fraude dans une banque des Emirats," *AFP,* March 30, 1998.

33. *AP News,* 09/99.

34. See Chapter 12.

10. LIBYA 1994: A TERRORIST IS BORN

1. The document is marked *Confidential intended only for police and judicial authorities.* Given the importance of this notice, we decided to reproduce it in its entirety at the end of the book. See Appendix II.

2. "U.S. Cites Saudi Businessman as Leading Terrorist," Associated Press, August 14, 1996.

3. See *Maghreb Confidential,* No. 184, April 21, 1994.

4. Great Britain also suffered economic losses in the defense industry. See Eric Gerdan's sinister and very accurate dossier, *A Comme armes* (Paris: Alain Moreau, 1975).

5. For a thorough account of Great Britain's actions, see Stephen Dorrill's excellent work, *M16: Inside the Covert World of Her Majesty's Secret Intelligence Service* (New York: Free Press, 2000).

6. See Mark Hollingsworth and Nick Fielding's report *Defending the Realm, MI5 and the Shayler Affair* (London: Editions Andre Deutsch, 1999).

7. This version of the events was confirmed by the descendant of King Idriss al-Senoussi in an interview with the press agency Washington Compass Middle East Wire. Stephen Dorrill's research (see above) also supported this conclusion.

8. This discussion was confirmed by the Libyan ambassador in London, Mohammed Azwai, in an interview with the *Guardian*, October 7, 2001.

11. FAMILY SUPPORT

1. "Bin Laden Family Distances Itself from Osama," *APS Diplomat Recorder*, March 5, 1994.

2. "Saudi elite tied to money groups linked to bin Laden," *Boston Herald*, October 14, 2001.

3. "Family ties; The Bin Ladens," *Sunday Herald*, October 7, 2001.

4. "John Major Link to Bin Laden Dynasty," *Sunday Herald*, October 7, 2001.

5. IAC Company Intelligence, 2001; Saudi Binladin Group.

6. Source: declassified memo from the CIA on Osama bin Laden (undated). See Appendix V.

7. "The Most Wanted Man in the World," *Time*, November 1, 2001.

8. "Bin Laden Is Tied to US Group," *Wall Street Journal*, September 27, 2001.

9. "US President's Father Was in Business with Bin Laden's Family," *Sunday Business Post*, September 30, 2001.

10. "Behind the Veil," *Jerusalem Report*, June 3, 1993.

11. Unpublished interview for *France Soir*, 1995, cited in "Ben Laden, le milliardaire diabolique," *Le Point*, No. 1513, September 14, 2001

12. THE BANKER OF TERROR

1. "NCB net profit edges up in 1998," *Middle East Economic Digest*, July 9, 1999; "NCB names twenty owners under new arrangement," *Moneyclips*, June 18, 1997; "NCB moves towards public ownership," *Financial Times*, May 5, 1997.

2. Arab Bankers Association of North America, 2000.

3. *Forbes*, March 18, 2002.

4. *Banker*, March 1, 2001.

5. "The Saudi Connection: The Next Best Thing to Mecca Is Houston; Houston as the Mecca for the Saudis," *Washington Post*, April 19, 1981.

6. *Bankers Almanack*, 1999.

7. ICC Directors, 1999; "Saudi Aramco-Nimir Petroleum Company Limited," *APS Review Downstream Trends*, November 24, 1997.

8. ICC Directors, 1998; "The BCCI Affair," Report to the Committee on Foreign Relations, United States Senate, Senator John Kerry and Senator Hank Brown, December 1992-102d Congress, 2d Session, Senate Print 102-140.

9. "A rich man whose reputation was on the rocks," *Irish Times*, October 4, 1997.

10. Manhattan district attorney, July 2, 1992.

11. See James Adams and Douglas Frantz's *A Full Service Bank: How BCCI stole billions around the world.* (New York: Pocket Books, 1992).

12. "The BCCI Affair," Report to the Committee on Foreign Relations, United States Senate, Senator John Kerry and Senator Hank Brown, December 1992-102d Congress, 2d Session, Senate Print 102-140.

13. Ibid.

14. "Saudi Money Aiding Bin Laden Businessmen Are Financing Front Groups," *USA Today,* October 29, 1999.

15. James Woolsey hearing, US Counterterrorism strategy, Senate Judiciary Committee, US Senate, September 3, 1998.

16. "State ousts Bin Mahfouz from NCB," *Middle East Economic Digest,* June 11, 1999; "Africa, Middle East," *Forbes,* July 5, 1999.

17. IAC Company Intelligence, 1997.

18. *Moneyclips,* July 8, 1992.

19. ICC Directors, 1998; *ICC Directory of UK Companies,* 1998.

20. ICC Directors, 2001.

21. *Irish Independent,* September 30, 2001.

22. "More Assets on Hold in Anti-Terror Effort; 39 Parties Added to List of Al Qaeda Supporters," *Washington Post,* October 13, 2001.

23. *New York Times,* October 13, 2001.

AFTERWORD

1. *Christian Science Monitor,* May 31, 2001.

2. *Los Angeles Times,* April 25, 2002.

3. *Oil and Gas Journal,* April 29, 2002.

4. Ibid.

5. *Los Angeles Times,* May 30, 2002.

APPENDIX VII

1. IAC Company Intelligence, 1997; Saudi Binladin Group.

2. Unclassified memo from the CIA on Osama bin Laden (undated). See Appendix.

3. "Bin Laden Family Distances Itself From Osama," *APS Diplomat Recorder,* March 5, 1994.

4. ICC Directors, 1998.

5. *ICC Directory of UK Companies,* 1997; ICC Directors, 1998.

6. IAC Company Intelligence, 1997.

7. IAC Company Intelligence, 1997.

8. IAC Company Intelligence, 1997.

9. IAC Company Intelligence, 1997.

10. *ICC Directory of UK Companies,* 1998; ICC Directors, 1998.

11. ICC Directors, 1998.

12. ICC Directors, 1998.

13. ICC Financial Analysis Reports, 1996.

14. Office of the Tribunal de Commerce de Paris, 1998.

15. ICC *Directory of UK Companies,* 1998; ICC Directors, 1998.

16. Office of the Tribunal de Commerce de Paris, 1998.

17. *Mideast Mirror,* May 17, 1994.

18. "The State of the Arab Nation," *Mideast Mirror,* May 17, 1994.

19. ICC Financial Analysis Reports, 1998.

20. Office of the Tribunal de Commerce de Paris, 1998.

21. Creditreform Swiss Companies, 1999.

22. Creditreform German Companies, 1999.

23. MASAI, 1998.

24. Creditreform German Companies, 1999.

25. ICC Directors, 1998.

26. IAC Company Intelligence, 1997.

27. ICC Directors, 1998.

28. IAC Company Intelligence, 1997.

29. "South Africa's Pariah Cost to Get Oil Likely Higher Due to Gulf Crisis," *Platt's Oilgram News,* September 12, 1990.

30. "Inquiry hears fund MD horrified by bribe he did not report," *Africa News,* June 23, 1998; "South Africa: New order follows the bad old ways," *Africa News,* December 12, 1997.

31. "Sheik Down," *Time,* March 21, 1983.

32. "The BCCI Affair," Report to the Committee on Foreign Relations, United States Senate, Senator John Kerry and Senator Hank Brown, December 1992—102d Congress, 2d Session, Senate Print 102-140.

33. Creditreform Swiss Companies, 1999; *Bankers Almanack,* 1999.

34. *ICC Directory of UK Companies,* 1999.

35. Association of Banks in Lebanon, database, 1999.

36. Creditreform Swiss Companies, 1999.

37. International Professional Biographies, Martindale-Hubbell Law Directory, 1999.

38. Annual Report 1993; IAC Company Intelligence, 1997.

39. IAC Company Intelligence, 1997.

40. Annual Report 1992 and 1993; IAC Company Intelligence, 1997; *Investment Dealers Digest,* 1998.

41. Worldscope, 1999; Extel Cards Database, 1996; *ICC Financial Analysis Reports,* 1998; ICC Directors, 1998.

42. US Securities and Exchange Commission, form S1, December 23, 1998; form SC13E4, February 6, 1998.

43. Office of the Tribunal de Commerce de Paris, 1999; ICC Directors 1998.

44. "The BCCI Affair," Report to the Committee on Foreign Relations, United States Senate, Senator John Kerry and Senator Hank Brown, December 1992—102d Congress, 2d Session, Senate Print 102-140.

45. IAC Company Intelligence, 1997.

46. IAC Company Intelligence, 1997.

47. IAC Company Intelligence, 1997.

48. ICC Directors, 1998; *ICC Directory of UK Companies,* 1998.

49. *Bankers Almanack,* 1999.

50. Bank of Credit and Commerce International SA, ICC Directors, 1998.

51. *Who's Who in International Banking,* 1997.

52. "Billionaires," *Forbes,* July 28, 1997, and July 5, 1999.

53. ICC Directors, 1998; "The BCCI Affair," Report to the Committee on Foreign Relations, United States Senate, Senator John Kerry and Senator Hank Brown, December 1992, 102d Congress, 2d Session, Senate Print 102-140.

54. "A Rich Man Whose Reputation Was on the Rocks," *Irish Times,* October 4, 1997.

55. Manhattan district attorney, July 2, 1992.

56. "NCB Net Profit Edges Up in 1998," *Middle East Economic Digest,* July 9, 1999; "NCB names twenty owners under new arrangement," *Moneyclips,* June 18, 1997; "NCB Moves Towards Public Ownership," *Financial Times,* May 5, 1997.

57. "State Ousts bin Mahfouz from NCB," *Middle East Economic Digest,* June 11, 1999; "Africa, Middle East," *Forbes,* July 5, 1999.

58. Arab Bankers Association of North America, 2000.

59. *Bankers Almanack,* 1999

60. ICC Directors, 1999; "Saudi Aramco-Nimir Petroleum Company Limited," *APS Review Downstream Trends,* November 24, 1997.

61. ICC Directors, 1998.

62. ICC Directors, 1998.

63. "Bin Mahfouz Family," *Forbes,* July 25, 1988.

64. "Bin Mahfouz Family," *Forbes,* July 25, 1988.

65. *Bankers Almanack,* 1999.

66. IAC Company Intelligence, 1997.

67. IAC Company Intelligence, 1997.

68. MECG, 1999.

69. "Dubai Group Invests in Lebanese Bank," *Middle East Economic Digest,* February 13, 1998.

70. IAC Company Intelligence, 1997.

71. Prime Commercial Bank, 1999; *Bankers Almanack,* 1999.

72. *Bankers Almanack,* 1999.
73. IAC Company Intelligence, 1997.
74. "PSA Takes Equity Stake in Aden Terminal Project," *Business Times Singapore,* October 22, 1997.
75. "Family Firms Start to Share their Riches," *Middle East Economic Digest,* July 31, 1998.
76. IAC Company Intelligence, 1997.
77. IAC Company Intelligence, 1997.
78. IAC Company Intelligence, 1997.
79. IAC Company Intelligence, 1997.
80. IAC Company Intelligence, 1997.
81. IAC Company Intelligence, 1997.
82. IAC Company Intelligence, 1997.
83. *Bankers Almanack,* 1999.
84. ICC Directors, 1999.
85. Standard & Poor, 1999; SEC filings.
86. ICC Directors, 1999.
87. *Bankers Almanack,* 1999; IAC Company Intelligence, 1997.
88. James Woolsey hearing, US counterterrorism strategy, Senate Judiciary Committee, US Senate, September 3, 1998.
89. Hoover's Company Profile, 2001.
90. Mergers & Acquisitions Database, December 3, 1987; SEC Document 13D—Amendment 1, December 3, 1987.
91. Directory of Corporate Affiliations, National Register, 1999; *S & P Daily News,* November 2, 1993; Reuters, December 6, 1991.
92. MEPC, 1999.
93. United Financial Group, SEC 1993.
94. "Feds Investigate Entrepreneur Allegedly Tied to Saudis," *Houston Chronicle,* June 4, 1992.
95. ICC Directors, 2001.
96. ICC Directors, 1999.
97. Hybridon Inc. press release, December 21, 1999.
98. Creditreform Swiss Companies, 1999.
99. Creditreform Swiss Companies, 1999; "One-Stop Service Center for Private Planes Expand to Gulf," *Moneyclips,* December 8, 1994.
100. Creditreform Swiss Companies, 1999.
101. Creditreform Swiss Companies, 1999.
102. Creditreform Swiss Companies, 1999.
103. Creditreform Swiss Companies, 1999.
104. Creditreform Swiss Companies, 1999.
105. Creditreform Swiss Companies, 1999.
106. Creditreform Swiss Companies, 1999.
107. Creditreform Swiss Companies, 1999.

108. Creditreform Swiss Companies, 1999.
109. Creditreform Swiss Companies, 1999.
110. Creditreform Swiss Companies, 1999.
111. Office of the Tribunal de Commerce de Paris, 1999.
112. Office of the Tribunal de Commerce de Paris, 1999.
113. Office of the Tribunal de Commerce de Paris, 1999.
114. Office of the Tribunal de Commerce de Paris, 1999.
115. Office of the Tribunal de Commerce de Paris, 1999.
116. "Arab Investor Cites Kaiser's Expertise," *New York Times,* March 26, 1981.
117. ICC Financial Analysis Reports, 1998.
118. ICC Financial Analysis Reports, 1998; ICC Directors, 1998.
119. ICC Financial Analysis Reports, 1997; ICC Directors, 1998.
120. *ICC Directory of UK Companies,* 1998; ICC Directors, 1998.
121. "No Link Between Firm and Osama," *New Straits Times Malaysia,* December 17, 1998.
122. ICC Financial Analysis Reports, 1998; ICC Directors, 1998.
123. ICC Directors, 1998.
124. *ICC Directory of UK Companies,* 1998; ICC Directors, 1998.
125. *ICC Directory of UK Companies,* 1998; ICC Directors, 1998.
126. *ICC Directory of UK Companies,* 1998; ICC Directors, 1998.
127. *ICC Directory of UK Companies,* 1998; ICC Directors, 1998.
128. U.S. grand jury indictment (USA v. Osama bin Laden), S2 98 Cr. 1023, point 10d, 05/11/98; "Bin Laden Reportedly Severed Financial Ties with Sudan, Saudi Arabia," BBC Summary of World Broadcast, August 25, 1998.
129. *African Economic Digest,* August 29, 1994.
130. U.S. grand jury indictment (USA v. Osama bin Laden), S2 98 Cr. 1023, point 10d, 05/11/98; "A Global, Pan-Islamic Network," *Washington Post,* August 23, 1998.
131. *Bankers Almanack,* 1998.
132. Bin Laden trial transcript, U.S. District Court, Southern District of New York, 05/01.
133. IAC Company Intelligence, 2001; *Bankers Almanack,* 2000.
134. *Bankers Almanack,* 2000.
135. IAC Company Intelligence, 1997.
136. Creditreform Swiss Companies, 1999.
137. IAC Company Intelligence, 1997.
138. ABC for Commerce and Industry, 1997.
139. *Wer Liefert Was,* 1998.
140. *Hoppenstedt Companies and Executives in Austria,* 1998.
141. ICC Directors, 1998.
142. *Bankers Almanack,* 1999.

143. *Who's Who in International Banking,* 1997.
144. IAC Company Intelligence, 1997.
145. IAC Company Intelligence, 1997.
146. "Worldspace Reveals Identity of Investors," *Space Business News,* February 3, 1999.
147. *Africa News,* June 5, 1998.
148. "Many in Sudan Dispute Plant's Tie with Bomber," *Washington Post,* October 22, 1998; "Sudan Invites UN to Inspect Factory," *Independent,* August 24, 1998; "A Case of Mistaken Identity," *Economist,* August 29, 1998; Interview with Tom Carnaffin, technical director of the Al Shifa factory, World Socialist Website, September 12, 1998; "Embassy Bombing Suspects Charged in US," *World News Digest,* September 3, 1998.
149. IAC Company Intelligence, 1997.
150. IAC Company Intelligence, 1997.
151. ICC Directors, 1998; ICC Financial Analysis Reports, 1997.
152. IAC Company Intelligence, 1997.
153. IAC Company Intelligence, 1997.
154. IAC Company Intelligence, 1997.
155. IAC Company Intelligence, 1997.
156. IAC Company Intelligence, 1997.
157. AFP, May 19, 1995.
158. Creditreform Swiss Companies, 1999.
159. Creditreform Swiss Companies, 1999.
160. ICC Financial Analysis Reports, 1997.
161. IAC Company Intelligence, 1997.
162. IAC Company Intelligence, 1997.
163. *Bankers Almanack,* 1999; IAC Company Intelligence, 1997.
164. *Bankers Almanack,* 1999.
165. *Bankers Almanack,* 1999.
166. "Dubai Bank Withstands BCCI Collapse," UPI, June 3, 1996; "Closing in on Baba," *Miami New Times,* April 8, 1999; "Islamic Bank Rocked by Allegations of Massive Fraud," *AFP,* March 30, 1998; "BCCI Payout, Islamic Bank Dividend Tied," UPI, May 19, 1996; "BCCI Deal Buoys UAE Stocks," Inter Press Service, February 6, 1995; "Arab Bank's Objections May Put BCCI Deal in Jeopardy," *Financial Times,* May 6, 1992; "Baba's Big Bucks," *Miami New Times,* July 30, 1998; "Nouvelle Affaire de Fraude dans une Banque des Emirats," *AFP,* March 30, 1998. *AP News,* 09/99
167. ICC Financial Analysis Reports, 1998; ICC Directors, 1998; ICC Directory of UK Companies, 1998.
168. ICC Directors, 1998.
169. Africa Online, 1998.

170. *Bankers Almanack,* 1999.
171. *Bankers Almanack,* 1999.
172. *Complete Marquis Who's Who,* 1986.
173. U.S. State Department Factsheet 08/96; Congressional Research Service Issue Brief 08/27/98; U.S. v. Usama Bin Laden trial transcript, U.S. District Court, Southern District of New York, 05/01.
174. Unclassified memo from the CIA on Osama bin Laden (undated). See Appendix.

BIOGRAPHICAL NOTES

Jean-Charles Brisard is a consultant on business, corporate, and diplomatic intelligence who was special advisor and Vice President of Business Intelligence for Vivendi Universal. His report, "The Economic Network of the bin Laden Family," was commissioned by the French intelligence community and was used by the French parliament to close down fraudulent Islamic charities. His work has appeared in numerous professional journals as well as *Salon* magazine. He was educated at Georgetown University and in Paris, where he gained advanced degrees in comparative law, international finance and a Ph.D. in International Law.

Guillaume Dasquié is an investigative journalist who is the editor-in-chief of the respected intelligence newsletter, *Intelligence Online* (www.intelligenceonline.com). He has worked for several radio and television stations, and has published an investigative work titled, *Secret Affaires: les Services Secrets Infiltrent les Entreprises* and (with Jean Guisnel) *L'Effroyable mensonage: these et foutaises sur les attentats du 11 septembre (The Appalling Lie: Theories and Fantasies about the September 11 Attacks)*. He has a degree in law and a graduate degree in political science and sociology from the Sorbonne.

Joseph Trento has spent more than thirty years as an investigative journalist and has written three books on the CIA, including the recent *Secret History of the CIA* (Random House) and two on NASA. He has worked for Jack Anderson, the

Wilmington News Journal (where he received six Pulitzer nominations), CNN's Special Assignment Unit and consulted with CBS, NBC, ABC, MSNBC, NHK and others. He is the Managing Director of the D.C.-based National Security News Service.

Wayne Madsen is the Washington correspondent for Intelligence Online. He has written for the *Village Voice, The Progressive, In These Times, Multinational Monitor,* and *CounterPunch.* He was a U.S. naval officer and worked for the National Security Agency as a communications security analyst. He has appeared on ABC News, *60 Minutes, Nightline,* Fox News Channel, *20/20,* CNN, MSNBC, CNBC and NPR. He is the author of *Genocide and Covert Activities in Africa 1993-1999* and a Senior Fellow of the Electronic Privacy Information Center (EPIC), a non-partisan privacy public advocacy group in Washington, D.C.